Romanticism and Form

Also by Alan Rawes

BYRON'S POETIC EXPERIMENTATION: *Childe Harold,* the Tales and the Quest for Comedy

ENGLISH ROMANTICISM AND THE CELTIC WORLD (*co-edited with Gerard Carruthers*)

ROMANTIC BIOGRAPHY (*co-edited with Arthur Bradley*)

Romanticism and Form

Edited by

Alan Rawes

First published 2007 by
PALGRAVE MACMILLAN
Houndmills, Basingstoke, Hampshire RG21 6XS and
175 Fifth Avenue, New York, N.Y. 10010
Companies and representatives throughout the world

PALGRAVE MACMILLAN is the global academic imprint of the Palgrave
Macmillan division of St. Martin's Press, LLC and of Palgrave Macmillan Ltd.
Macmillan® is a registered trademark in the United States, United Kingdom
and other countries. Palgrave is a registered trademark in the European
Union and other countries.

ISBN-13: 978–1–4039–9472–1 hardback
ISBN-10: 1–4039–9472–2 hardback

This book is printed on paper suitable for recycling and made from fully
managed and sustained forest sources. Logging, pulping and manufacturing
processes are expected to conform to the environmental regulations of the
country of origin.

A catalogue record for this book is available from the British Library.

Library of Congress Cataloging-in-Publication Data
Romanticism and form/edited by Alan Rawes.
        p. cm.
    Includes bibliographical references (p.) and index.
    ISBN-13: 978–1–4039–9472–1
    ISBN-10: 1–4039–9472–2
    1. English poetry—19th century—History and criticism. 2. English
poetry—18th century—History and criticism. 3. Romanticism—Great
Britain. 4. Literary form—History—19th century. 5. Literary form—
History—18th century. 6. Poetry—Authorship—History—
19th century. 7. Poetry—Authorship—History—18th century.
    I. Rawes, Alan.
    PR590.R597 2007
    821.009—dc22   2006053012

10   9   8   7   6   5   4   3   2   1
16 15 14 13 12 11 10 09 08 07

Printed and bound in Great Britain by
Antony Rowe Ltd, Chippenham and Eastbourne

Contents

v

List of Illustrations

Notes on Contributors

Bernard Beatty is Senior Fellow at the University of Liverpool. He is the author of *Byron's Don Juan* and *Byron's Don Juan and Other Poems*, has edited three collections of essays on Byron and written widely on Romanticism, Restoration literature and the Scriptures. He was editor of the *Byron Journal* from 1988 to 2005.

Maria Nella Carminati was born and educated in Italy, where she took a first degree in English and German language and literature. After that, she spent many years in English-speaking countries, working as a teacher of English and studying language-related disciplines. In 1984 she obtained her MPhil in theoretical linguistics from Cambridge University and in 2002 a PhD in psycholinguistics from the University of Massachusetts, Amherst. For the last two years she has been a lecturer in linguistics and psycholinguistics at the University of Milan Bicocca, while at the same time pursuing experimental research in language comprehension and production.

Paul M. Curtis teaches English language and literature at l'Université de Moncton, Canada, and has published several articles on Byron, digression and wordplay. He has also edited the volume of selected proceedings from the 30th International Byron Conference, which goes by the title *Byron and the Romantic Sublime* (2005).

Martin H. Fischer, after obtaining his first degree in Germany, spent five years in Amherst/Massachusetts, working on motor control and reading research. He was at the University of Munich for three years before accepting the post in Dundee in November 1999. His diverse research interests are driven by the idea that there are direct perception–action links. He is Consulting Editor for the *Journal of General Psychology* and the *Quarterly Journal of Experimental Psychology*. He is a member of the Psychonomic Society, the European Society for Cognitive Psychology and the Experimental Psychology Society.

Caroline Franklin is Professor of English at University of Wales, Swansea. She has published widely on Romantic-period writing, and her books include *Byron's Heroines* (1992), *Byron: A Literary Life* (2000), *Mary Wollstonecraft: A Literary Life* (2004), *Women's Travel Writing 1750–1850* (2006) and *Byron* (2007).

Gavin Hopps has been Lecturer in English at the Universities of Aachen, Oxford and Canterbury Christ Church, and is currently an Academic Fellow at the University of St Andrews. His recent and forthcoming publications include: *Romanticism and Religion from William Cowper to Wallace Stevens*, co-edited with Jane Stabler; *Romantic Invocations*; *Morrissey: The Pageant of his Bleeding Heart*.

Steven E. Jones is Professor of English at Loyola University, Chicago. He is co-creator and co-editor of the *Romantic Circles* Website, author of *Satire and Romanticism* (2000) and *Against Technology: From the Luddites to Neo-Luddism* (2006), and editor of *The Satiric Eye: Forms of Satire in the Romantic Period* (2003).

Professor **Jacqueline M. Labbe** teaches at the University of Warwick, where she specialises in Romantic poetry. She is the author of several books, the latest of which is *Charlotte Smith: Romanticism, Poetry and the Culture of Gender* (2003), and many articles. Her edition of Smith's *Poems* for *The Works of Charlotte Smith* (Pickering & Chatto, 2005–7) will be out in 2007 and she is currently researching a monograph on Smith, Wordsworth and the establishment of a Romantic style.

Michael O'Neill is Professor of English at Durham University, where he is Director of the University's Institute of Advanced Study. His single-authored publications include *The Human Mind's Imaginings: Conflict and Achievement in Shelley's Poetry* (1989) and *Romanticism and the Self-Conscious Poem* (1997). His editorial publications include, with Zachary Leader, *Percy Bysshe Shelley: The Major Works* (2003) and, with Mark Sandy, the four-volume *Romanticism: Critical Concepts in Literary and Cultural Studies* (2006). His book, *The All-Sustaining Air: Romantic Legacies and Renewals in British, American, and Irish Poetry since 1900*, and *Romantic Poetry: An Annotated Anthology*, co-edited with Charles Mahoney, are forthcoming.

Alan Rawes is Lecturer in Romanticism in the School of Arts, Histories and Cultures at the University of Manchester. He is the author of *Byron's Poetic Experimentation* (2000) and co-editor of *English Romanticism and the Celtic World* (2003) and *Romantic Biography* (2003). He also edits the *British Association for Romantic Studies Bulletin and Review* and is the Academic Editor of the *Byron Journal*.

Andrew Michael Roberts is Reader in English in the School of Humanities at the University of Dundee, where he teaches twentieth- and twenty-first-century literature and culture. His research interests include: poetry since 1950, especially the work of Geoffrey Hill and avant-garde/'linguistically innovative' poetry; Modernist poetry and fiction, especially the works of Mina Loy and Joseph Conrad; theories of masculinity and psychoanalytical theory; poetry and cognitive processes. His books include *Conrad and Masculinity*, *Geoffrey Hill* and (with Jonathan Allison) *Poetry and Contemporary Culture: the Question of Value*. He is currently completing a book entitled *Poetry & Ethics*.

Mark Sandy is Lecturer in English Studies at Durham University. He is author of *Poetics of Self and Form in Keats and Shelley: Nietzschean Subjectivity and Genre* (2005) and co-editor (with Michael O'Neill) of four volumes on *Romanticism: Critical Concepts in Literary and Cultural Studies* (2006). He is currently co-editing (with Andrew Radford) a collection of critical essays on Romantic echoes in the Victorian era.

Jane Stabler is Reader in Romanticism in the School of English, University of St Andrews. Her interests include poetic form and intertextuality in the Romantic period. She is currently researching a study of the ways in which the writings of the Byron–Shelley circle influenced the next generation of English poetic exiles in Italy and working on an edition of Byron for the Longman Annotated English Poet Series. Her publications include *Byron, Poetics and History*, which was awarded the British Academy's Rose Mary Crawshay Prize in 2003.

Nicola Trott is Head of the Department of English Literature, University of Glasgow. Among her recent publications in the Romantic period are an annotated edition of Issac D'Israeli's *Vaurien*, in the Anti-Jacobin Novels series for Pickering & Chatto, and an essay in *Robert Southey and the Contexts of English Romanticism*, edited by Lynda Pratt (2006).

Susan J. Wolfson is Professor of English at Princeton University, and the author of *The Questioning Presence: Wordsworth, Keats, and the Interrogative Modes of Romantic Poetry* (1986), *Formal Charges: The Shaping of British Romantic Poetry* (1997) and *Borderlines: The Shiftings of Gender in British Romanticism* (2006). She is co-editor, with Peter Manning, of

Selected Poems of Lord Byron, Selected Poems of Hood, Praed and Beddoes, and *The Romantics and Their Contemporaries* (Volume 2a of *The Longman Anthology of British Literature)*, and, with Marshall Brown, of *Reading for Form* (2000). On her own she has produced innovative editions of Felicia Hemans (2000) and John Keats (2007).

Introduction

Alan Rawes

The study of form, in Romantic Studies as elsewhere, had a rough ride in the 1970s and 1980s. Most leading Romanticists distanced themselves, for various reasons (and with varying success), from the formalism of New Criticism.[1] Marxist theorists such as Terry Eagleton and Fredric Jameson taught Romanticists to consider literary form as the means by which writers, in Jameson's words, 'invent [...] imaginary or formal "solutions" to unresolvable social contradictions'.[2] Exposing these 'unresolvable social contradictions' became more and more central to the study of Romantic-period culture, while the study of form found itself increasingly pushed to the margins of the major critical debates of the period.

The 1990s and early years of this century saw a reaction against this marginalisation of form. Radical reconsiderations of the aesthetic, coupled with various kinds of 'New Formalism', began to exert an influence on Romantic Studies.[3] Books such as Michael O'Neill's *Romanticism and the Self-Conscious Poem* (1997) – with its emphasis on the ways in which Romantic poems 'are energized and subtilized by their consciousness of themselves as poems' – and, particularly, Susan Wolfson's *Formal Charges: The Shaping of Poetry in British Romanticism* (1997) – offering 'a contextualized formalist criticism that remaps New Criticism (especially its claims of literary autonomy and its paradigms of unity and coherence) but frankly retains its commitment to close reading and its care for poetic form' – helped to make form a focus of critical attention once again.[4] Interest in form has now re-entered the mainstream of Romantic Studies – so much so that one of the latest introductory guides to the study of Romanticism, *An Oxford Guide to Romanticism* (2005), devotes over 300 of its 743 pages to 'Romantic Forms'.[5]

Faced with the increasing amount of formalist activity in Romantic Studies today, this collection gathers together a number of leading scholars of Romanticism and some relative newcomers to offer a snapshot of what and where we are currently up to with the study of form in the Romantic period. Many of the contributors are authors or editors of recent formalist studies of Romantic literature or studies of Romantic literary forms, and, while each focuses on his or her own particular topic (see Susan Wolfson's Afterword for an overview of each chapter), taken together their chapters tell us a great deal about what formalism currently looks like, and of what it is already doing, in Romantic Studies, as well as offering glimpses of possible future directions for the study of Romanticism and form.

So what are we currently up to with the study of form in the Romantic period? To begin negatively, but emphatically, we are not up to New Criticism's old tricks. In this book, Wimsatt and Brooks *et al.* barely get a mention and there is little interest in what Wolfson calls in her Afterword the 'iconicity, unity and intrinsic totality' so dear to New Critics. Where an interest in unity and totality does surface, these are thought about at arm's length from New Criticism and in the context of very different traditions of thought. However, much more evident – and here the influence of deconstruction rather than New Criticism is visible – is an interest in and attention to formal indirection, instability, fragmentation, irregularity, illegitimacy, gratuity, multiplicity, doubleness, combination, foldedness, indeterminacy, artifice, openness to contingency and playfulness. Among the results are new analyses of canonical texts, explorations of vibrant Romantic-period cultures entirely detached from the Romantic aesthetics of organicism and studies of a literary culture working to contain and diffuse the 'Romantic' eruptions within itself.

The new interest in form in the Romantic period is also often historicist. Chapters in this book, uncovering alternative formal priorities to 'organic unity' and 'sincerity' in both canonical and non-canonical texts, go on to explore the implications of these alternative priorities in relation to, for example, war, nationalism, propaganda, empire and urbanisation.

An attention to form is also opening up new ways of reassessing and rehabilitating neglected and marginalised writers, including, in the chapters that follow, Thomas Lovell Beddoes, Felicia Hemans, John Clare, Ann Batten Cristall, Charlotte Smith and, most visibly, Robert Southey. Much is revealed here about these writers and their work but also much that enriches our knowledge and understanding of the interactions between literature and the wider culture in the Romantic period. In the case of Southey, for example, attention to his linguistic inventiveness brings into view aspects of the fertile and dynamic interrelations between literary practices, science, religion, slavery and empire.

Other contributors are keen to explore the relationship between form and reader. The indirection, fragmentation, multiplicity and indeterminacy being here uncovered across Romantic-period literature and beyond naturally throw up questions about the effects – intended and otherwise – these have on readers. For some contributors, what we are confronted with is the use of (as well as ideas about the power of) formal strategies to force readers into various kinds of imaginative acts – co-authoring the text and its meanings, making ethical choices, providing poets with some sort of posthumous existence. For others, new ways of measuring the physical responses of actual readers to particular literary forms open up a very different can of worms.

Where, then, are we up to with form in the Romantic period? No new theory of Romantic form, or single 'New Formalism', emerges from the pages that follow, but signs that literary form in the Romantic period is being radically reconceived are everywhere. Our understanding of form is rapidly evolving to discover and meet new challenges. The contributors to this book are developing approaches to form in Romantic-period literature that are, on the one hand, distanced from Romantic organicism and New Criticism and, on the other hand, informed by the revolutions in Romantic Studies that have occurred since the 1960s. Deconstruction and new historicism are certainly exerting their influence on this process, shaping very different understandings of form from those of New Criticism, not least in terms of what forms warrant attention – in this book we see formal analysis extended to fragments, the invention of words, the combination of image and text in satirical prints and paratexts. The influence of feminism is clearly evident too, but even more prominent are the turn to liturgical and other religious traditions as possible models for understanding literary forms and practices and the impact of new technology on the ways in which we can now approach the study of form. And, while the kinds of formalist criticism at work in Romantic Studies today have clearly learnt a lot from, and freely draw on, those schools of thought that marginalised the study of form in the 1970s and 1980s, they are mounting powerful challenges not only to that marginalisation but also to the agendas upon which it was based.

As Bernard Beatty says in Chapter 8, 'form is not an invention of formalists'. While we might disagree with the ways in which form has been studied in the past, by neglecting form we run the risk of making fundamental errors in the study of any literature. The chapters that follow highlight just how much there is to be gained – and how much is already being gained – by attending particularly to Romanticism and form.

Notes

1. See, for example: Geoffrey Hartman, *Beyond Formalism: Literary Essays 1958–1970* (New Haven and London: Yale University Press, 1970), pp. ix–xiii;

Harold Bloom, 'The Breaking of Form', in *Deconstruction and Criticism* (New York: Seabury Press, 1979), pp. 1–38, where Bloom announces his complete 'lack of interest in most aspects of what is called "form in poetry" ' (p. 2); Paul de Man, 'The Dead-End of Formalist Criticism', in *Blindness and Insight: Essays in the Rhetoric of Contemporary Criticism*, 2nd edn (London: Routledge, 1983), pp. 229–44; Jerome J. McGann, *The Beauty of Inflections: Literary Investigations in Historical Method and Theory* (Oxford: Oxford University Press, 1985), pp. 4–10, 15–66, 69–89.

2. Fredrick Jameson, *The Political Unconscious: Narrative as a Socially Symbolic Act* (Ithaca: Cornell University Press, 1981), p. 79.
3. See, for example: George Levine (ed.), *Aesthetics and Ideology* (New Brunswick: Rutgers University Press, 1994); James Soderholm (ed.), *Beauty and the Critic: Aesthetics in an Age of Cultural Studies* (Tuscaloose: University of Alabama Press, 1997); Tilottama Rajan and Julia M. Wright (eds), *Romanticism, History and the Possibilities of Genre* (Cambridge: Cambridge University Press, 1998); David H. Richter (ed.), *Ideology and Form in Eighteenth-Century Literature* (Lubbock: Texas Tech University Press, 1999); Isobel Armstrong, *The Radical Aesthetic* (Oxford: Blackwell, 2000); Michael P. Clark (ed.), *Revenge of the Aesthetic: The Place of Literature in Theory Today* (Berkeley: University of California Press, 2000); Susan J. Wolfson and Marshall Brown (eds), *Reading for Form*, Special issue of *Modern Language Quarterly*, 61:1 (March 2000).
4. Micheal O'Neill, *Romanticism and the Self-Conscious Poem* (Oxford: Clarendon Press, 1997), p. xv; Susan J. Wolfson, *Formal Charges: The Shaping of Poetry in British Romanticism* (Stanford: Stanford University Press, 1997), p. 2.
5. Nicholas Roe (ed.), *Romanticism: An Oxford Guide* (Oxford: Oxford University Press, 2005), pp. 273–590.

1
Romantic Indirection
Paul M. Curtis

One of the many significant pleasures available to readers of Romantic poetry is the uncertainty of not knowing exactly *where* one is as one proceeds through a poem. In so many Romantic lyrics, the reader becomes aware that he has become positively *mal*adjusted, perhaps even lost, *vis-à-vis* a poem's beginning, middle and end. Furthermore, and perhaps this is the key to the pleasure, this maladjustment, once apprehended by the reader, is there to be welcomed rather than resisted. To speak generally of English *belles-lettres* in the eighteenth and early nineteenth centuries, the pleasure of maladjustment is the result of complex changes in the poetical and philosophical attitudes to the sequence of ideas in the mind. The principal source of this pleasure is 'indirection', a word used to denote the deliberately dilatory progress through a poem which is particular to the poetry of English Romanticism. If one accepts that the reader is aware of his progress through a poem, even at first reading, then progress must be marked in some manner. Various poetical features such as prosody and rhyme, rhetorical features such as syntax and metaphor, and ideas of form through mythos (plot) serve as markers of progress.

Plot is often lazily described according to clichés of linearity: story-line or plot-line. In popular discourse we hear questions such as 'How does the story go?' or 'Did you follow the story?'. In examples such as these, not-so-neutral notions of space, of following the story through, carry the burden of summary. Such clichés, and the unfortunate habits of reading they tacitly encourage, are largely the result of a powerful but largely unquestioned notion of the linearity of plot. Assumptions of linearity beg the question that progress through a work conforms to a line abstracted from the plot. This Lockean notion is parodied rigorously by Sterne: 'In a word, my work is digressive and *progressive* too, – *and*

1

at the same time.'[1] Coleridge questions sequential hierarchies in 'The Eolian Harp' by describing the 'notes' of the harp as being 'long' and 'sequacious' (18).[2] What precisely might these adjectives of duration and order mean if the beginning or ending of each musical note is the function of the 'desultory breeze' (14)? The sequacious indirection of the harp becomes the model for the imaginative coalescences of present and past time in the poem. This is a long way from Paul Ricoeur's answer to the simple but important question, 'What does it mean to follow a story?': 'To follow a story, in effect, is to understand the successive actions, thoughts, and feelings in the story inasmuch as they present a particular "directedness" '.[3] Such an abstract notion of a story's linearity arranges expectations of directedness on the part of the reader. And the elements that are 'off' or that 'stray' from such a line are somehow secondary and so less worthy of critical regard. Not so in Romantic lyric poetry.

One consequence of rhetorical indirection, apart from the purely pleasurable, is its effect on habits of reading. In reference to the epigraph to *Childe Harold's Pilgrimage*, canto I, Frederick Garber makes the point that the 'job of any reader is to seek to possess the text, to take it up within himself. Put in a different perspective, reading is like traveling in that it is based on the desire to make the foreign part of oneself.'[4] However appropriate Garber's metaphor of travel for reading Byron might be, we might extend the job of the reader of Romantic lyrics to one beyond that of possession. Instead of reading simply as readers, Romantic poetry frequently compels us to read as writers would read. By placing the reader in a situation of uncertainty, mystery and doubt, without the crutch of 'consequitive reasoning', as Keats puts it, the reader invests more significantly in the consideration of form rather than the simpler notion of followability.[5] And this investment bears the fruit of pleasure.

This chapter seeks to identify how the rhetoric of Romantic-period verse 'moves' indirectly and to account, in part at least, for the pleasure of reading without spoiling it by doing so.

Polonius

The first Act of *Hamlet* comes to an end with Hamlet's ominous conclusion, 'The time is out of joint' (I, v, 196).[6] The context shifts in the next scene to offer a respite from the macabre supernaturalism of Act One. Polonius, concerned with the reputation of his son now in Paris, commands Reynaldo to spy on Laertes. As we have rapidly come to expect from Polonius, he uses puffed up language. In other

words, he uses a circumlocutory description of circumlocution: 'By
[...] encompassment and drift of question' (II, i, 10). On the one
hand, Shakespeare in this scene seeks to dramatise indirection. Intention and resolution, however, are comically mismatched in Polonius
since he has trouble controlling words disingenuously gone 'astray'.
On the other hand, and more to our purpose here, Shakespeare seeks
to dramatise the linguistic potential of indirection. Indirection is not
simply the ironic obliquity of double-entendre, innuendo, or of speaking
asklent. It is through the copiousness and plenitude implied by indirection, we suspect, that the 'full stretch of human sensibility' might be
expressed.[7]

The rhetorical effectiveness of Polonius' speech increases consider-
ably because its syntactical sequence enacts its meaning. With imaginative literalism, the reader's eyes and ears pass in and then out of line
68.[8] Shakespeare employs the figure of chiasmus, whereby a pair of
syntactical elements appears to cross each other as the verse proceeds
from beginning to end: 'By indirections find directions out' (II, i, 66).[9]
Each half of the line's syntax mirrors the sequence of the other. The
mirroring is not semantic, of course, since the prefix 'in' aligns with its
opposite 'out' and vice versa. Such is the shape of the line's teasing asym-
metry. Shakespeare names and performs indirection through a chiastic
and equilibrated syntax. The line's syntactical logic, its direction from
left to right, is also anti-logical, due to its criss-cross indirection. The
second half of the line works backward to reconstitute the first. Although
opposites in meaning, 'in' and 'out' are syntactical equals as units of
a chiastic pair; and, as befits opposites, the prepositions are situated at
either 'end' of the line giving it the illusion of spatial volume. 'Out',
moreover, appears at the terminal limit of the line and calls attention
to itself as limit, 'making the preposition a directive for reading'.[10] We
have here, therefore, a directive for reading indirection. The movements
in and out direct the reader to the potential of indirection in poetical
language beyond the immediate references within this line. The formal
wit in the chiasmus here is a function of an order heightened to an artful
disorder.[11]

Much of the formal innovation in Romantic poetry is due to indirection, which we might define for the moment as a poetical playing
with the sequencing of ideas. At the level of the micro-argument,
which is the level of the line, is an etymological pun on the Latin
word for a line of poetry, *versus*. Even though the unit of the poem's
script is the line, and lines proceed in orderly and grammatical fashion
from left to right, from line to line, and down the page, the words

often work 'versus' or against the linear notions of sequence of the line in which they appear. The experience of reading Polonius on indirection occurs at the level of the line of verse, the motion of which is straightforward but the significance of which is not. The poetic line as a unit of meaning for Romantic poetry assumes less and less a linear form. One useful example of a perfectly linear and therefore dysfunctional language occurs by way of satiric attack on Castlereagh in Byron's *Don Juan*:

> Oh, gentle ladies! should you seek to know
>   The import of this diplomatic phrase,
> Bid Ireland's Londonderry's Marquess show
>   His parts of speech; and in the strange displays
> Of that odd string of words, all in a row,
>   Which none divine, and every one obeys,
> Perhaps you may pick out some queer *no*-meaning,
> Of that weak wordy harvest the sole gleaning. (IX, st. 49)[12]

The death of language as a vital force of communication and the expression of Byron's humanism is imaged here by the linearity of Castlereagh's odd string of words. And the hit is palpable since Byron's neologistic '*no*-meaning' ridicules the string of words that, precisely because of its linearity, signifies 'queerly' below the absolute zero of *un*-meaning.[13] Intellectual eunuchs are prisoners of the straight line, it would seem, whereas Romantic poets create indirect ones.

Pope

Contrary to the poetry of Romantic indirection, the reader knows exactly 'where' s/he is in a poem by Pope due to several types of sequence generated by, among other things, metaphor, narrative and syntax.[14] The nuances of Pope's metaphoric, narrative and allusive syntax also serve to situate Pope the artist and the art of his poems *vis-à-vis* tradition. This is the case, for example, in Pope's first published poem, his pastoral 'Spring' (1709). Here, as in the *Pastorals* generally, we see Pope's complex consideration of what the pastoral form is; and, in a more profound sense, of the forms that creativity assumes in poetry at large. In this way, the first subject of Pope's *Pastorals* is poetic creativity.[15]

The narrative frame of reference of 'Spring' is dual since Pope introduces the Arcadian locale with a dedicatory wink at one of his contemporaries, Sir William Trumbull. The 'Two Swains', Daphnis and Strephon, 'whom love kept wakeful' (18–19), appear at line 18.[16] The two duel in song for two prizes under the watchful eye and attentive ear of Damon, the sub-titular hero of the poem and Pope's first critic of pastoral poetry. Since the songs of the shepherds alternate, the formal progress through the narration is antiphonal and strongly directed.

STREPHON

> Sing then, and *Damon* shall attend the Strain,
> While yon slow Oxen turn the furrow'd Plain.
> Here the bright Crocus and blue Vi'let glow;
> Here Western Winds on breathing Roses blow.
> I'll stake yon' Lamb that near the Fountain plays,
> And from the Brink his dancing Shade surveys. (29–34)

A lamb capable of *surveying* his own reflection in the water is striking. A poetic syntax that seems to anticipate its own progress across the verse paragraphs is more so. For example, every contest must have its rules, and a contest in song is no exception. The very form of Pope's syntax, however, assumes the shape of these rules thanks to his use of chiasmus in way very different from Shakespeare's Polonius:

DAMON

> Then sing by turns, by turns the Muses sing,
> Now Hawthorns blossom, now the Daisies spring,
> Now Leaves the Trees, and Flow'rs adorn the Ground;
> Begin, the Vales shall ev'ry Note rebound. (41–4)

The imperative of Damon's first line is performative since the contest begins with the utterance of his command. Whereas our Shakespearean example of chiasmus accommodates the opposites of direction and indirection, Pope's chiasmus leads into the contest and implies thereby the ineluctable harmonies of sequence. And since the image of the Lamb mirrored in the fountain is in turn 'reflected' in the aural image of an echo, 'ev'ry Note rebound', Pope's syntax gives the impression of watching, hearing and recapitulating itself as it proceeds. In the poem's last stanza Damon generously offers each contestant the other's wager. His chiastic conclusion caps the sequence of the competition leaving the songs of each player in perfect synchrony:

DAMON

Cease to contend, for (*Daphnis*) I decree
The Bowl to *Strephon*, and the Lamb to thee:
Blest Swains, whose Nymphs in ev'ry Grace excell;
Blest Nymphs, whose Swains those Graces sing so well! (93–6)

The couplet's chiasmus images the symmetry of a tie, but also the notion of a tie that dispenses with the rules of the contest. Daphnis and Strephon are reflections of each other, reflections of a single ideal. Since Damon is the referee of the pastoral competition, Pope gives his name to the poem's subtitle signifying the simultaneous birth of poetry and criticism.

Coleridge

In *Biographia Literaria*, Coleridge gives his reaction to eighteenth-century poetry in general and to Pope's couplet art in particular. Coleridge objected to the heroic couplet because the reader looks for a '*point* [...] at the end of each second line' (9).[17] Although the term 'point' is here a geometrical abstraction in the service of literary criticism, it implies a triple hiatus of grammar, logic and meaning. The couplet is a formal arrangement of lines on the space of the page which encourages a momentary pause permitting rhyme and reason to catch each other up. This terminal point makes the progress of reading the poem rigidly cumulative, similar to that of crossing a stream with the help of equidistant stepping stones. Before taking the step into the next couplet, one's 'footing' in the couplet of the moment must be firm.[18] Coleridge uses the phrase 'conjunction-disjunctive' to describe the effect of the couplet as one of 'thoughts *translated* into the language of poetry'; and he introduces the phrase as a 'grammatical metaphor, a *conjunction-disjunctive* of epigrams' (9, his emphasis). Since Coleridge denotes his metaphor as grammatical, his metaphor *identifies* a couplet's internal grammatical coherence with an incoherence in motion from one couplet to the next. The motion of Pope's couplets is highly sequential within each couplet, but arbitrary across couplets. Northrop Frye has observed that 'what words do best, do most accurately, and do most powerfully, is hang together'.[19] Coleridge would agree that they hang together in sequences within

Pope's couplets; the disjunction he disdains occurs between Pope's couplets.

Just prior to his critique of Pope's couplet, Coleridge discusses his intellectual debt to the teachings of the Rev. James Bowyer, who taught him that

> poetry, even of the loftiest and, seemingly, that of the wildest odes, had a logic of its own as severe as that of science; and more difficult, because more subtle, more complex, and dependent upon more and more fugitive causes. In the truly great poets, he would say, there is a reason assignable, not only for every word, but for the *position* of every word. (3, my emphasis)

On the one hand, then, we see in *Biographia Literaria* Coleridge's sensitivity to the reading experience as one that is at every moment directed by a logic of composition, and, on the other hand and more particularly, Coleridge's Romantic critique of the 'pointed' direction of Pope's couplet art. Elsewhere in the *Biographia*, as we shall see presently, Coleridge offers the image of his own mind in the act of composition. It is here that images of indirection elucidate the mysteries of composition.

Coleridge's critique of Hartley in *Biographia Literaria* offers the curious instance of a polemic that produces additional philosophical insights for its author, insights gained, we have the impression, as a result of the complex associative process that shapes the *Biographia* itself. In Chapter 7, Coleridge reacts against the 'paralogisms' – the fallacious reasoning – he finds in Hartley's treatment of time. Coleridge's analogy of the water-beetle demonstrates how the iconography of the mind had changed by his time from a linear configuration to one that acknowledges discontinuity, indirection and alternating sequence. Thinking for Coleridge is a constant action against the force of the present and a function of associations. To jump requires an active voluntary movement up against gravity, which is followed by a 'partly voluntary' movement down to land on the spot already chosen. These actions require both active and passive states of mind and body. Coleridge continues the analogy to include the act of composition; and then offers an image he believes could be called 'the emblem of the mind's self experience in the act of thinking':

> Now let a man watch his mind while he is composing; or, to take a still more common case, while he is trying to recollect a name; and he

will find the process completely analogous. Most of my readers will have observed a small water-insect on the surface of rivulets which throws a cinque-spotted shadow fringed with prismatic colours on the sunny bottom of the brook; and will have noticed how the little animal wins its way up against the stream, by alternate pulses of active and passive motion, now resisting the current, and now yielding to it in order to gather strength and a momentary fulcrum for a further propulsion. This is no unapt emblem of the mind's self experience in the act of thinking. (72)

Coleridge images the aleatory progress of the mind and demonstrates such progress stylistically. Coleridge's prose moves from the mental world to the physical by way of associative analogy. The active/passive motion of Coleridge's water-boatman creates progress out of its struggle against a contrary current. Analogously, the mind struggles against the force of contemporaneity in the acts of memory or composition, alternately resisting and releasing to produce an erratic sort of progress. The faculty that mediates between this active/passive action is the 'imagination', more particularly, 'on the subject of poetry [...] a superior degree of [that] faculty, joined to a superior voluntary controul over it' (72). The image the insect gives us is one of repetitiveness but not repetition. Progress is gained, lost, retraced; and the insect's motion overlays the motion of the stream. The force expended is much greater by virtue of the resistance against it. As a complex image of contrary motions, the insect seems static on the surface of the brook since he must 'move' at least as fast as the water to stay 'still'. As an image of progress, mere stasis signifies considerable movement. Coleridge's insect suggests how rich a static moment is, and how each is hard-won instead of following automatically in succession.[20] The water-boatman casts its shadow into the brook, suggesting the 'depth' of a moment. Its diminutive size casts a grand shadow; and, taken altogether, the image artfully explores the temporal and spatial relationships essential to contemporaneity. Coleridge's analogy for the mind in the act of composition helps the reader read as a writer writes.

Cadiz

This chapter began with a discussion of the impression of sequence produced by a poem and, in particular, the pleasure of maladjustment produced in the reader by the sequential indirection of many Romantic poems. Polonius's chiasmus on indirection alerted us to the possibilities of reading indirectly. We then construed indirection as implying a copiousness or plenitude inherent in language, one that exists beyond rectilinear sequences of language. The discussion turned to examples of the intellectual texts of the eighteenth century by way of understanding the importance of sequence in the association of ideas. Before turning to examples of Romantic poetry, we should note that our initial question of where the reader is in a poem has evolved. The question has broadened from being one about where the reader is in the poem to one about the reader's relation to the figure of time the poem creates. Keats's 'green-rob'd senators' in *Hyperion: A Fragment* (73) or Coleridge's 'Ancestral voices prophesying war' in 'Kubla Khan' (30) are examples of indirection in time.[21] Figuring 'green-rob'd' trees as *senators* within the temporal context of a Titan's fall anticipates a Rome that is in the poet's past but in his poem's future. Our progress through the chronography of the poem is at odds with the sequence of chronology that we share, in part at least, with Keats. The question, therefore, becomes not only one of 'where' the reader is in the poem but also one of 'when' the reader is. The solecism might be truer to the purpose since Romantic indirection interrogates the various spatial concepts of ideas 'moving' through the mind that are used – from Aristotle to Augustine and Locke – to generate the idea of time. We know less where we are in a Romantic poem because of the temporal uncertainties within it. The fictive experience generated in Romantic poetry depends in part upon temporal forms, and temporal indirection affects the reader's notion of time. Ricoeur pursues the thesis that *'time becomes human to the extent that it is articulated through a narrative mode, and narrative attains its full meaning when it becomes a condition of temporal existence'*.[22] Ricoeur, we note, employs chiasmus in order to communicate the retrospective nature of any conceptual movement forward.

In many well-known Romantic poems, the reader is silently urged, even compelled, to question his/her situation *vis-à-vis* a poem or, rather, what that situation might be, as a result of the progress from idea to idea, and this even at first reading. Keats's sonnet on Chapman's Homer, for example, begins with the idea of the reality of a book, Chapman's translation. It proceeds to the world of Chapman's source – more specifically, how that world would appear in Homer's head – via the Homeric epithet 'deep-browed Homer' (6). The poem concludes with the idea of water via Cortez as he 'stared at the Pacific' (12). The speed and scope of the transitions are remarkable, and the reader is pleasurably maladjusted within these transitions, all the while, however, searching out the clue to the poem's logic. The uncertainty we feel about where or when we are at line 14 is one powerful attraction of reading. According to Frye, we are drawn to read because we find in books precisely what cannot be found in reality.[23] And in Keats's Chapman sonnet, the poem's indirection creates a form of time never yet experienced in the real world but which might serve to make sense of that world. The utility of contrasting the direction of Pope's pastoral 'Spring' to the indirection of Romantic lyric poetry here might seem dubious. Yet Keats's 'Ode on a Grecian Urn' invokes the pastoral genre – 'Cold Pastoral!' (st. 5) – and Coleridge's 'Frost at Midnight' invokes the imminent futurity of 'all seasons' (65), while in both poems chiasmus is key. Here, however, chiasmus becomes a scheme of indirection that provides a climax of prophetic amplitude.

Keats's ode tests the limits of two art forms: the ode as a verbal medium which occurs in time and the urn as a plastic medium which occurs in space. The where and when of the reader are therefore engaged with to an unusually high degree. The poem moves from one stanza to the next despite the stasis of the urn. Is there a directedness that determines this movement, or do we simply follow the motion of the speaker's eye over the surface of the urn, or beyond, in, for example, Stanza 4?

> Who are these coming to the sacrifice?
>   To what green altar, O mysterious priest,
> Lead'st thou that heifer lowing at the skies,
>   And all her silken flanks with garlands drest?
> What little town by river or sea shore,
>   Or mountain-built with peaceful citadel,
>   Is emptied of this folk, this pious morn?
> And, little town, thy streets for evermore
>   Will silent be; and not a soul to tell
>   Why thou art desolate, can e'er return.

As Helen Vendler comments, 'Three times the poet "enters" a scene on the urn: but, as I see the progress of the poem, he enters each successive scene with a different view, as spectator, of what the urn is and what it does'.[24] Following the many questions and the many images of movement, stanza 4 sharpens the focus on where and when since it is a meditation upon the impossibility of return. The notion of chronological sequence becomes inadequate. Without a before or an after, the chronology becomes 'aching time! [...] moments big as years!'(*Hyperion*, I, 64). Keats, given the fugacity of things, would stop time at the still centre of his ode.[25]

With a deft variation upon the pastoral antiphony we discussed in Pope, the chiastic utterance of the urn completes the question–answer circuit:

> Cold Pastoral!
> When old age shall this generation waste,
> Thou shalt remain, in midst of other woe
> Than ours, a friend to man, to whom thou say'st,
> 'Beauty is truth, truth beauty, – that is all
>   Ye know on earth, and all ye need to know'. (st. 5)

The third-person present tense of the verb 'to be' is understood through ellipsis in the second element of the chiasmus 'Beauty is truth, truth beauty'. In the previous examples of chiasmus that we have noted, the second half reconfigures the first. In this case, the erasure of the verb in its second clause reconfigures truth and beauty without the prior verb and the time it signifies. Thus freed from chronological time, the urn's utterance, imagined in some obscure future, is heard 'now'.

In Coleridge's 'Frost at Midnight', the reader follows the speaker's meditations upon the burning 'film' in his grate (15). These meditations take the reader from Coleridge's reminiscences of his boyhood to his prophetic utterance before his infant boy. The frost of the poem's title is mentioned only twice in the 74-line body of the poem, in lines 1 and 72. If we arrange the two lines one after another in isolation, they form the sequence: 'The Frost performs its secret ministry [...] Or if the secret ministry of frost'. Although this arrangement is not, strictly speaking, an example of rhetorical chiasmus, it arranges a chiastic frame around the poem. The forward-backwardness of chiasmus recalls Coleridge's analogy of the mind in the act of composition in the *Biographia* and illustrates the formal indirection of the poem as a whole. As we read between lines 1 and 72, attentive to the meditations of the speaker before us, the frost performs its secret ministry beyond our awareness. The 'flame [in the grate] burns and consumes, eating away at time, the frost, absent but not forgotten, builds ice palaces'.[26] Within the broadly chiastic strategy of the poem, these palaces of ice are brought to the reader's mind only after the prophecy is uttered:

> so shalt thou see and hear
> The lovely shapes and sounds intelligible
> Of that eternal language, which thy God
> Utters, who from eternity doth teach

Himself in all, and all things in himself.
Great universal Teacher! He shall mould
Thy spirit, and by giving make it ask. (58–64, my emphasis)

The chiasmus (in italics) occurs within the context of God's 'eternal language', which is the subject of the speaker's prophecy. The speaker's meditations, therefore, are to the secret ministry of frost as his concluding prophecy is to God's eternal language.

In *The Rhetoric of Romantic Prophecy*, Ian Balfour makes important distinctions between the specific genre of prophecy, spanning but 200 years in the context of the Old Testament, and the diverse examples of it in the history of nineteenth- and twentieth-century Western literatures. The easiest understanding of prophecy – the prediction of events in future time – is, according to Balfour, erroneous. Prophecy is not simply prediction but a type of discourse that is at once highly metaphorical, often highly obscure, uniquely repetitive and, finally, one in which the effects might diverge from the content. In the prophetic books of the Old Testament, a prophet utters a word that is original to the divinity. In effect the prophet repeats the words of another. And the idea of repetition is crucial here in the sense that the utterance delivered by the prophet is a form of citation but without the quotation marks.[27] Despite the apparent immediacy in the 'now' of a prophetic utterance, the temporal frame of the words uttered by the prophet belongs to some prior or past tense. Discourse pertaining to the future, through its repetition as a 'citation', is, therefore, a function of the past. 'Prophecy', Balfour summarises, 'is a call and a claim much more than it is a prediction, a call oriented towards a present that is not present'.[28] At the conclusions of such poems as Coleridge's 'Frost at Midnight' and Keats's 'Ode on a Grecian Urn' prophecy *aims* at a future that is imagined in a present context that is yet to be.[29]

As Alan Rawes has pointed out, however, in *Childe Harold's Pilgrimage*, I and II,

> Like Wordsworth, Byron can write lyrical sequences in a meditative mode which foregrounds the speaker and which creates the impression of moving freely and intimately with the 'thought ... and feeling' of that speaker. But where Wordsworth necessarily limits himself to a single experience, or the achievement of a particular mood, Byron's lyricism can and does move perpetually between multiple experiences and multiple moods.[30]

Whereas Keats and Coleridge, and Wordsworth for that matter, seek through temporal indirection what I have called a prophetic amplitude, the speakers of Byron's *ottava rima* poems rely upon the weight and pith of human experience. Even the reliance upon this experience threatens, however, to swell beyond the limits of any sort of linear plot. Byron chooses the terminal line of *Beppo* to maximise the retrospective irony: 'stories somehow lengthen when begun'. They do lengthen, especially in *Don Juan*, as narrative indirection produces a verbal world of unprecedented copiousness and plenitude.

The Byron of *Don Juan*, as opposed to his much admired Pope, writes a type of poetry where dislocations of sequence, as Garber notes, produce rhetorical liberation:

If there is a sense in which we are prey to linearity there is another in which we can play with linearity, divert its incessant energies, if only for a while. We can unmake linearity just as it unmakes us, and we can do so in a place, the stanza, that we ourselves have made. In Byron's mature ironic mode the mind has found its proper vocation: it mocks linearity by mimicking its effects upon us, and as it mocks its natural enemy it frees itself, temporarily, from full subservience to linearity.[31]

Balachandra Rajan compresses into one sentence a summary of the entire poem: 'He falls from innocence, is shipwrecked into paradise, is sold into slavery after the obliteration of that paradise, survives harem intrigues, war, the lusts of an empress, and the manners of English society.'[32] The summary, however extreme in its reduction, does describe the poem's astonishing sequence. Rajan comments further that *Don Juan* is the poem (in his survey of the English fragment) that most closely approaches the condition of 'sheer succession'. 'Somewhere', he says,

in the field we are surveying there should be a place for a poem based on sheer succession, which is not approximative, transformational or developmental, which is not propelled by its nature to the magnetic north of a final cause, and which is not driven forward by the prospect of emergent understandings or even the hunger for those understandings. *Don Juan* comes closest to being such a poem. The patterns in *Don Juan* are coalescences brought about by the repetitiousness of events, but the repetitions do not accumulate sufficiently to support a theory of repetitiousness. The whole is not privileged since there is insufficient evidence that any whole is being sought, either by the protagonist or by the increasingly dominant authorial voice. On the other hand the fragment is not privileged, except implicitly. Explicit privileging would arise out of the fragment's successful resistance to incorporation. In *Don Juan* there is no clearly discernible incorporative effort.[33]

While Garber insists upon Byron's scepticism of an organic totality and much of Rajan's commentary contributes significantly to the debate about the poem's unfinished form, I cannot accept the argument that 'there is insufficient evidence that any whole is being sought'. Granted, Byron would deny the legitimacy of any whole that is the product of systemic thought.[34] He seeks, however, to include in *Don Juan* 'life's infinite variety' (XV, st. 19), a whole much grander than that which literary commentary generally seeks to quantify. Byron's inclusiveness is more daring, therefore, and the affective texture of the verse invites the risk of a magnificent failure rather than the satisfactions of a mediocre success. Recalling the etched lines that organise the seasons on Pope's pastoral bowl, Byron's marshalling of infinite variety does not abide by a line of discerning that would delineate a whole or set one off against another. Garber's and Rajan's scepticism regarding closure, and the theories this implies, makes them reluctant to recognise the incorporative efforts that do exist in the poem despite its non-linearity. In the English cantos, the architectural form of 'Norman Abbey', with all its flaws, disproportions and recollections of Newstead, could rightly serve as an allegory of the form of *Don Juan* in its entirety:

> Huge halls, long galleries, spacious chambers, join'd
>   By no quite lawful marriage of the Arts,
> Might shock a Connoisseur; but when combined,
>   Form'd a whole which, irregular in parts,
> Yet left a grand impression on the mind,
>   At least of those whose eyes are in their hearts.
> We gaze upon a Giant for his stature,
> Nor judge at first if all be true to Nature. (XIII, st. 67)

Almost everywhere behind the verse we sense the force of thought, the wisdom of hope and the vast comprehension of a mind engaged in the creation of an 'anatomy' (II, st. 216). For this 'Giant' of a poem to be complete or whole would deny its aspiration to an unceasing inclusiveness and changeability.

Each emotion or action in the poem is a discrete particular held before the reader's attention, and this notwithstanding the panorama which serves as a backdrop to each. Without the hierarchical patterning of a cumulative logic, these particulars are often presented within a digression or within the context of imminent futurity. Through verses in a parallel structure, images turn back on themselves, a sharply indirect motion which gives the impression of the speaker's knowledge coming in a rush rather than with the pre-meditated retrospection of repetition:

> Haidee was Nature's bride, and knew not this;
>   Haidee was Passion's child, born where the sun
> Showers triple light, and scorches even the kiss
>   Of his gazelle-eyed daughters; she was one
> Made but to love, to feel that she was his
>   Who was her chosen: what was said or done
> Elsewhere was nothing – She had nought to fear,
> Hope, care, nor love beyond, her heart beat *here*. (II, st. 202)

In the stanza's first two lines, the metaphors identifying Haidee as Passion's child and Nature's bride are in parallel. The repetition of the syntax emphasises but, in so doing, attenuates the grammatical function of bride and child. The genitives associate unencumbered by causality, as it were, signifying desire and possession as functions of each other: 'to feel that she was his / Who was her chosen'. With a fine irony, the spatial clarity that we usually expect of the deictic 'here', the stanza's last word, dissolves into the emotion that defines space as a condition of that emotion. In this way, parallelism performs an incantatory attack upon sequence rather than merely repeating syntactical patterns.

As opposed to the couplet of Pope, moreover, Byron's line is the narrative unit but without the control of the Popean caesura. The lines are often choppy, communicating emotion and appearing as if, reminiscent of Berkeley's idealist philosophy, they were created in an instant:

> But words are things, and a small drop of ink,
>   Falling like dew, upon a thought, produces
> That which makes thousands, perhaps millions, think;
>   'Tis strange, the shortest letter which man uses
> Instead of speech, may form a lasting link

> Of ages; to what straits old Time reduces
> Frail man, when paper – even a rag like this,
> Survives himself, his tomb, and all that's his. (III, st. 88)

Despite the poem's wealth of historical anecdote and despite the power of an organising mind behind it all, *Don Juan* does not cultivate a sense of cumulative knowledge. Its allusions do not organise a monumental regression through the literary tradition as Pope's seem to do in every line. Byron's mammoth fragment is at times obscure, as if it were written by one of the first 'bards' (I, st. 221). Despite its lack of cumulative knowledge, the poem boasts the comprehensiveness of an 'anatomy', but one that is composed of 'A non-descript and ever-varying rhyme, / A versified Aurora Borealis' (VII, st. 2). *Don Juan's* persona, with sublime nonchalance, flaunts the poem's capacity to contain life's infinite variety and flouts the conventions of the genre of his own devising, the 'Epic Satire' (XIV, st. 99):

> I perch upon an humbler promontory,
> Amidst life's infinite variety:
> With no great care for what is nicknamed glory,
> But speculating as I cast mine eye
> On what may suit or may not suit my story,
> And never straining hard to versify,
> I rattle on exactly as I'd talk
> With any body in a ride or walk. (XV, st. 19)

Whereas the reader is secure within the sequential progress of the poetry of Pope, the first-time reader of Byron is never sure what will happen next, and this uncertainty – however irrational it may feel at the moment – is at the root of Byron's rhetoric of liberation. The rhetoric of liberation is not confined to a political expression of Byron's liberalism even though many examples of such expressions are readily available. Byron's rhetoric of liberation is embedded in his use of the English language in which he took such pride. It extends as well to the improvised way his words 'hang together'. The momentum of the rhetoric renders plot a subordinate level of signification. In the midst of this liberation, the poem's indirection communicates the freedom of the creative imagination thanks to its freedom from the exigencies of cause and effect.

In what might well seem a paradox, by indirection Byron finds directions out to connections that have rhetorical power precisely because they are non-linear or out of sequence. He even taunts the reader to find them. One such example is the Cadiz sequence in canto II. Early in the second canto, we visit Cadiz:

5

I said, that Juan had been sent to Cadiz –
A pretty town, I recollect it well –
'Tis there a mart of the colonial trade is,
(Or was, before Peru learn'd to rebel)
And such sweet girls – I mean, such graceful ladies,
Their very walk would make your bosom swell;
I can't describe it, though so much it strike,
Nor liken it – I never saw the like:

6

An Arab horse, a stately stag, a barb
New broke, a cameleopard, a gazelle,
No – none of these will do; – and then their garb!
Their veil and petticoat – Alas! to dwell
Upon such things would very near absorb
A canto – then their feet and ankles – well,
Thank heaven I've got no metaphor quite ready,
(And so my sober Muse – come, let's be steady –

7

Chaste Muse! – well, if you must, you must) – the veil
Thrown back a moment with the glancing hand,
While the o'erpowering eye, that turns you pale,
Flashes into the heart: – All sunny land
Of love! When I forget you, may I fail
To – say my prayers – but never was there plann'd
A dress through which the eyes give such a volley,
Excepting the Venetian Fazzioli.

8

But to our tale: the Donna Inez sent
Her son to Cadiz only to embark;
To stay there had not answer'd her intent,

But why? – we leave the reader in the dark –
'Twas for a voyage that the young man was meant,
    As if a Spanish ship were Noah's ark,
To wean him from the wickedness of earth,
And send him like a dove of promise forth.

9

Don Juan bade his valet pack his things
    According to direction, then received
A lecture and some money: for four springs
    He was to travel.

With lascivious innuendo, Byron wrote of Cadiz as 'the first spot in the creation',[35] and its reputation in his poetry is one of notoriety.[36] Cadiz is a place of strong (and 'swelling') impressions, so strong that the speaker retreats disingenuously from description: 'I can't describe it'. Since its powerful attractions are passed over, Cadiz seems to barely register. It has all the substance of a theatrical flat in a way similar to Haidee's island. The Greek isle of the Haidee-Juan segment serves Byron as a prop to demonstrate that an ideal and a real love are really much the same since they are both products of the human imagination. On the one hand, Cadiz serves Byron as a trigger for a digression on the semiotics of seduction. On the other, it figures in a larger sequence of indirection, the knowledge of which must be kept from the reader by leaving him 'in the dark'. The Cadiz digression ends with an allusion to Polonius's advice to Laertes as he sets off to Paris.[37] The city of Cadiz resurfaces, as it were, in the subsequent episode of Juan's shipwreck. Tragedy does not preclude farce in Byron's world; neither does disease humour:

And next they thought upon the master's mate,
    As fattest; but he saved himself, because,
Besides being much averse from such a fate,
    There were some other reasons; the first was,
He had been rather indisposed of late,
    And that which chiefly proved his saving clause,
Was a small present made to him at Cadiz,
By general subscription of the ladies. (II, st. 81)

The legacy of Cadiz, for the master's mate at least, gives pause to the basest instinct for human survival. By indirections find directions out.

In the midst of infinite variety, Byron creates a peculiar logic in which he dwells upon the odd 'conjunction of vista and particular'.[38] In the Cadiz sequence, Byron forgoes loco-description for the wisdom and, dare one say, the hope of irony.

Envoi

In his famous letter of 16 October 1819, Byron performs an aggressive and self-serving bit of ventriloquism upon his interlocutor, Douglas Kinnaird. Byron's letter is the written version of how he insists Kinnaird construe *Don Juan*. 'As to "Don Juan" – confess – confess – you dog – and be candid – that it is the sublime of *that there* sort of writing – it may be bawdy – but is it not good English? – it may be profligate – but is it not life, is it not *the thing*?'[39] Byron's command to confess and be candid is followed first by the oblique confession that the poem is bawdy and profligate and secondly by the 'candid' estimation of poem's three criteria of achievement. The poem's good English, its representation of life and its being *the thing* are the one-two-three triple constituents of the sublime of *that there* sort of writing. The first and third of these criteria might appear to be cancelled out in the sense that the third, the noun 'thing', is the least differentiated word in the entire language. Yet, Byron insists first and firmly upon the poem's good English. In most examples of usage, the noun 'thing' is slack English because of its catch-all convenience. Byron renders 'thing' specific, however, by means of the definite article which gives the phrase the idiomatic force of flash language. His poem is the catch-all thing precisely because it sets a standard so inclusive that this standard can only be suggested rather than named. Moreover, in the metre of Byron's epistolary prose, the pyrrhic 'the thing' chimes with the previous pyrrhic 'that there', another example of Byronic rhetorical obliquity, yet another and this time more specific reference to genre. As a generic label, 'that there sort of writing' is specifically vague; but as is the case with 'is it not the thing', the reader understands how the indirection of the phrase is *apropos*. Byron uses the sublime to describe the experimental *Don Juan* as the highest of the comic or the highest of the low type of writing. Clear in Byron's usage of a term of classical literary criticism is the implication that Byron's 'low' writing surpasses the highest of the high type – which leaves us with the poem's 'is it not life'. As the second of the three criteria, it is the 'centre' of the sequence and partakes of the other two. 'Is it not life' refers doubly to the scope, the 'thingness' of humanity represented in the poem, as well as to the poem's tremendous vitality, its good English, in the portrayal of humanity. And its 'life', like the manner of its representation, is perhaps the only genre that matters – the genre of the versified Aurora Borealis.

Notes

1. Laurence Sterne, *The Life and Opinions of Tristram Shandy, Gentleman*, ed. by Ian Watt (Boston: Houghton Mifflin, 1965), pp. 54–5.
2. Quotations from Coleridge's poetry are taken from *Coleridge: Poetical Works*, ed. by Ernest Hartley Coleridge (Oxford: Oxford University Press, 1969). Line references are given after quotations in the text.
3. Paul Ricoeur, *Time and Narrative*, trans. by Kathleen McLaughlin and David Pellauer, 3 vols (Chicago and London: University of Chicago Press, 1984), I, p. 150.
4. Frederick Garber, *Self, Text, and Romantic Irony: The Example of Byron* (Princeton: Princeton University Press, 1988), p. 4. Elsewhere, and opposed to the argument here, Garber describes the rhythm of Harold's acts as 'linear, an incessant forward drive' (p. 24).
5. Keats's 'uncertainties, Mysteries, doubts' appears in the famous passage on 'Negative Capability' in the letter to George and Thomas Keats of December 1817, 'Consequitive reasoning' in the letter to Benjamin Bailey of 22 November 1817 (*The Letters of John Keats 1814–1821*, ed. by H. E. Robbins, 2 vols (Cambridge, Mass.: Harvard University Press, 1958), I, pp. 183–5, 192–3).
6. All quotations from *Hamlet* are taken from the Arden Shakespeare, 3rd series, ed. by Harold Jenkins (London: Methuen, 1982). Act, scene and line references follow quotations in the text.
7. 'The full stretch of human sensibility' is a phrase I have adapted from the Canadian poet Don Coles' first novel, *Doctor Bloom's Story* (Toronto: Alfred A. Knopf, 2004), p. 279, itself a study in narrative indirection.
8. On performatives see J. L. Austin's *How to Do Things with Words* (Cambridge, Mass.: Harvard University Press, 1967), as well as Derrida's critique of Austin in his 'Signature Event Context' (*Margins of Philosophy*, trans. by Alan Bass (Chicago: University of Chicago Press, 1982), pp. 307–30). Christopher Ricks writes on allusion as performative in his *Allusion to the Poets* (Oxford: Oxford University Press, 2002).
9. 'Chiasmus': a 'grammatical "crossing" in which the order of words in one of two parallel clauses is inverted in the other' (*OED*). Also see Lee A. Sonnino, *A Handbook to Sixteenth-Century Rhetoric* (London: Routledge & Kegan Paul, 1968), p. 199.
10. Susan J. Wolfson, *Formal Charges: The Shaping of Poetry in British Romanticism* (Stanford: Stanford University Press, 1997), p. 38. The context of the discussion is the preposition 'down' in 'To Spring' from Blake's *Poetical Sketches*.
11. Jacques Derrida speaks of the 'chiasmus effect' in the context of Condillac's *Essay*. According to the effect, Condillac's metaphysics, which is the second member in the chiastic pair of Western philosophy, 'methodically reconstitute[s] the generative principles' of the 'unconscious empiricism' of Aristotle's first philosophy (*The Archaeology of the Frivolous:*

Reading Condillac, trans. by John P. Leavey Jr (Pittsburgh: Duquesne University Press, 1980), p. 35). For our purposes, syntactical movement forward is not only retrospective – it also refigures the antecedent clause.

12. All quotations from *Don Juan* are taken from *Lord Byron: The Complete Poetical Works*, ed. by Jerome J. McGann, 7 vols (Oxford: Clarendon Press, 1980–93), V. Canto and stanza references are given in the text.

13. See Frederick Garber's fine discussion of this passage as satire in *Self, Text, and Romantic Irony: The Example of Byron*, pp. 277–82.

14. See as well 'knot' and 'plot' in Paul de Man's 'Epistemology of Metaphor', *Critical Inquiry*, 5 (1978), pp. 13–30.

15. See Paul Alpers, 'What is Pastoral?', *Critical Inquiry*, 8 (1982), pp. 437–60, for a summary of the critical history of the term.

16. Quotations from Pope are taken from *The Poems of Alexander Pope*, ed. by John Butt (London: Methuen, 1965). Line references are given in the text.

17. Quotations from *Biographia Literaria* are taken from *Biographia Literaria, or the Biographical Sketches of my Literary Life and Opinions*, ed. by George Watson (London: Dent & Sons, 1975). Page references follow quotations in the text.

18. See Ruth Salvaggio's 'Time, Space, and the Couplet', *Philological Quarterly*, 62 (1983), pp. 95–108. Salvaggio approaches the couplet from the perspective of 'sequential reading' (p. 98) and demonstrates its efficacy by contrasting *Absalom and Achitophel* and *Essay on Criticism*.

19. See 'The Responsibilities of the Critic', in Northrop Frye, *Myth and Metaphor: Selected Essays 1974–88*, ed. by Robert D. Denham (Charlottesville and London: University Press of Virginia, 2000), pp. 124–40 (p. 128).

20. Coleridge considered the etymology of the word 'mind' to signify the oscillating motion of a scythe (see James K. McKusick, *Coleridge's Philosophy of Language* (New Haven: Yale University Press, 1986), p. 45).

21. Quotations from Keats's poetry are taken from *John Keats: The Complete Poems*, ed. by John Barnard (Harmondsworth: Penguin, 1973). Line or stanza references follow quotations in the text.

22. Paul Ricoeur, *Time and Narrative*, I, p. 52, Ricoeur's emphasis.

23. 'What we'd never see except in a book is often what we go to books to find' (*The Educated Imagination* (Bloomington and Indianapolis: Indiana University Press, 1964), p. 91).

24. Helen Vendler, *The Odes of John Keats* (Cambridge, Mass.: Harvard University Press, 1983), p. 118.

25. 'In the great moments of Dante and Shakespeare, in, say *The Tempest* or the climax of the *Purgatorio*, we have a feeling of converging significance, the feeling that we are close to seeing what our whole literary experience has been about, the feeling that we have moved into the still center of the order of words' (*Anatomy of Criticism* (Princeton: Princeton University Press, 1957; repr. 1973), p. 117).

26. Brian Hepworth, *The Rise of Romanticism* (Manchester: Carcanet, 1978), p. 335.

27. The model that I'm using here is put forward by Balfour in an essay that precedes the publication of his book: 'The Future of Citation: Blake,

Wordsworth, and the Rhetoric of Romantic Prophecy', in David Wood (ed.), *Writing the Future* (London and New York: Routledge, 1990), pp. 115–28.

28. Ian Balfour, *The Rhetoric of Romantic Prophecy* (Stanford: Stanford University Press, 2002), p. 18.

29. For aiming, see for example Byron's *The Prophecy of Dante*: 'Many are Poets but without the name; / For what is Poesy, but to create / From overfeeling Good or Ill, and *aim* / At an external life beyond our fate' (IV, lines 10–13, my emphasis).

30. Alan Rawes, *Byron's Poetic Experimentation: Childe Harold, the Tales and the Quest for Comedy* (Aldershot: Ashgate, 2000), pp. 24–5.

31. Garber, *Self, Text, and Romantic Irony*, p. 181. On the progress of the verse is Jerome McGann's description – 'radically, aggressively episodic and meandering' – in *Don Juan in Context* (Chicago: Chicago University Press, 1976), p. 3.

32. Balachandra Rajan, *The Form of the Unfinished: English Poetics from Spenser to Pound* (Princeton: Princeton University Press, 1985), p. 162. One wonders if this is Rajan's parody of Aristotle's famous one sentence plot summary (in the original Greek) of the *Odyssey* in his *Poetics*.

33. Ibid., pp. 16–17.

34. In reference to Leigh Hunt's claim to a 'system' in *The Story of Rimini*, Byron writes to Thomas Moore on 1 June 1818: 'his style was a system, or *upon system*, or some such cant; and, when a man talks of system, his case is hopeless: so I said no more to [Hunt], and very little to any one else' (*Byron's Letters and Journals*, ed. by Leslie A. Marchand, 12 vols (London: John Murray, 1973–82), VI, p. 46.)

35. Letter to Francis Hodgson, 6 August 1809, in *Byron's Letters and Journals*, I, p. 216.

36. Cadiz figures as well in *Childe Harold's Pilgrimage*, I, 65, and 'The Girl of Cadiz' (1809). See Peter Cochran's notes to canto II in his electronic edition of *Don Juan*. Follow the links from the website of the International Byron Society (www.internationalbyronsociety.com).

37. Peter Cochran glosses the allusion to *Hamlet* I, iii, 68 (ibid.).

38. The felicitous phrase belongs to Bernard Beatty: see ' "An awful wish to plunge within it": Byron's Critique of the Sublime', in Paul M. Curtis (ed.), *Byron and the Romantic Sublime* (Moncton: Revue de l'Université de Moncton, 2005), pp. 265–76 (p. 274).

39. *Byron's Letters and Journals*, VI, p. 232.

2
'Conscript Fathers and Shuffling Recruits': Formal Self-awareness in Romantic Poetry

Michael O'Neill

In a letter sent to Southey in 1815, Wordsworth discusses the requirements which poetry needs to satisfy if it is to attain the status of 'epic'. With *Jerusalem Delivered* in mind, he expresses reservations about 'the movement of Tasso's poem', faults ascribable to the fact it is 'written in stanzas'. For Wordsworth no stanzaic form is equal to blank verse where epic is concerned:

> Spenser's stanza is infinitely finer than the *ottava rima*, but even Spenser's will not allow the epic movement as exhibited by Homer, Virgil and Milton. How noble is the first paragraph of the *Aeneid* in point of sound, compared with the first paragraph of the *Jerusalem Delivered*! The one winds with the majesty of the Conscript Fathers entering the Senate House in solemn procession; and the other has the pace of a set of recruits shuffling on the drill-ground, and receiving from the adjutant or drill-serjeant the command to halt at every ten or twenty steps.[1]

Wordsworth invokes the senators of ancient Rome in support of his preference, in epic, for verse forms that eschew stanzaic compartmentalisation. The 'Conscript Fathers' were the senators of Rome, the term deriving from the fact that the original fathers (*patres*) were joined by new senators (*conscripti*). In time, the two categories became one, but Wordsworth makes us aware of the term's origin by uniting the original fathers of epic poetry (Homer and Virgil) with their most significant successor (Milton). His vivid, witty illustrations make clear how important, for him, is the movement of poetry. Indeed, the idea of poetic feet shadows the image of the 'set of recruits shuffling on the drill-ground', commanded to 'halt at every ten or twenty steps'. As critics such as Brennan O'Donnell have made clear, Wordsworth excels in the skilful deployment of stanzas as well as blank verse; and the anathema on stanzaic form applies strictly only to epic. But his comment is of wider suggestiveness for considering the formal practice of Romantic poets, prompting, in this chapter, reflection on their choice and deployment of verse-forms, especially blank verse and *ottava rima* (Section I), rhyming couplets in iambic pentameter (Section II) and a variety of lyric stanza-forms (Section III).

I

Wordsworth writes *The Prelude*, an epic of consciousness, concerned with the growth of the poet's mind, in blank verse. The account of this mental growth privileges evocation and disdains reductive analysis. Such disdain communicates in lines which themselves constitute an implicit defence of blank verse. Attacking 'that false secondary power, by which / In weakness we create distinctions, then / Believe our puny boundaries are things / Which we perceive, and not which we have made' (1805, II, 221–4),[2] Wordsworth outflanks the creator of false distinctions with distinctions of his own, but his own necessary contrast between perception and creation, borne along on the current of the caesura-shifting verse, abolishes the setting up of 'puny boundaries'. With the penultimate line in mind, Christopher Ricks observes that 'Wordsworth uses the line-ending here to crystallise his contempt', his point being that we are brought up short by 'things', a word claiming a stake in reality, before that claim is outflanked by the clause into which we pass in the next line.[3] The blank verse enacts a freeing of consciousness from self-created prisons of thought:

> Hard task to analyse a soul, in which
> Not only general habits and desires,
> But each most obvious and particular thought,
> Not in a mystical and idle sense,
> But in the words of reason deeply weighed,
> Hath no beginning. (II, 232–7)

Blank verse here is a means of staging highly deliberated recoils of sense and qualifications of meaning. Analysis is dismissed in favour of the 'words of reason deeply weighed'. The rhythms mimic a journey back towards a point of origin which recedes as it is approached and about whose determinate existence the poetry is deeply sceptical. As Jonathan

Wordsworth has pointed out,[4] Wordsworth's 'Hard task' nods in the direction of Milton's use of the phrase 'Sad task and hard' (*Paradise Lost*, V, 564) to depict the war in Heaven, and the echo allies Wordsworth's sense of his task with that of the greatest epic poet in English.[5]

Often intent on establishing himself as Wordsworth's poetic adversary, Byron composes *Don Juan*, the other major Romantic-period poem with epic pretensions, in *ottava rima*. It feels like a rebuke, on Byron's part, to do so, since the use of stanzaic measure acts as a sharp retort to Wordsworth's practice in *The Excursion*. Indeed, one of the benefits of writing in a form that thrives on the chimes and contrasts set going by a rhyming stanza is that another poet's titles can be the object of satirical scorn: so, Byron refers in canto III to 'A drowsy frowsy poem, call'd the "Excursion," / Writ in a manner which is my aversion' (st. 94). Linking *The Excursion* to a state of 'aversion', Byron uses rhyme's capacity for put-downs to devastating effect.[6] He accuses Wordsworth of building up, in *The Excursion*, 'a formidable dyke / Between his own and others' intellect' (III, st. 95), and yet Wordsworth devotes the majestic blank verse of his poem's prefatory lines to breaking down such dykes, to images of uniting and marrying. His is a 'spousal verse' (57) by virtue of complexities resolving themselves into affirmations.[7]

For Byron, such affirmations seem willed and to ignore design-ruffling particulars that refuse to prove 'how exquisitely' 'The external World is fitted to the Mind' (66, 68). Byron's is an epic that is consciously, mockingly belated; it builds itself out of the ruins of epic exemplars, out of nothing so much as the poet's wish regularly to change his ground, albeit less like a shuffling recruit than a master strategist. Throughout, difference from previous epic models turns out to serve Byron's advantage. The poem opens by alluding to Virgil's *Aeneid*. Whereas Virgil begins by singing of arms and the man, Byron starts with a comic lack, which invites a compensating virtuosity: 'I want a hero', he says in the poem's first line, before alighting on Don Juan, seemingly *faute de mieux*. The poet 'can't find any [brave men] in the present age / Fit for my poem (that is, for my new one), / So, as I said, I'll take my friend Don Juan' (I, st. 5). Casting about for a subject emerges as Byron's subject and reinforces his poetic credentials. He has, that final rhyme quietly reminds us, cornered the contemporary market in heroes, the 'Byronic hero' being a knowingly ersatz addition to a lineage that goes back to 'Agamemnon' (I, st. 5).

Byron's 'new' hero will, in fact, be his own narrative voice, a voice suited to the medium of *ottava rima*. His 'movement' may be more infernal than 'celestial', to borrow Wordsworth's term for the movement necessary in 'the highest class' of epic poetry, namely, that which has a 'religious' subject'.[8] But even this distinction is less than clear when we enter the 'English' cantos, and their fascination with the enigmatic figure of Aurora Raby, who 'look'd as if she sat by Eden's door, / And grieved for those who could return no more' (XV, st. 45). Rhyme points up possibility, even as the 'as if' construction stays in the realm of guesswork. The local effect is typical of the larger design; a design that defeats the claims of single explanations. So, here, Byron is attracted by Aurora's air of being 'seated on a throne / Apart from the surrounding world' (XV, st. 47), where 'world', as often in Byron, glances at its social meaning, referring to a privileged elite, 'The twice two thousand, for whom earth was made', as he says sardonically if a little wistfully in canto XIII (st. 49). But whether Aurora can re-open the door that leads back to Eden is doubtful, as is the indirectly hinted-at thought that the 'fallen worship' (XV, st. 46) of Catholicism might reassert itself in England – or, indeed, that a Romantic poet can recreate the epic in its pristine form.

At the poem's start, Byron's *sprezzatura* emerges as his main way of challenging for epic laurels. He rejects epic convention with nonchalant ease, characterising the canonical – 'Most epic poets plunge "in medias res", / (Horace makes this the heroic turnpike road)' – only to subvert it:

> That is the usual method, but not mine –
> My way is to begin with the beginning;
> The regularity of my design
> Forbids all wandering as the worst of sinning,
> And therefore I shall open with a line
> (Although it cost me half an hour in spinning)
> Narrating somewhat of Don Juan's father,
> And also of his mother, if you'd rather. (I, sts 6–7)

Wordsworth uses blank verse to chart the growth of a soul that can, without mystical idleness, be said to have had no 'beginning'. In saying this, Wordsworth alludes to Christian notions of the soul's immortality. Byron's inexhaustible epic also challenges the idea of closure and definition; but he openly concedes or boasts that he is engaged in an artificial pursuit, the writing of a poem. Ricks comments on Wordsworth's self-reflexive use of the word 'end', and connects it to the idea of beginnings as well as endings, and to the fact that 'Poetry is involved, more than prose, in persistently stopping and starting – and yet it must not be a thing of stops and starts'.[9] But whereas the writer of blank verse will have no qualms about ending lines with the word 'end', there may be more hesitation over placing the word 'beginning' in so prominent a place since, positioned thus, the word cries out for a feminine rhyme. Wordsworth wishes his blank verse to blend with the flow of his thought-processes in such a way as to subtilise our awareness that he is writing a poem; Byron delights in thrusting upon the reader the fact that he is composing. He debunks what Edward Said calls 'the tyranny of starting a work *in medias res*, a convention that burdens the beginning with the pretense that it is not one': that is, neither a 'convention' nor a 'beginning'.[10] Evidently Byron jokes when he claims that 'The regularity of my design / Forbids all wandering as the worst of sinning'; the poem's 'design' embraces all manner of 'wandering'. Wandering from thought to thought positively propels it. And yet, playing against such thematic lawlessness is the endlessly 'regular' chiming of the rhymes in the *ottava rima* stanza. The 'half an hour' spent 'spinning' a line rebukes the 'sinning' involved in 'wandering' and confirms that, at a formal level, the poem is always 'beginning' again, always reverting to a pattern that, first and foremost, acquaints us intimately with the present-tense of composition. At the same time, this stanzaic discipline brings into play and thrives on any amount of contingency, as is suggested by the final rhyme, where the poet offers to speak 'somewhat of Don Juan's father, / And also of his mother, if you'd rather'. Amusingly 'if you'd rather' presents subject matter as infinitely open to alteration, depending on the supposed whim of the reader, but really the wish of the poet. For Wordsworth, there is one story and one story only: his growth to poetic maturity. His poem can engage in 'wandering', sure that it cannot miss its way; its blank verse is 'Joyous, nor scared at its own liberty' (*The Prelude*, 1805, I, 16), able to convey with apparently unpremeditated art the oncoming of 'Trances of thought and mountings of the mind' (*The Prelude*, 1805, I, 20).

Not, of course, that Byron's embrace of artifice prevents him from, in places, performing with great skill the workings of sincerity.[11] Nor does blank verse give Wordsworth the kind of liberty dreamed of by a poetry that has dispensed with the line as its staple unit. In Book IV of *The Prelude*, he describes composing while out walking with his dog, 'an attendant and a friend', 'Obsequious to my steps, early and late, / Though often of such dilatory walk / Tired, and uneasy at the halts I made' (97, 98–100). The passage reveals Wordsworth's underestimated sense of humour as he stages a comically self-reflexive scenario; the dog follows in the poet's footsteps, at once 'Obsequious' and 'uneasy at the halts I made'. A few lines later, Wordsworth offers a more self-admiring image of the composing self in the presence of his faithful terrier as he speaks of himself 'like a river murmuring / And talking to itself' (110–11). But his formal skill lies not merely in his ability to mimic through his rhythms 'a river murmuring', central as that metaphor is to the poem's myth of mysterious development; it subsists, too, in his sensitivity to 'halts', impediments to onward flow. In his prefatory note to *Paradise Lost*, Milton locates 'true musical delight' in blank verse when it exhibits 'apt numbers, fit quantity of syllables, and the sense variously drawn out from one verse into another'.[12] For Wordsworth, drawing 'the sense [...] from one verse into another' is a means of approaching 'The perfect image of a mighty Mind, / Of one that feeds upon infinity, / That is exalted by an underpresence, / The sense of God, or whatso'er is dim / Or vast in its own being' (*The Prelude*, 1805, XIII, 69–73). The drawn-out sense here moves from 'a mighty Mind' to attempts to evoke the nature of its might, attempts that convey the indefinable sublimity of the mind's own being. Feeding upon infinity mixes an elemental, physical verb with an augustly abstract noun, but Wordsworth's use of apposition rarely cedes primacy to any force beyond the mind. Shelley uses the same verb in a lyric from the first act of *Prometheus Unbound*, where a poet 'feeds on the aerial kisses / Of shapes that haunt thought's wildernesses' (741–2), lines that illustrate how sense can be drawn out through rhyme, in this case a series of triplets which continually postpone limits, until one is driven into 'thought's wildernesses'.[13] Wordsworthian feeding on infinity sounds more robustly appetising than the more famishing fare of 'aerial kisses' on which Shelley's poet thrives. But both poets keep body and soul together in the act of focusing, through their formal devices, on possible gaps between the physical and the metaphysical.

II

Wordsworthian blank verse and Byronic *ottava rima* offer alternatives to the heroic couplet, still very much alive in the Romantic period. Ideologies ghost Romantic uses of verse-forms, though there are many ways in which it can be simplistic to read form in terms of political inclination or allegiance. That said, Keats and Hunt deploy the couplet form to calculatedly unAugustan effect, freeing the form up to express, through a range of practices, a mood of escape from oppression, as in the opening to *Endymion*. There, Keats achieves something of the continuous flow of blank verse while retaining the ear-soothing consistency of rhyme associated with the couplet. The opening line, 'A thing of beauty is a joy for ever', gathers to itself the aphoristic precision normally effected by both lines in the Popean couplet, before passing into a passage that eschews the closed couplet; only at line 24 does a full stop coincide with the close of a couplet.[14]

Romantic poets are drawn to and delight in formal self-awareness. Such self-awareness may enhance awareness of the poem's subject. It may itself become the poem's subject, in which case one would wish to make a distinction: between a self-awareness that is vigilant and one that is complacent about the dangers of mere poetic narcissism. Here consideration of formal matters leads towards the labyrinth of ambivalences explored by Paul de Man in a discussion of Rilkean 'inwardness', a term which, according to de Man, 'designates the impossibility for the language of poetry to appropriate anything, be it as consciousness, as object, or as a synthesis of both'.[15] In *Epipsychidion* Shelley, possibly influenced by *Endymion*, anticipates such 'inwardness' as he employs couplets that take on something of the momentum of blank verse, and both delight in and worry about the 'impossibility' of 'appropriation'. Rejecting closure and finding a poetic form for the workings of love as want, he celebrates the pursuit of 'this soul out of my soul' (237) through ever-regrouping alliances of sound that mimic 'thought's melody' (560). The poem builds from an opening declaration of its own inadequacy as it speaks of offering 'votive wreaths of withered memory' (4) by means of a series of self-kindled surges of poetic enthusiasm. The couplet form provides Shelley with a default position for his longing for harmony; its very existence as sonic echo provides a provisional ballast after the intricacies of aspiration mimed, for example, in the passage from line 91 to 123.

In this passage, Shelley scarcely closes a single couplet, certainly not in the manner that an ear trained on Pope would expect. Its opening lines –

> The glory of her being, issuing thence,
> Stains the dead, blank, cold air with a warm shade
> Of unentangled intermixture, made
> By Love, of light and motion. (91–4)

– characterise a poetic procedure that makes new a traditional form. Stress-shifts combine with changing caesurae to convey Shelley's sense of the mobile, hardly definable nature of the 'glory of her being'. The voice falls on 'Stains', the first syllable of line 92, with unexpected force, pointing up the semantic richness of the word in context; it can mean to 'impart a new colour to', but it can also suggest that the staining in some ways represents a sullying of the glory's original purity: even in being expressed, that is, the 'glory' can never fully convey its true nature, just as the poet's language, however inspired, must always confess its 'infirmity' (71). Shelley's practice in the poem, one conjectures, may have earned Wordsworth's 'detestation', quoted by Ricks,

> of couplets running into each other, merely because it is convenient to the writer [...]. Reading such verse produces in me a sensation like that of toiling in a dream, under the night-mair. The Couplet promises rest at agreeable intervals; but here it is never attained – you are mocked and disappointed from paragraph to paragraph.[16]

If in the passage starting at line 91 'rest' is 'never attained', the effect of the poetry is to make one hope that the poet can sustain his sense of Emily's indefinability. The poetry does not play gimmicky tricks with ideas of expressiveness, and one would not wish to claim for it any banal mimicking of sense by sound and syntax. However, Shelley's formal adroitness results in writing that has the onward propulsion associated with paragraphs of blank verse, along with the intimations of harmony produced by couplets. Certainly, the reader searching for an uncomplicated definition of Emily's 'glory' will be 'mocked and disappointed', but it is arguable that the writing, with due calculation, commits itself to 'toiling in a dream': the 'dream' being the view that Emily is the embodiment of the poet's previously unsatisfied ideas of perfection. The writing grows self-reflexive as so often in *Epipsychidion*, as much about itself as it is about Emily. Indeed, the two subjects converge as Shelley puts into the foreground the task of seeking to capture Emily's identity, or seeking to imagine a state of Utopian bliss. Here, the lines of the poem as well as Emily's 'flowing outlines' (96) create an effect of being 'Continuously prolonged, and ending never' (101), where 'Continuously' irradiates throughout surrounding lines its suggestion of uninterrupted process: in part, through a feminine rhyme ('never') that is hostile to the idea of completion, closure, 'ending'; in part, through devices of syntax that continually oppose 'ending'. Throughout the poem, 'till' serves to postpone the ending to which it looks forward. So, in this passage, Shelley writes, 'Till they [the flowing outlines] are lost, and in that Beauty furled / Which penetrates and clasps and fills the world' (102–3). If 'that Beauty' announces an absolute, it is one that is in intimate, even erotic contact with the world of process.

Language in the passage shimmers with uncoverings, delvings, movements 'Beyond the sense' (110) that stay in touch with sensuous experience. This is not to deny that Shelley places, and knows that he is placing, on Emily a near-insupportable burden of significance, 'a mortal shape indued / With love and life and light and deity' (112–13). Inevitably, the brilliant coal of inspiration mimes its fading as swift interplay passes into impassioned declaration; when he describes Emily as 'An image of some bright Eternity' (115), Shelley imitates the collapse of imaginative apprehension of 'the before unapprehended relations of things' into that state when words become 'signs for portions or classes of thoughts, instead of pictures of integral thoughts'.[17] It is finely and precisely done, this laying bare of the poet's activity; Shelley concedes that he has portrayed Emily as 'A Metaphor of Spring and Youth and Morning' (120). The poem's formal devices are attuned to the miming of imaginative entropy going on in the verse, the feminine rhymes now seeming like a failed protest against the ongoing demands of the couplet before the passage comes to a halt, mid-line, with the image of a 'summer grave' (123). That image ostensibly depicts a triumph over 'Frost the Anatomy' (122), but Emily, 'incarnate April' (121) though she be, has also suffered a kind of burial.

In his 'Pygmalion: The Cyprian Statuary', Thomas Lovell Beddoes seeks to resurrect, not to bury, to animate the inanimate. He subtly counterpoints form with content in his use of the couplet as his poem meditates on opposites and their possible reconciliation. The couplets promise harmony; however, the poem's plot offers ironic over-balancings. Galatea comes to life at the apparent cost of Pygmalion's imminent death. Moreover, the poetry locks itself in a palace of art, a maze of sounds and images. Pygmalion, able to create forms that are 'Alike too beautiful for life and death' (27), longs for his sculpture of Galatea to live since, as he says in his prayer to Venus, 'is there not gone / My life into her which I pasture on?' (191–2).[18] Again, the image of feeding occurs; here, it conveys the mind's longing to bite on something other than its own workings. In a fine discussion, Michael Bradshaw sees the poem as concerned (among other things) with the 'incarnation of spirit into material form'.[19] Yet the more Pygmalion longs for such 'incarnation', the more virtuosic Beddoes's verse seems. Themes prominent in Keats and Shelley are present, as Bradshaw observes,[20] but Beddoes brings to such themes a quietly sumptuous awareness that creation is always a question of artifice; his couplets reject Augustan pointedness and what might be called 'primary' Romantic expansiveness. In their place, he offers a more 'secondary' Romanticism, one which does not so much turn on its own desires as concede their existence as verbal phenomena. When Galatea trembles on the verge of 'incarnation', she is described thus: 'And she was smooth and full, as if one gush / Of life had washed her' (128–9). That surmised 'gush / Of life' is mimicked to perfection, 'mimicked' being the operative word for the overflow of sense effected by the line-ending. The greater the desire to escape from art into life, in this poem, the more equably usurpatory seem the claims of art. Even when Pygmalion's chisel is imagined working with magical spontaneity, the language rivals the supposed power of the sculpture less to move towards the real than to increase the reader's awareness of the poem as being 'self inhabited', to use Beddoes's suggestive description of 'Lonely Pygmalion' (35). And yet, for a brief moment, Beddoes marries art and life:

> The winged tool as digging out a spell
> Followed a magnet, whereso'er it fell,
> That sucked and led it right – and for the rest
> The living form with which the stone be blest
> Was the loved image stepping from his breast. (148–52)

The artist's 'winged tool' passively 'follows', while his material actively 'sucked' and 'led it right', an image whose sub-textual eroticism seeks to banish the merely auto-erotic. In the final line Beddoes finds an answer to the predicament of narcissism explored by Shelley, say, in *Alastor*, and the passage achieves its own kind of 'living form' as the triplet induces a temporary sense of 'rest'. Still, the answer is wish-fulfilling; Galatea is neither more nor less than 'a loving image stepping from his breast', and the oddly conditional locution 'be blest' suggests that longing is still present as the possibility of incarnation dawns.[21]

III

In his judicious account of Wordsworth's formal practice, O'Donnell notes that the use of longer stanzas in poems such as 'The Complaint of a Forsaken Indian Woman' corresponds to 'The poet's ability to embody [...] complexity of pleasure and pain'.[22] The poem illustrates the way lyric form can suspend arrival at some supposed conclusion, how it thrives on the gap between near-exhaustion and finality, how that gap, in fact, serves as the catalyst for poetic speech. 'And yet I am alive' (8) is a sentiment that beats through the lyric of extreme emotion, examples of which are examined in this section. Cast as a monologue, Wordsworth's poem makes something unvarnished and original out of the traditional form of the complaint, here associated less with erotic than with social abandonment. Left to die, the forsaken speaker never quite commits herself fully to the wish to 'let my body die away!' (10). Complexities of feeling criss-cross the poem even as the initial two couplets of each stanza pass into a more complicated quatrain with alternate rhymes before the concluding couplet seeks to pull feeling into a coherent cry. Wordsworth shows how stanza form lends itself to the rendering of obsession. All the odd-numbered stanzas end with an 'ay' (as in 'day') rhyme. They do not, however, merely repeat the opening stanza's wish for death. In Stanza 3, the final couplet asserts the speaker's strength after being left and implicit regret that she had not been taken with her tribe; in Stanza 5, the speaker declares her need for speech: 'Too soon, my friends, you went away, / For I had many things to say' (49–50), almost a rationale for the poem's own continuance and survival; and in Stanza 7, the last of the poem, the initial wish to die has moved into something closer to stoical acceptance: 'I feel my body die away, / I shall not see another day' (69–70). The poem's form allows emotion to live at a pitch of intensity, and yet to qualify and complicate itself through changes of emphasis; it guides its lyric canoe down rapids of feeling and manages to stay afloat.

Felicia Hemans, in her 'Indian Woman's Death Song', places the reader in a less problematic place. Here the poem's spacious fourteeners conjure a breathing space between imminent death and hoped-for release. In his poem, Wordsworth offers a psychological study, a 'feeling [...] developed' (599), to use his phrase from the Preface to *Lyrical Ballads* (1802). On Wordsworth's own account in the Preface, the poem explores 'the last struggles of a human being, at the approach of death, cleaving in solitude to life and society' (598). Nothing human is alien from Wordsworth, and this fascination with human emotion and its 'subtle windings' constitutes the true political charge of his contributions to *Lyrical Ballads* (598). His poetic forms are democratic by insisting on the uniqueness of each person. Hemans conveys in her poem a characteristic eloquent melancholy coupled with a refusal to complain that has its own repressed feminist edge: 'And thou, my babe, though born, like me, for woman's weary lot, / Smile – to that wasting of the heart, my own! I leave thee not' (36–7).[23] The movement of the verse mimes the onward flowing which the speaker continually recommends, but here it accommodates a semi-bitter stress-shift in 'Smile'; it houses, too, an ingenious syntax that momentarily makes the baby endure 'woman's weary lot' and 'that wasting of the heart' before the speaker asserts that she will spare her baby such suffering (by ensuring that she and her child will die). Wordsworth's speaker cleaves to 'life and society'; Hemans's speaker puts her faith in an imagined 'realm' (43) 'where none are heard to weep' (40), part sentimentalised fantasy, part feminist Utopia. 'In the wildest of ecstasies his self-anatomising intellect is equal to itself':[24] Walter Bagehot's praise for Shelley might be applied to many Romantic lyrics which haunt the space between what is barely sayable and what lies the other side of words. One thinks, in particular, of poems in stanzaic form that do not aspire to the grand designs and licensed returns of the Ode, but that develop with an elusive alertness. In John Clare's 'I Am', the poem's form, a six-line stanza of iambic pentameters rhyming *ababab*, shapes itself out of the impossibility of definition: 'I am – yet what I am, none cares or knows; / My friends forsake me like a memory lost: – / I am the self-consumer of my woes' (1–3).[25] 'I am' betokens the bare fact of existence rather than any God-like power or even Cartesian ability to disengage consciousness from its object, and the poem records a process whereby the self consumes itself. The fascination of its development lies in Clare's refusal to budge from the brutally unignorable, 'And yet I am, and live' (6), in the process of imagining two forms of escape, each cancelled or severely qualified as it is uttered. The first is despairingly nihilist; it involves a comparison between his mode of living and 'vapours tost // Into the nothingness of scorn and noise, – / Into the living sea of waking dreams, / Where there is neither sense of life or joys, / But the vast shipwreck of my lifes esteems' (6–10). The comparison transgresses the stanza boundary as if to mime the violence of feeling that compares what it is to 'live' with 'vapours tost // Into [...] nothingness'. Each successive line offers a tantalising glimpse of something better, before denying the existence of that something. So, the 'living sea of waking dreams' might suggest a kind of imaginative vitality, until the next line exposes the 'living sea' as a place devoid of any 'sense of life'. The second form of escape is that adumbrated in the final stanza. Here the imaginative scenario changes from shipwreck to a state that is 'untroubled' (17). Yet the stanza's opening words, 'I long' (13), expose what follows as wish-fulfilment, while the longing to 'sleep as I in childhood, sweetly slept' (16) knows, by way of 'as', about the gap between 'childhood' and adult life, and implies a new kind of sleep. The poem limns a poetic biography, yes, but it also records with fevered precision a permanent Romantic state. Jonathan Bate comments shrewdly, 'He longs at once for childhood and the grave'; if, in Bate's words, 'Poetry took him to a better place', allowing him to 'complete the circle of vision', it does so, in this case, with a keen sense that the circle described by the three stanzas is a frail formal device.[26]

Romantic lyric, then, frequently aligns its deployment of stanzaic form into what Susan Wolfson calls a 'meta-rhyme with *storm*', where 'storm' might suggest the ravages of private and public experience.[27] Although, in 'Stanzas to [Augusta]', Byron begins with a line that posits aftermath and failure – 'Though the day of my destiny's over' (1) – the bounce of the anapaests and rhyming, along with the alliterative verve, help to retrieve value from the shipwreck of his life's esteems. In various drafts, Byron wrote, 'days of my Glory' rather than 'day of my destiny's'.[28] 'Destiny', like 'Glory', works to establish a self-fashioning link between Byron and Napoleon, subject of complex elegiac and self-mirroring reflections in *Childe Harold's Pilgrimage*, canto III, also composed in 1816. Like Napoleon, Byron has experienced 'destiny' in the sense of 'what is destined to happen to a particular person' (*Oxford English Reference Dictionary*), but, whereas (for Byron) Napoleon masters destiny through stoic courage and hauteur, Byron does so through poetic form. The fact that the worst has happened which can befall allows him a spirited respite. 'The day of my destiny's over' is an expression that has, hidden within it, a comfort of sorts: the poet is now beyond the control of his destiny since its day is over.

The verse sets the hostile opinion of most people towards Byron against the love for him of one person, who valiantly 'refused to discover / The faults which so many could find' (3–4). Form works wryly here. Byron suggests that the compulsion to rhyme mirrors a compulsion to 'discover' and 'find' fault and that such fault-finders are as guilty of unthinking glibness as a shoddy rhymester. Through an adroit knowingness, Byron puts distance between himself and such shoddiness until, in the stanza's final rhyme, he works in a less jaundiced way, bringing together 'me' (6) and '*thee*' (8). The italicisation of 'thee', repeated a further four times in the poem (16, 24, 40, 48), picks out Augusta as the poet's significant other in a way that makes the precise nature of otherness significant. Byron's rhymes come close to saying, as Shelley will declare in *Epipsychidion*, 'I am a part of *thee*' (52), his rhyme between 'me' and 'thee' betokening less a marriage than an incestuous union. Certainly Byron felt that he was 'at war "with all the world and his wife"; or, rather, [that] "all the world and *my* wife" are at war with me', turning a commonplace phrase on its head and using italics to single out his principal adversary rather as he uses them in the poem to denote his champion.[29]

Byron's naming of 'thee' partakes of the obsessive character associated with Romantic longing. An implicit self-ironising may be at work, in which the poet, so to speak, watches himself construct an image of the perfectly loyal supporter out of evidences of others' betrayal. In the fourth stanza, Augusta's perfection shapes itself into near-epigrammatic form, and consists in not doing what 'the world' (33) has done. If Byron is 'watchful' (31), his vigilance has an eye as much on the 'world' as it does on his ostensible subject. Indeed, admiration for Augusta is the whetstone on which the poet sharpens his aggression towards his enemies: 'Though human, thou didst not deceive me', he writes; 'Though woman, thou dost not forsake; / Though loved, thou forborest to grieve me; / Though slandered, thou never could'st shake' (25–8). Through deftly antithetical turns of phrase, Augusta materialises as the opposite of the poet's foes. Poetic form, thus, operates, as often in Romantic poetry, as a mode of fighting back, of redress for injuries sustained. At the same time, the ending concedes through its phrasing that such redress may be confined to the realm of the virtual: 'In the desert a fountain is springing, / In the wide waste there still is a tree, / And a bird in the solitude singing, / Which speaks to my spirit of *thee*' (45–8). These lines underpin the explicit prayer with which Auden concludes his elegy for Yeats ('In the deserts of the heart / Let the healing fountain start'), and have themselves the inflection of desire as much as statement.[30] If the poem's 'thee' identifies the possibility of love and hope, she quickly passes into images that seem to spring from longing and to 'sing' because the poem's metre dictates so. The 'desert' and 'fountain' generate one another, while the image of the 'tree' derives sustenance from Wordsworth's broken-hearted recognition in his 'Ode: Intimations of Immortality', 'But there's a Tree, of many one' (51): sustenance and yet possible rebuke, since Wordsworth's line breaks through the web of figurative speech to refer to a 'single' tree, whereas Byron's tree remains fluently literary. Byron consciously refuses to disengage his image from a self-validating figurative scheme.

To say so much is less to deconstruct the workings of form in 'Stanzas to [Augusta]' than to argue that, in common with much Romantic poetry, it incites and indeed itself exhibits attentiveness to such workings. Hemans is also drawn to stanzaic forms that permit poetic eloquence to emerge from a state of extremity. In 'Second Sight' the poem's balladic verse-form – alternating four- and three-stress quatrains – is the vehicle of what Stuart Curran calls 'generic self-reflexiveness'.[31] The poem assumes the posture of the (female) poet as reluctant prophet of her culture's future desolations. The very alternation of rhythmical units (four- and three-stress lines) corresponds to the antithetical play between present and future, between 'the triumph's hour' (5) and 'the coming woe' (6), 'The shadow in the sunny hour, / The wail in the mirthful song' (35–6), where the extra syllable in line 36 disrupts expressively the harmony of 'mirthful song'. Form, however, is the source of fortitude in the poem. In the face of impending sorrow, Hemans, like Wordsworth in 'Ode: Intimations of Immortality', ranges the active power of the poet to 'see' (11, 13, 17) and to 'hear' (21, 25), and she extends this capacity to 'all deep souls' (34). Ultimately, 'heaven' (40), not for the only time in Hemans, turns out to be the 'home' (40) where 'repose' (39) will be found. But in the meantime, as is frequently the case in Romantic poetry, an emotional and spiritual 'home', however provisional, is supplied 'here' (39), in the poem. And its architect is poetic form.

Notes

1. Letter to Robert Southey, autumn (?) 1815, in *Letters of William Wordsworth: A New Selection*, ed. by Alan G. Hill (Oxford: Oxford University Press, 1984), pp. 184, 185.
2. Unless noted otherwise, Wordsworth's poetry and prose are quoted from *The Oxford Authors: William Wordsworth*, ed. by Stephen Gill (Oxford: Oxford University Press, 1984). Line/page references are given in the text.
3. In 'William Wordsworth 1: "A Pure Organic Pleasure from the Lines"', *Essays in Criticism*, 21 (1971); reprinted in Christopher Ricks, *The Force of Poetry* (Oxford: Oxford University Press, 1984), pp. 89–116 (p. 100).
4. See William Wordsworth, *The Prelude: The Four Texts (1798, 1799, 1805, 1850)*, ed. by Jonathan Wordsworth (London: Penguin, 1995). Jonathan Wordsworth writes, 'Tacitly Wordsworth is claiming for his own task an importance comparable to Milton's' (p. 564).
5. *Paradise Lost* is quoted from *Milton: Poetical Works*, ed. by Douglas Bush (Oxford: Oxford University Press, 1966).
6. Byron's poetry is quoted from *Lord Byron: The Complete Poetical Works*, ed. by Jerome J. McGann, 7 vols (Oxford: Oxford University Press, 1980–1993). Stanza/line references are given in the text.
7. Quoted from the Preface to the 1814 edition of *The Excursion*, in *Wordsworth: Poetical Works*, ed. by Thomas Hutchinson, new edn, rev. by Ernest De Selincourt (London: Oxford University Press, 1936), pp. 754–5. Line references follow quotations in the text.
8. Letter to Southey, autumn (?) 1815, in *Letters of William Wordsworth: A New Selection*, p. 184.
9. 'Wordsworth 1: "A Pure Organic Pleasure from the Lines"', p. 107.
10. Edward W. Said, *Beginnings: Intention and Method*, new edn (London: Granta, 1998), p. 43.

11. See Jerome McGann, *Byron and Wordsworth: The Annual Byron Lecture, Given in the University of Nottingham on 27 May 1998* (Nottingham: School of English Studies, University of Nottingham, 1999), for a stimulating contrast between *Manfred* as a poem in which, unlike 'Tintern Abbey' and *Childe Harold's Pilgrimage*, III, 'the determining stylistic move' is 'self-consciousness rather than sincerity' (p. 24). For further reflection on difference and affinity between the poets, see Philip Shaw, 'Wordsworth or Byron?', *Byron Journal*, 31 (2003), pp. 38–50.

12. John Milton, *Paradise Lost*, 'The Verse', *Milton: Poetical Works*, p. 211.

13. Shelley's poetry is quoted from *Percy Bysshe Shelley: The Major Works*, ed. by Zachary Leader and Michael O'Neill (Oxford: Oxford University Press, 2003). Line references are given in the text.

14. Keats's poetry is quoted from *The Oxford Authors: John Keats*, ed. by Elizabeth Cook (Oxford: Oxford University Press, 1990). Line references are given in the text. For more on the question of Romantic couplets and their possible political significances, see William Keach, 'Cockney Couplets: Keats and the Politics of Style', *Studies in Romanticism*, 24 (1986), pp. 182–96. See also Susan J. Wolfson's chapter on Byron's *The Corsair* in *Formal Charges: The Shaping of Poetry in British Romanticism* (Stanford: Stanford University Press, 1997).

15. 'Tropes (Rilke)', in Paul de Man, *Allegories of Reading: Figural Language in Rousseau, Nietzsche, Rilke, and Proust* (New Haven: Yale University Press, 1979), pp. 20–56 (p. 47).

16. Letter to Hans Busk, 6 July 1819, quoted in 'Wordsworth 1: "A Pure Organic Pleasure from the Lines"', pp. 93–4.

17. *A Defence of Poetry*, in *Percy Bysshe Shelley: The Major Works*, p. 676.

18. Quotations from Beddoes are taken from *Plays and Poems of Thomas Lovell Beddoes*, ed. by H. W. Donner (London: Routledge & Kegan Paul, 1950). Line references follow quotations in the text.

19. Michael Bradshaw, *Resurrection Songs: The Poetry of Thomas Lovell Beddoes* (Aldershot: Ashgate, 2001), p. 38.

20. Ibid., pp. 39–40.

21. Donner's 1950 and 1935 editions both read 'be blest', but in his critical study *Thomas Lovell Beddoes: The Making of a Poet* (Oxford: Basil Blackwell, 1935), one finds the more straightforwardly sense-making reading, 'he blest' (p. 175).

22. Brennan O'Donnell, *The Passion of Meter: A Study of Wordsworth's Metrical Art* (Kent, Ohio: Kent State University Press, 1995), p. 127. 'The Complaint of a Forsaken Indian Woman' is quoted from *Romanticism: An Anthology*, ed. by Duncan Wu, 3rd edn (Oxford: Blackwell, 2006). Line references follow quotations in the text.

23. Quotations from Hemans' poetry are taken from *Romantic Women Poets*, ed. by Duncan Wu (Oxford: Blackwell, 1997). Line references follow quotations in the text.

24. 'Percy Bysshe Shelley' (1856), in *Literary Studies*, 2 vols (London: Dent, 1911), I, p. 111.

25. Clare is quoted from *The Oxford Authors: John Clare*, ed. by Eric Robinson and David Powell (Oxford: Oxford University Press, 1984). Line references are given in the text.

26. Jonathan Bate, *John Clare: A Biography* (London: Picador, 2003), p. 505.

27. Susan J. Wolfson, 'What Good is Formalist Criticism? Or: *Forms* and *Storms* and the Critical Register of Romantic Poetry', *Studies in Romanticism*, 37 (1988), pp. 77–94 (p. 77).

28. See *Lord Byron: The Complete Poetical Works*, IV, p. 33n.

29. Letter to Thomas Moore, 29 February 1816, in *Byron's Letters and Journals*, ed. by Leslie A. Marchand, 12 vols (London: John Murray, 1973–94), V, p. 35.

30. Quoted from W. H. Auden, *Collected Poems*, ed. by Edward Mendelson (London: Faber, 1976). The echo is pointed out by Jerome J. McGann in *Fiery Dust: Byron's Poetic Development* (Chicago: University of Chicago Press, 1968), p. 93.

31. Stuart Curran, *Poetic Form and British Romanticism* (New York: Oxford University Press, 1986), p. 132.

3
Romantic Invocation: A Form of Impossibility

Gavin Hopps

Who, if I cried out, would hear me among the angelic orders?

(Rilke, Duino Elegies, I, 1)[1]

Rilke's *Duineser Elegien* begin with a stepping *away* from invocation: *'Wer wenn ich schriee, hörte mich'*. The invocation, which conventionally announces the beginning of epic poetry, is suspended in the amber of a conditional clause embedded in a question about the efficacy of invocation. This stepping away is, however, complicated by the fact that the question is itself a sort of invocation – calling out in asking about the point of calling out – so that it in a sense argues against its own argument against invocation and suggests an attachment to as well as doubts or anxieties about the act of calling out to a transcendent other. In this chapter, I wish to suggest that this 'oxymoronic' combination of aversion and attachment – which pulls the poet simultaneously in opposite directions – is not peculiar to Rilke but is, rather, more generally representative of the Romantics' attitude towards this conventional poetic form of calling out, which leaves the post-Miltonic speaker 'stammer[ing] where old Chaucer used to sing' (Keats, *Endymion*, I, 134).[2]

To contend, with respect to belief in the transcendent, that the Romantics found themselves in an oxymoronic or in-between space and seem to have felt as it were in a limb they no longer possessed is relatively uncontroversial;[3] yet it is still perhaps necessary in order to counter the persistent tendency to assume that as modernity unfolded invocatory forms in poetry simply disappeared or were condemned to a pantomime afterlife of parody or satire. The larger and more controversial argument ventured in this chapter concerns the possibility of transcendence as such – a matter that crucially affects our interpretation of Romantic practice but tends to be settled by presupposition and brushed under the carpet – and the related possibility that this underwrites alternative construals of such invocatory stammering. This more general consideration of the failure or efficacy of invocation as a form of transcendence is prompted by and fundamentally challenges new historicist readings of the Romantic enterprise – such as Jerome McGann's hugely influential *The Romantic Ideology* – which have attempted to wipe away the horizon of transcendence, and instead see the literary utterance as imprisoned even as it is enabled by the material circumstances of its production. Whilst focusing on a single and apparently marginal poetic form – namely invocation – this chapter thus takes issue more generally with the new historicist project and its policing of the possible.

I

To begin with, however, it may be instructive to investigate the apparent death of the Muse. According to John Hollander, 'after Milton, no major poem could ever again straightforwardly or even deviously command the muse to sing, save satirically'.[4] This view is endorsed by Jonathan Culler, who sees the act of invoking the transcendent in poetry as an embarrassing 'relic of archaic beliefs', by which speakers pretentiously 'constitute themselves as sublime poets or as visionary'.[5] The readings which these comments condense have helpfully drawn attention to the shortcomings of more traditional ways of looking at the act of invocation, but both, I think, are in need of qualification. It is certainly true that the ancient practice of invoking the Muse has dramatically declined since the Enlightenment, and it is also apparent that it is and has for a long time been a source of embarrassment to the modern mind. Nevertheless, this decline is not as straightforward or complete as Hollander claims, and embarrassment is not the same as indifference or simple antipathy, but is rather, I suggest – to cite the poet who understood that emotion so well – 'a thing of yes and no' (Keats, *Endymion*, IV, 898). Since in logic one contradiction is sufficient to discredit a general proposition, a few illustrations of non-satirical invocation should suffice to challenge the validity of Hollander's general claim.

If we consider the early stirrings of Romantic practice, we find, for example, obviously conventional but non-satirical invocations in Thomson's *The Seasons*. The first invocation of 'Summer' will serve as an illustration:

> Come, Inspiration! From thy hermit-seat,
> By mortal seldom found: may fancy dare,

> From thy fixed serious eye and raptured glance
> Shot on surrounding Heaven, to steal one look
> Creative of the poet, every power
> Exalting to an ecstasy of soul. (15–20)[6]

If, in spite of its enormous popularity and importance to the Romantics, Thomson's *The Seasons* has lost something of its canonical status and is thereby exempted as a counter-example, what about the epic writings of Blake, whom Hollander for some reason completely ignores? Here, for instance, is the first invocation from *Jerusalem* – in which, we might note, the speaker acknowledges but carries on in spite of the embarrassment his calling, in both senses, causes:

> Trembling I sit day and night; my friends are astonish'd at me;
> Yet they forgive my wanderings. I rest not from my great task,
> To open the Eternal Worlds, to open the immortal Eyes
> Of Man inwards into the Worlds of Thought, into Eternity
> Ever expanding in the Bosom of God, the Human Imagination.
> O Saviour! pour upon me thy Spirit of meekness & love.
> Annihilate the Selfhood in me! be thou all my life!
> Guide thou my hand which trembles exceedingly
>   upon the rock of ages. (I, Plate 5, 16–23)[7]

Or what about Wordsworth's invocation in *The Recluse*, which, as Harold Bloom points out, 'like Blake's [invocation] to the Daughters of Beulah in his epic *Milton*, is a deliberate address to powers higher than those that inspired *Paradise Lost*'?[8] Here are a couple of short extracts:

> Urania, I shall need
> Thy guidance, or a greater muse (if such
> Descend to earth, or dwell in highest heaven),
> For I must tread on shadowy ground, must sink
> Deep, and ascend aloft, and breathe in worlds
> To which the heaven of heavens is but a veil.
> [...]
> Descend, prophetic Spirit! that inspir'st
> The human Soul of universal earth,
> Dreaming on things to come. (25–30, 83–5)[9]

Or, finally, what about the sustained invocation of Clare's 'To the Rural Muse' – the proem to *The Midsummer Cushion* – which for 16 stanzas, and with foregrounded reverence, addresses the Muse? I cite a single stanza by way of example:

> Muse of the cottage hearth oft did I tell
> My hopes to thee, nor feared to plead in vain
> But felt around my heart thy witching spell
> That bade me as thy worshipper remain
> I did & and worship on – O once again
> Smile on my offerings and so keep them green
> Bedeck my fancies like the clouds of heaven
> Mingling all hues which thou from heaven dost glean
> To me a portion of thy power be given
> If theme so mean as mine may merit aught of heaven. (21–30)[10]

It is perhaps important enough in the wake of revisionist accounts of the poet's calling such as Hollander's and Culler's simply to note the persistence of formalised, non-ironic invocation – albeit residually – within Romantic poetry. What I wish to focus on in more detail, however, is the less conspicuous and more intriguing occurrence of what I have referred to as invocatory stammering – that is, all the halting, spectral and virtual forms as well as all sorts of hybrids, mutations and surrogates – that we find 'after Milton' and most especially in Romantic verse.[11]

One of the most obvious forms of invocatory stammering is an elegiac calling which, in addressing that which is perceived as deceased or absent as though it were living and present, appears to be born of and to conjure up out of the fabric of its own yearning a sense of presence which sunders the absence it simultaneously bespeaks. This sort of elegiac stammering is common in Byron. Let us take, for example, the remarkable invocatory to-ing and fro-ing that irrupts in the midst of the narrative of *Childe Harold's Pilgrimage*, canto I (which I quote in part):

> Oh, thou Parnassus! whom I now survey
> [...]
> What marvel if I thus essay to sing?
> The humblest of thy pilgrims passing by
> Would gladly woo thine Echoes with his string,
> Though from thy heights no more one Muse will wave her wing.
> [...]
> Shall I unmov'd behold the hallow'd scene,
> Which others rave of, though they know it not?

> Though here no more Apollo haunts his grot,
> And thou, the Muses' seat, art now their grave,
> Some gentle Spirit still pervades the spot,
> Sighs in the gale, keeps silence in the cave,
> And glides with glassy foot o'er yon melodious Wave.   (sts 60–2)[12]

The poet's invocatory havering – which continues in spite of his repeated attempts to use the local closure of the poem's form to settle the matter one way or another – reveals the simultaneous pull of equal and opposite claims. He is at once manifestly convinced of the Muses' decease ('And thou, the Muses' seat, art now their grave') and yet has an equally affective sense of their ghostly persistence *in spite of* their decease ('Some gentle Spirit still pervades the spot'). The stanzas' syntax – which threatens to subvert even as it sustains the formal apostrophe which deictically marks the act of invocation – is constantly turning against itself and undermining any apparently settled position with its 'though's and 'but's. In this way, the lines figure a posture of stammering and suggest, however counter-rational the idea may seem, the abiding coexistence of a yes and a no in the act of invoking the Muse.

Keats's use of invocation in *Endymion* is also 'a thing of yes and no', though the poet's stammering in this case is caused by a radical sense of unworthiness conjoined with an equally strong sense of poetic vocation. As a result, he is recurrently unable straightforwardly to invoke the Muse, yet unable to stop *talking about* his inability to invoke her. Like someone continually walking past a shop they claim they do not want to enter, he keeps returning to and dancing around but backing away from the subject. Moreover, it is the Muse herself that he talks to about his inability to invoke her. The following faltering invocation, for example, is found at the start of Book IV:

> Muse of my native land! loftiest Muse!
> [...] thou know'st what prison
> Of flesh and bone, curbs, and confines, and frets
> Our spirit's wings. Despondency besets
> Our pillows; and the fresh tomorrow morn
> Seems to give forth its light in very scorn
> Of our dull, uninspired, snail-pacèd lives.
> To thee! But then I thought on poets gone,
> And could not pray – nor can I now – so on
> I move to the end in lowliness of heart. (1, 20–9)

The poem is littered with aborted, stammering and hypothetical invocations of this sort – utterances which seem in their humility to retreat from and seek to pave the way for themselves, without quite pulling themselves out of being, and whose convoluted concessive syntax, like Byron's, gives rise to a pirouetting stasis on the threshold of invocation. Having briefly identified examples of conflictual and reluctant invocations, which appear in some way to fall short of themselves – in backing away from their own asking or in doubting the existence of that to which they call – if we turn to Shelley's 'Ode to the West Wind', to look at one further example of invoking 'awry', we find an illustration of what Jonathan Culler in his brief but brilliant comments on the poem describes as 'hyperbolic' invocation.[13] Let us consider the well-known opening section:

> O wild West Wind, thou breath of Autumn's being,
> Thou, from whose unseen presence the leaves dead
> Are driven, like ghosts from an enchanter fleeing,
>
> Yellow, and black, and pale, and hectic red,
> Pestilence-stricken multitudes: O Thou
> Who chariotest to their dark wintry bed
>
> The winged seeds, where they lie cold and low,
> Each like a corpse within its grave, until
> Thine azure sister of the Spring shall blow
>
> Her clarion o'er the dreaming earth, and fill
> (Driving sweet buds like flocks to feed in air)
> With living hues and odours plain and hill:
>
> Wild Spirit, which art moving everywhere;
> Destroyer and Preserver; hear, O hear! (1–14)[14]

According to Culler, Shelley's invocation is an act of *ritual* calling.[15] It calls in order to be in calling and seeks its own perpetuation.[16] The extraordinary predicative burden the vocative is made to carry is radically in excess of its ostensible purpose, while seeming to be careless of its own redundancy. If the Spirit addressed in the poem is capable of hearing and responding as the speaker apparently hopes, it presumably already knows everything he is telling it about itself and does not need all the elaborate modification to know that it in particular, as opposed to other wild West Winds, is being addressed. Matthew Arnold once noted that we are made to wait until the 39th word of Milton's invocation in

Paradise Lost before we arrive at the main verb and realise what's going on.[17] In Shelley's ode, the proliferation of subordinate constructions staves off the invoking verb – which in the end turns out to ask only for what the act of calling always implicitly asks – for a hundred and five words or the whole of the poem's first sonnet stanza. This astonishing vocative water-treading, which advertises its own gratuity, might be described as the stammering of excessive asking. Rather than reticently backing away from calling or having its calling sundered by a sense of its inefficacy, Shelley's invocation *only* and insistently calls – indeed, it calls *too much* and thus, as it were, 'overtakes' its aim – and is in a sense turned towards itself, since it seems to yearn above all to keep itself in being. This reflexive 'fold' within Shelley's invocation, which complicates without subverting its purported aim, is what makes it – like the foregoing forms of invocatory stammering – 'a thing of yes and no'.

Before elaborating on the ways in which my reading of such stammering, after extensive agreement, radically diverges from Jonathan Culler's, it will be helpful to widen our focus and consider explicitly what is at stake.

II

It might at this point be reasonably objected that what I have shown so far, even if my analysis is accepted, is not of very much consequence. True, it may be conceded, the readings I have offered counter the prevalent but impoverishing tendency to assume that the act of invocation disappeared completely or became a figure of fun during the Romantic period. Yet these modifications of the received reading are overshadowed and appear to be rendered effectively irrelevant by two other general arguments that discredit the transcendent aspirations of the figure, and which my account so far has not addressed. The first of these holds that the act of invocation in poetry is not doing what it purports to do, the second that it is not *able* to do what it purports to do. How bound are we to accept these claims?

In spite of the widespread endorsement of the former reading, and in spite of my own indebtedness to many of its insights, I want to suggest that there are grounds for questioning the inevitability of its conclusions and its displacement of more traditional readings. Let us remind ourselves of the claims on which it is based, some of which have been touched upon already. Here is Jonathan Culler's account of the act of calling out:

invocation is a figure of vocation. This is obvious when one thinks how often invocations seek pity or assistance for projects and situations specifically related to the poetic vocation, but it can also be inferred from the functionally gratuitous invocations which mark so many poems. If asking winds to blow or seasons to stay their coming or mountains to hear one's cries is a ritualistic, practically gratuitous action, that emphasizes that voice calls in order to be calling, to dramatize its calling, to summon images of its power so as to establish its identity as poetical and prophetic voice. [...] The poet makes himself a poetic presence through an image of voice, and nothing figures voice better than the pure O of undifferentiated voicing [...]. Devoid of semantic reference, the O of apostrophe refers to other apostrophes and thus to the lineage and conventions of sublime poetry. [...] the pun [in Baudelaire's 'Le Cygné'] identifies the potential addressee of every apostrophe as the apostrophic 'O' itself and makes every apostrophe an invocation of invocation.[18]

And here is how John Hollander explains the figure's ulterior function. 'In either case', he argues, speaking of different sorts of imperative,

we are to be considering metaphoric commands and urgings, schemes of the imperative that are designed not literally to enact, but poetically to bring a fiction into being. To take a poetic command literally [...] is trivially to misread the poetry. [...] On the other hand, throughout ['Ode to the West Wind'], we can and do absorb the spill, as it were, of the first three strophes' concluding imperatives, 'Oh, hear!' [...] We, as oblique listeners, are also attending to a figurative command: what we are in fact made to listen to is a polemically moralizing description of the 'You'. All that material has been smuggled into any listener's hearing in the lining of the manifest subject of the imperative.[19]

Taking these two accounts together, we can identify a number of general characteristics which might lead us to conclude that the act of invocation in poetry is not doing what it purports to do. These may be summarised as follows. Invocation, according to this reading,

1. is a hyperbolic gesture which is conspicuously removed from quotidian models of language use;
2. is concerned with its own gratuitous perpetuation – in that it 'calls in order to be calling';

3. is in some sense directed towards and postpones itself – in that it is 'an invocation of invocation';
4. is a descriptive utterance *about* a vocative, since it swerves away from its putative orientation in speaking askance to its overhearing audience.

Accepting these claims – as I emphatically do – might seem irresistibly to commit us to an anti-realist reading of the figure. But, as Catherine Pickstock's account of the act of invocation in the liturgy makes clear, it is possible to concur with all of these claims and yet arrive at radically different conclusions. Here is how Pickstock describes invocation or the apostrophic voice, taking the pre-conciliar Roman rite as her liturgical paradigm:

> In the Roman Rite there are two main types of apostrophe. First, there are invocations which seek assistance for projects related to the vocation of the liturgical journey. [...] Secondly, there are functionally gratuitous apostrophic identifications. Because this latter type is removed from the economy of utility, it is more readily assimilable to the character of language as gift [...] and takes the form not of a petition but a calling which, like music, both *invokes* and *attracts*. It instantiates a sensual calling which, without instrumental purpose, represents a dislodging of language from diurnal orders of reasoning. The apostrophic voice calls in order to be calling, or in the hope of a further calling, and is thus situated within an expectant and passionate order of language [...].
>
> The gift-character of the second type of apostrophic address is very similar to the structure of liturgy itself, in its perpetual acts of postponement, and casting as the hope that there might be a liturgy. In the same way, apostrophe is an invocation of invocation, a sacrifice which hopes for a repetition [...]. Devoid of mundane reference to an object, the cry of invocation is a physical event, a desire for proximity, in the pure 'O!' of undifferentiated voicing. In thus dispossessing himself, the worshipper calls upon God to enter him, in a double movement of ecstasy and attraction which is a supreme expression of desire.[20]

How, then, might the hyperbole, gratuity, reflexivity and covert swerving of invocation, as identified in the secular readings of Culler and Hollander, be explained from a theological point of view?

A prefatory word about the 'oddity' of liturgical speech will be helpful here. The liturgy confronts us with a radically alternative world, which it at once fashions and reveals. One of the most important ways in which it gives form to this alternative world is by means of a voice that self-consciously seeks to set itself apart and advertise its difference from quotidian speech. It does this by way of chanting, generic and intertextual hybridity, its strictly scripted and unspontaneous character, and various forms of extravagance and redundancy – such as litany, repetition and melismata (the dwelling on or stretching out of a single syllable by singing it to several notes). By means of such 'acrobatics and juggling', the liturgical voice interrupts the mundane 'horizontal' flow of speech and appears to be dancing to different music, which it metonymically gives to visibility.[21] From a quotidian perspective, such radically uneconomic caesuras will obviously seem mad or embarrassing and like standing on one's head. Yet in this way, liturgical semiotics hold out a challenge to that perspective – reminding it of, by speaking from within and seeking proleptically to give form to, another world and an alternative perspective, from which *quotidian* behaviour seems like madness and standing on one's head. In the first place, then, we should simply note – *pace* Jonathan Culler – that there *are* extra-literary speech acts to which the formally extravagant invocations of Romantic poetry may be said to correspond.[22] And, secondly, we should notice that whilst from an exclusively secular point of view, such gestures may seem to speak only of their own aberration – and hence in poetry will inevitably be read as a form of metapoesis – from a believer's perspective, these gestures point beyond themselves to a world in which they proleptically participate and of which they are the manifestation. In this way, the liturgical gesture – of which invocation is a pre-eminent example – 'gives visibility to a transgression',[23] and may therefore be described as a form of transcendence.[24] These thoughts will be useful to us as we progress. How, then, to return to our more particular questions, might we account for the hyperbole of the act of calling?

The excessive gesture of liturgical invocation may be seen as a sort of stammering, which adverts to the burden of attempting to speak of that which is infinite by means of the finite ('hyperbole', literally, means to throw – *ballō* – over or beyond, and 'extra-vagance', as its etymology reminds us, is an extreme form of vagrancy or wandering, which implies a lack of arrival) and which is characteristic of prophetic speech.[25] Its extravagance, in this case, would be a form of apophasis – a way of speaking which proceeds by saying what is not – which acknowledges, by saying *too much*, not only the radical inadequacy of finite attempts to figure the ineffable but also the impropriety of the attempt (as this would involve idolatrously presuming that something finite could adequately comprehend the divine). Hyperbole may therefore be seen as a way of outwitting the covetousness of quotidian speech.

If the act of invocation is liberated by virtue of its extravagance from the aspirations of quotidian speech, what is its purpose or justification? One way of explaining its apparent gratuity, as Pickstock points out, is in terms of its gift or sacrificial character. Relinquishing the project of predication frees invocation to become an act of doxology or discourse of praise – calling attention to, in its stammering and enumeratively giving praise to, the inexhaustible plenitude and unnameable supereminence of that which it invokes. Such giving, if everything comes from God, is obviously and, in a sense, ludicrously superfluous. Yet, like the presents small children give their parents, paid for with money their parents gave them, it is in another sense the most valuable and meaningful of gifts. And neither is it devoid of our own contribution, since, in doing so, we give our giving. Something else takes place in such acts of gratuitously calling out to the transcendent. Invocation, crucially, instantiates a mode of relation: as Pickstock writes, it restores 'to time and physicality that which cannot be seen, and exteriorizes that which is contained within ideality'.[26] The act of calling thus narrows or helps us traverse the distance between the caller and that which is called.[27] Furthermore, in making manifest or giving form to – after the manner of an icon – that which is but 'is' without being, invocation also allows 'the final to shine through in advance in the provisional'.[28] If, then, the act of invocation establishes – by intensifying or unveiling – a mode of relation, and gives to visibility – in an anticipatory fashion and through a glass darkly – that which at the same time remains invisible, its apparent gratuity and the desire it betokens to dwell in calling make sense in a way that has been ignored by Culler.

The foregoing remarks also help us to reinterpret the self-reflexive character of invocation. Whilst Culler's observation that 'every apostrophe [is] an invocation of invocation' leads him to conclude that the poet's calling is self-consuming and a case of poetry narcissistically imitating itself, Pickstock's account of liturgical practice again reveals the possibility of arriving at alternative conclusions from the same observations. According to the latter, the act of calling out to the transcendent is, to be sure, an invocation of invocation, which involves a deferral of its own activity. Yet the utterance's shying away from itself does not, according to a theological reading, necessarily entail the kind of meta-poetic short-circuiting of its ostensible orientation that Culler's reading proposes. On the contrary, its perpetual supplementation of itself is a sign of humility and a petitioning for its own possibility, which, like Rilke's question about the point of calling out, is still a calling out, and which, from a religious perspective, paradoxically *contributes* to even as it impedes its own purposes, for it is this very sense of unworthiness that renders us worthy (to seek remission of our unworthiness) and turns the act of invocation into a sort of prefatorial stammering which calls in the hope that there may be calling.

How, finally, might the covert sideways orientation of invocation, described by Hollander, be explained from a theological point of view? An examination of liturgical practice once again reveals that the customary conclusions are not necessarily entailed by their premises. It is certainly the case that the liturgical utterance, like its poetic equivalent, has what Roman Jakobson refers to as a 'split addressee' and in the act of calling speaks as it were behind its hand to an overhearing third-party audience.[29] Indeed, the liturgical voice may be said to be orientated 'backwards' as well as sideways – which is to say, it speaks in front of and for the benefit of the *self* as well as a third-party audience. There are two crucial differences, however, between Hollander's account of such covert swervings in poetry and the construal that emerges from liturgical practice. First, liturgical speech is an *affective* rather than an *expressive* discourse. That is to say, it reverses the customary understanding of the relationship between the self and the language, so that whereas, according to the dominant model, it is the interior motions of thinking, willing and feeling that precipitate speech (and we might add 'only' and 'authentic' if we wish to highlight the Romantic provenance of this model), in liturgical practice it is *the act of speech* – which involves standing in and speaking with the words of another – that is supposed to incite the interior motions of self, which is thus performatively constituted. Secondly, whilst the liturgical utterance is implicitly orientated back towards its speaker and sideways towards its third-party auditors, this does not mean that it may not also be orientated towards its ostensible addressee, and that the call cannot be heard as well as overheard. Each time Mass is said, the prayers of the Celebrant are manifestly orientated towards – and intended to influence – the overhearing congregation, yet they are still also hopefully addressed towards the divine. The sideways comportment of the act of calling need not, therefore, as liturgical practice suggests, annul or occur at the expense of its avowed orientation. Rather, it is intended contagiously to involve those who overhear in its orientation towards the divine and hoist them jointly with its own petard.

A more general objection – concerning the relationship between poetry and the liturgy – looms large at this point and needs to be addressed before we draw some conclusions. If we accept that there are substantive parallels in the *form* the act of calling takes in poetry and the liturgy, the obvious retort that this invites is that the context makes all the difference. Thus, whilst in the liturgy it may be granted that all the worshipper's acts of address to people and things might be – or might be intended as – real communications of meaning, such utterances in poetry in an age of non-belief will be a sort of playing at meanings which poets can no longer really mean. Therefore, it will be argued, the same formula that in a liturgy of believers is interpreted as a directed vocative will in a literary context be merely a contemplated vocative. If, then, as I am arguing, Culler's account of invocation involves an illicit secular elision of poetic and liturgical utterances – viewing all calling as parodic and self-contemplating – is not the alternative account I am putting forward guilty of an equally unwarranted religious elision – suggesting that all calling is because of an I–Thou relation? So far, my argument may appear to be tending in this direction; though it is precisely this sort of elision that I wish to rebut – along with the secular elision effected by Culler – without, however, this making it necessary to accept an absolute discontinuity of contexts either. How, then, might the relationship between liturgical and poetic calling be explained?

A proper response would require more space, but the following may serve to indicate one possible avenue of approach. All of the positions canvassed so far – that all calling is parodic and self-contemplating, that all calling is a real and meaningful response to a Thou, that there is an absolute separation between liturgical and poetic calling – are, I think, on to something important but are nonetheless in themselves mistaken. Yet it may be possible to counter this mistakenness by holding on to *all* of these apparently contradictory claims. This may at first seem somewhat illogical or eccentric, but it resembles the way differences in divine presence are traditionally explained by theological, and in particular Catholic, tradition. Whilst, for the believer, it is true that only in the Mass do we find the fullness of Christ and the fullness of reciprocal mediation (to us and from us), it does not follow from this that the divine is absent from, or that there is no mediation available in, other ecclesiastical structures or outside the church. Hence, it might similarly be argued, in the first place, that it is only in the liturgy that signs and things signified are uniquely identical and that the crossover between divine and human worlds is at its authorising apogee – in other words, that only in the liturgy is there a real and meaningful response to a Thou. Nevertheless, it is at the same time possible with consistency to hold, as de Lubac and von Balthasar so powerfully argued, that whilst the world of the human is indeed wholly transformed by, and dependent upon, grace from without, it always already had this latency within it – which permits this transformation as its ultimate fulfilment, unreachable by itself but not foreign to it – so that without depriving the creaturely of its independence or integrity, it follows that nothing in creation is untouched by grace. Therefore, even in unredeemed human nature there will be everywhere traces of the deification for which it is intended. Similarly, latent in all calling, there will be traces of the supreme call – which is God's utterance of himself – in which all calling stands, which will be both the thing into which all calling could turn and, more importantly, the foundation of its possibility, since creaturely calling only has being by virtue of its participation in the being which is the calling of God. In this way, we might, without contradiction, on the one hand stress the unparalleled difference of the liturgy and what it makes present, and on the other hand insist that it uncovers *in all that is* an innate interlacement, both potential and actual, of the natural and supernatural – which lures us towards what we already in a sense latently possess – in revealing the hidden 'self-exceeding' nature of created phenomena, by means of which the created order is para-doxically elevated above itself in being itself. Likewise, it thus becomes possible – and makes sense – to maintain, however contradictory it may seem, that (i) there is an absolute difference between liturgical and poetic calling, (ii) all calling will to some extent be self-contemplating and parodic in character – perhaps most of all for the believer, for whom poetic calling is an echo of an echo, as liturgical calling is itself an answering and imperfect imitation of the ongoing call that is creation (and the re-creation that is redemption) and (iii) all calling will nonethe-less be redolent of and open to the possibility of becoming – in latently bearing within itself a trace of – a real and meaningful response to a Thou. This will mean that the believer can register non-liturgical calling as precisely that, whilst at the same time seeing it as implicitly rendered possible and ultimately directed by a ground of dialogue only fully used up in the liturgy. The non-believer, who will of course remain sceptical about such claims, may nevertheless grant that they have rational force and the potential to throw real light on the ground, direction and intel-ligibility of all invocation, insofar as no one – believer or non-believer – can fully specify the origin and reach of human and aesthetic calling out.

Certain interim conclusions may now be drawn from the foregoing discussion. To begin with, Culler's identification of the ritual char-acter of invocation in poetry does not, in spite of his own conclusions, necessarily argue against the utterance's aspirations. On the contrary, it brings into view a model of usage in which the speaker's hyperbolic calling, gratuitously sustained stammering and invocatory postpone-ment of invocation paradoxically *assist* the utterance's reaching out towards – even as it appears to languish away from – its addressee. Additionally, Culler's pointing up of the analogy between certain poetic invocations and ritual practice calls into question the related conten-tion, put forward by John Hollander, that in speaking sideways to its eavesdropping audience or as it were backwards to its own speaker, the invocation is not also addressing its addressee. The affinity noted by Culler between poetic and ritual invocation, whilst apparently intended to endorse his metapoetic reading of the figure, therefore seems to back-fire in that it brings to light a model of invocation in which the utter-ance's multiple orientation, profligate gestures and preparatory deferral or prefacing of itself form part of a larger referential strategy, and thereby suggests (bearing in mind the caveat concerning their differ-ence) that the ritualised act of invocation in poetry may, in spite of its self-referentiality, gratuity and excess and in spite of its surrepti-tiously split addressee, also be a hopeful and, perhaps, efficacious act of address.

So far, I have attempted to establish, against the accounts of invoca-tion put forward by Jonathan Culler and John Hollander, first of all that whilst there has been a dramatic decline in the use of conventional forms of calling out in poetry, which is undoubtedly linked to larger cultural changes in attitudes towards religion, the act of invocation does not entirely disappear – nor does its waning form part of what is commonly assumed to be an inevitable unidirectional trajectory – but remains, in spite of the Romantics' suspicions and theatrical ventriloquising of its gestures, available for serious use and retrieval. Secondly, I have argued that the various forms of invocatory stammering that burgeon as more straightforward invocation declines and seem to bespeak an embarrass-ment about the practice as such do not necessarily reflect a simple aversion or disbelief but may instead signify a complicated conjunction of *conflicting* impulses – including some sort of recalcitrant attachment – towards the act of calling out. Lastly, drawing on a theological account of invocation, and examining each of the customary objections, I have sought to show that such conflicts and apparent impediments may in fact be a normal feature of invocation, and need not mean that the voice in calling is not doing what it purports to do. In the concluding section of this chapter, I wish to consider in a more general sense the 'impossibility' of what invocation ventures.

III

In the preceding section, it was argued that the voice in calling is a form of transcendence. By this it was meant that the act of calling gives to visibility the transgression it performs. I say transgression in the singular, though it has also emerged that the voice in calling is the becoming visible of a plurality of transgressions. As the comments quoted from Denys and Pickstock – and Thompson's invocation – indicate, the act of calling is a form of ecstasy or wayfaring from self. In addition, it was noted that the act of calling synecdochically makes manifest another world in which it participates (in hoping it may do so), to which the stammering and excessive gestures of the liturgy seek, as it were, under erasure to give form. Finally, it has been argued by Jean-Louis Chrétien (following Heidegger and Levinas) that our calling out is a response to an anterior call – and prevenient transgression – which our answering call retroactively makes manifest.[30] Such claims are obviously not without opponents, and it is to their likely objections that I now wish to turn.

At the heart of Jerome McGann's new historicist reading of the Romantic enterprise set forth in *The Romantic Ideology* is the assumption that transcendence is an impossibility. It is this assumption that allows him to make the following kinds of claims:

> The grand illusion of Romantic *ideology* is that one may escape such a world [of suffering] through imagination and poetry. The great truth of Romantic *work* is that there is no escape.
> [...]
> This idea that poetry, or even consciousness, can set one free of the ruins of history and culture is the grand illusion of every Romantic poet.
> [...]
> In the end Byron's poetry discovers what all Romantic poems repeatedly discover: that there is no place of refuge, not in desire, not in the mind, not in imagination.[31]

The transcendent is thus turned into a sort of dream space or holiday home of the imagination, which is set over against, and where one goes to 'get away from', reality. Now it is of course entirely possible that this is the case – that any intimations we might have of 'worlds beyond this world's perplexing waste' (*Don Juan*, XVI, 48) are illusory. It is also true that the Romantics themselves suspected that turning away from the 'weariness, the fever, and the fret' meant culpably escaping into a 'waking dream' (Keats, 'Ode to a Nightingale', 23, 79). Yet surely it is more than a little presumptuous to speak as though the matter had been decided – to speak, that is, as though one could peek through the curtains of finitude and see what lies on the other side? Upon what authority – and from where – does McGann speak when he proclaims that such intimations are an illusion? Upon what principle is transcendence to be taboo-ed? Obviously, the Romantics themselves may be accused of invoking the transcendent without real belief or of popularising a rather anaemic transcendence – and in this respect McGann's sceptical reading is a necessary questioning of the more credulous readings that were hitherto dominant. Nevertheless, what he asserts as a matter of fact is in reality a matter of faith, but its contestability is kept out of view since this first stage of his argument takes place so to speak before it begins. One of the problems with such presuppositions – which appear to be unaware of themselves as such, and hence are ironically 'ideological' – is that they insidiously encourage a distortion of the object of study – Romantic writing – and an obfuscation of the claims of form, in that things that appear to confirm what has already been assumed are privileged as moments of truth and circularly used as interpretative vantage points. In McGann's case, this means seeing his own scepticism in Romanticism's mirror, and taking signs of doubt or anxiety about 'the one Life within us and abroad' ('The Eolian Harp', 26) or 'Intimations of Immortality' and declarations of disbelief as moments of truth in Romantic writing and viewing its more affirmative imaginings – moments, to quote Wordsworth, when its practitioners 'dare to hope' ('Tintern Abbey', 65) – as a matter of beautiful or tortured evasion. If, however, we could learn to be suspicious of our suspicions, and read as Martin Buber counsels – 'not believ[ing] anything a priori' and 'not disbeliev[ing] anything a priori'[32] – if, that is, we can be honest enough to bear in mind that the questions Romanticism asks are still open and can allow our assumptions to be challenged by its claims, instead of silencing its claims with our assumptions, such moments of doubt and disbelief will carry less authority – being matters of conjecture – and will seem less like Romanticism's underlying 'message' (even if such a message can be wrung from language itself). In worrying that transcendence might be an illusion and in hoping that this might not be the case – in 'leav[ing] the thing a problem' (*Don Juan*, XVII, st. 13), like Byron, and in *asking*, like Keats, is it 'a vision or a waking dream?' rather than somewhat hubristically assuming that the matter can be decided conclusively from our side of finitude – the Romantics are far more faithful to the mystery or undecidability of things, and also far more daring in being prepared to countenance the errancy *as well as* the truth of their intimations.

The act of invocation, I have been arguing in this chapter, is an exemplary sign of this daring acceptance, this wagering on the possibility of transcendence – which cannot be interdicted by decree, and may trouble as well as be troubled by our secular sensibilities. It is a reaching out which has only itself as its warrant and which phenomenologically precedes the faith that prompted it. It is a cry, like Rilke's, which is a question about its crying, in which faith and despair become difficult to distinguish. It is the voice in exodus, setting off recklessly into the wilderness, 'by envious winds / Blown vagabond or frustrate'.[33] Though for all this, the voice in calling is quintessentially a voice of hope; hope which unassailably 'forecloses closure',[34] which is the condition of its own possibility and which, in the words of Maurice Blanchot, 'bespeaks the possibility of what escapes the realm of the possible'.[35] To adopt a popular contemporary idiom, we might say that the voice in calling of Romantic invocation is a 'passion for the impossible';[36] a passion for that which infinitely exceeds our grasp, which overflows all containment, and which renders provisional the horizons of the possible. The voice in calling, I suggest, is a sign that the Romantics are keeping vigil for the impossible – perhaps desperately, embarrassingly, without foundation and in spite of themselves. Yet it is this that challenges new historicist attempts to prescribe and police the parameters of the possible in advance of its critique.

Notes

1. *The Selected Poetry of Rainer Maria Rilke*, trans. by Stephen Mitchell (London: Pan Books, 1987).
2. All quotations from Keats are taken from *The Poetical Works of John Keats*, ed. by H. W. Garrod (Oxford: Clarendon Press, 1958). Line references follow quotations in the text.
3. The burden of this predicament – in which belief has become something of a phantom limb – is beautifully rendered in Wordsworth's sonnet 'The world is too much with us'.
4. John Hollander, *Melodious Guile: Fictive Pattern in Poetic Language* (New Haven: Yale University Press, 1988), p. 72.
5. Jonathan Culler, *Literary Theory: A Very Short Introduction* (Oxford: Oxford University Press, 1997), p. 73; *The Pursuit of Signs: Semiotics, Literature, Deconstruction* (London: Routledge, 1981), p. 155. In both, Culler is discussing apostrophe, though he contends in the latter that apostrophe 'is perhaps always an indirect invocation of the muse' (p. 158).

6. Quoted from *The Complete Poetical Works of James Thomson*, ed. by J. Logie Robertson (London: Oxford University Press, 1908).

7. Quoted from *The Prophetic Writings of William Blake*, ed. by D. J. Sloss and J. P. R. Wallis, 2 vols (Oxford: Clarendon Press, 1957).

8. Harold Bloom, *The Visionary Company: A Reading of English Romantic Poetry* (Ithaca: Cornell University Press, 1971), p. 125.

9. Quoted from the Preface to the 1814 edition of *The Excursion*, in *Wordsworth: Poetical Works*, ed. by Thomas Hutchinson, new edn, rev. by Ernest De Selincourt (London: Oxford University Press, 1936), pp. 754–5. All quotations from Wordsworth are taken from this edition, and line references follow quotations in the text.

10. Quoted from *The Midsummer Cushion*, ed. by Anne Tibble (Manchester: Carcanet, 1978).

11. The term 'stammering' has been recently employed by Gilles Deleuze and Félix Guattari in *A Thousand Plateaus: Capitalism and Schizophrenia*, trans. by Brian Massumi (Minneapolis: University of Minnesota Press, 1987) as a way of describing the conjoined linguistic tendencies towards poverty and overload by means of which language itself is made to stammer (a 'creative' strategy they distinguish from stammering in language). I, too, in this chapter propose to view stammering as a sort of eloquence, though my usage owes more to Martin Buber (and the prophetic tradition), for whom it is an appropriate, if not the only, way of intimating divine 'excess'.

12. Quotations from Byron are taken from *Lord Byron: The Complete Poetical Works*, ed. by Jerome J. McGann, 7 vols (Oxford: Clarendon Press, 1980–93). Canto and stanza references are given in the text.

13. Culler, *Literary Theory*, p. 73.

14. Quoted from *Shelley's Poetry and Prose*, ed. by Donald H. Reiman and Neil Fraistat (New York: Norton, 2002).

15. Culler, *Literary Theory*, p. 73.

16. Ibid.

17. Matthew Arnold, *On the Classical Tradition* (New York: University of Michigan Press, 1960), p. 146.

18. Culler, *The Pursuit of Signs*, pp. 143–4.

19. Hollander, *Melodious Guile*, p. 65.

20. Catherine Pickstock, *After Writing: On the Liturgical Consummation of Philosophy* (Oxford: Blackwell, 1998), pp. 193–4.

21. The phrase 'acrobatics and juggling' alludes to St Bernard's description of the subversive counterpoise of monastic life, which he characterises as 'A good sort of playing which is ridiculous to men, but a very beautiful sight to the angels' (*The Letters of Saint Bernard of Clairvaux*, ed. by B. Scott James (London: Burns and Oates, 1953), p. 135).

22. This is not to imply that the Romantics consciously modelled their use of the form on liturgical practice, but to point out, along with Walter Schindler, that 'in its deepest historical roots, invocation is a religious, not a literary phenomenon, appearing as the original form of divine worship in all cultures' (*Voice and Crisis: Invocation in Milton's Poetry* (Connecticut: Archon Books, 1984), p. 6).

23. The phrase in quotation marks is taken from Jean-Yves Lacoste, 'Liturgy and Kenosis, from *Expérience et Absolu*', trans. by David H. Thompson, in

The Postmodern God: A Theological Reader, ed. by Graham Ward (Oxford: Blackwell, 1997), pp. 249–64 (p. 250).

24. According to Jean-Louis Chrétien, the act of calling gives visibility to transcendence in a chiastic sense, since he argues that our calling out is in fact a response, which is required to reveal this anterior call (*The Call and Response*, trans. by Anne A. Davenport (New York: Fordham University Press, 2004), p. 30).

25. See Herbert Marks, 'On Prophetic Stammering', *The Yale Journal of Criticism: Interpretation in the Humanities*, 1:1 (1987), pp. 1–20.

26. Pickstock, *After Writing*, p. 195.

27. This is not idolatrously to suppose that God is at our beck and call or that invocation is a sort of magic, for, as Denys reminds us, calling is not a matter of pulling the divine down towards us, but of 'stretch[ing] ourselves prayerfully upward' (*The Divine Names*, in *Pseudo-Dionysius: The Complete Works*, trans. by Colm Luibheid (New York: Paulist Press, 1987), pp. 47–131 (p. 68)).

28. Jean-Yves Lacoste, 'Liturgy and Kenosis', p. 253.

29. See 'Linguistics and Poetics', in Lucy Burke, Tony Crowley and Alan Girvan (eds), *The Routledge Language and Cultural Theory Reader* (London: Routledge, 2000), pp. 334–9.

30. *The Call and Response*, p. 30. See also in this connection, Jean-Luc Marion, *Being Given: Towards a Phenomenology of Givenness*, trans. by Jeffrey L. Kosky (Stanford: Stanford University Press, 2002).

31. Jerome McGann, *The Romantic Ideology: A Critical Investigation* (Chicago: University of Chicago Press, 1983), pp. 131, 137, 145.

32. *On the Bible: Eighteen Studies* (New York: Schocken Books, 1982), p. 5.

33. The quotation is taken from the description of the wayfaring of Adam and Eve's prayers in *Paradise Lost* (XI, 15–16).

34. Charles Winquist, Foreword to Clayton Crockett, *A Theology of the Sublime* (London: Routledge, 2001), p. xi.

35. *The Infinite Conversation*, trans. by Susan Hanson (Minneapolis: University of Minnesota Press, 1993), p. 41.

36. In the variously inflected writings of Derrida, Caputo, Kearney and others, the impossible is that which paradoxically *saves*, in preserving, the otherness of that which is to come. See, for example, John D. Caputo, 'Apostles of the Impossible', in John D. Caputo and Michael J. Scanlon (eds), *God, the Gift and Postmodernism* (Bloomington: Indiana University Press, 1999), pp. 185–222.

4
'Ruinous Perfection': Reading Authors and Writing Readers in Romantic Fragments

Mark Sandy

Romantic fragments, although readily identifiable, are as diffuse in kind as in form. Romanticism's fascination with the fragmentary is manifest in numerous works that are either textually fragmented (whether by dint of design or accident) or complete literary forms that treat ruins as a central subject. Interest in the fragment in the period transgresses traditional generic boundaries. This transcendence of formal categories necessitated the exclusion of Romantic fragments from Stuart Curran's survey of *Poetic Form and British Romanticism* and warranted their central place in Marjorie Levinson's study of *The Romantic Fragment Poem.*[1] Avoiding certain formal issues, Levinson's historicising method places poetic fragments of the Romantic period within their wider ideological, cultural and biographical context as a means of legitimatising these incomplete textual forms. Levinson's historicist sense of the social, cultural and political horizons of the nineteenth century regulates the dynamic between the author's text and the reader, but occludes those peculiar atemporal demands of a Romantic culture of posterity.[2] Breaking with this historicising tendency, this chapter shares an affinity with Balachandra Rajan's thematic reflections in *The Form of the Unfinished* and focuses on anachronistic posthumous exchanges between deceased author and future reader.[3]

I

Ruins of completion: Byron's *Manfred*

Byron in Faustian mode fantasises about surviving ahistorically beyond the confines of those recorded events that determine the figures and occurrences which become monumentalised as public history.[4] Byron's lyric drama, *Manfred*, epitomises the finished Romantic project that images its central anxieties over posthumous reputation through the fragmentary ruins of the historical past. In the opening scene of *Manfred*'s third and final act, a direct corollary exists between the hero's attempted evasion of historical reality and his intensely solitary recollection of youthful night ramblings:

> When I was wandering, – upon such a night
> I stood within the Coliseum's wall,
> 'Midst the chief relics of almighty Rome;
> The trees which grew along the broken arches
> Waved dark in the blue midnight, and the stars
> Shone through the rents of ruin; from afar
> The watchdog bayed beyond the Tiber; and
> More near from out of the Caesar's palace came
> The owl's long cry, and, interruptedly,
> Of distant sentinels the fitful song
> Begun and died upon the gentle wind.
> Some cypresses beyond the time-worn breach
> Appeared to skirt the horizon, yet they stood
> Within a bowshot – where the Caesars dwelt,
> And dwell the tuneless birds of night; amidst
> A grove which springs through levell'd battlements,
> And twines its roots with the imperial hearths,
> Ivy usurps the laurel's place of growth; –
> But the gladiators' bloody Circus stands,
> A noble wreck in ruinous perfection! (III, iv, 9–28)[5]

Manfred's description anticipates the demise of Roman civilisation envisaged in *Childe Harold's Pilgrimage*, canto IV. Manfred's chance reminiscence of stumbling upon this midnight scene, enchanted by the light of celestial bodies, is a reminder of the disparity between the terrible reality of the Coliseum's past and its moonlit transformation into the graceful tragic nobility of 'ruinous perfection'.[6]

On an introspective level, Manfred's moonlit adventure demonstrates how random and very different perceptions of the same observed object or figure can be, and instructs Manfred's recognition that his perfected image of Astarte is the product of only a single chance perception.[7] Manfred's nocturnal vigil is the key, for Jane Stabler, to his understanding and acceptance of what has already passed; however, acts of remembrance gaze towards futurity as frequently as they look back towards the past. Manfred's retrospective is not only focused on remembering events from the past but also on how the historical past will be remembered in, and for, the future. History is the foster-child of both remembrance and forgetfulness.[8] Manfred's verbal ingenuity contributes as much to the effect of the 'softened down [...] hoar austerity' as the transformative quality of the 'tender light' (III, iv, 32–3) does. This recount of the moonlit Coliseum becomes a wilful historical misreading which demands that Rome and all her accomplishments be honourably monumentalised, setting up a way of reading the past that would ensure that Manfred's own posthumous reputation of superior intellect, vision and prodigious feats is untainted by his own transgressions. History's recorded annals, Manfred is painfully aware, determine whether the Romans will be memorialised for their culture, technical innovations and empire-building or their cruelty, tyranny and barbarity.

The fate of Rome and her Coliseum correlates with Manfred's anxieties over whether those succeeding generations will associate his name with honour or disgrace. The restoration of Rome's reputation, Manfred's name and Byron's life and work reside with the interpretative choices that readers make in their reconstruction of an ambivalent remembrance of this 'ruinous' scene. Byron's indeterminate presentation of Rome creates a decisive break with temporality in a bid to excite a posthumous reputation and existence outside the historical moment of *Manfred*'s own inception and reception. Yet these thematic anxieties have been regularly legitimised through the sustained critical insistence on those contemporary biographical and historical circumstances surrounding *Manfred*'s composition. These include: concerns over the ineffectuality of the aristocracy in the wake of the French Revolution; Napoleon's temporary escape from Elba and subsequent internment on St Helena in 1815; Byron's banishment from polite English society, after rumours of the Augusta Leigh affair began to spread in the spring of 1816.[9] Even as part of a finished dramatic form, *Manfred*'s broken monuments of Rome, it seems, are only completed in the closed hermeneutic circle of historical readings that reassert the significance of these political, social, cultural and biographical crises at the precise moment they are forcibly evaded.

Historicising approaches resist textual free play within the fragmentary form. They ground the endless self-conscious spectacle of Byronic authorial performance in a transcendent historical realm. Formal and fragmentary instability is resolved by recourse to those public and personal events that first governed a text's indeterminate formal condition, and this is sanctioned by the literary work's disrupted form, which openly invites questions about provenance, the circumstances surrounding authorial composition and artistic purpose. Yet, even when Byron's poetic treatment of these fragmentary forms is conditioned by an anxiety of posterity, it ultimately valorises his future readers over an immediate historical audience and reality.

Byron's regulation of these anxieties over posterity through an indeterminacy of form aligns him, in poetic practice and perspective, with Keats and Shelley.[10] Mindful of current re-negotiations between formal and contextual criticism in Romantic Studies, the subsequent argument swerves away from restrictive conceptualisations of the historical to foreground the significance of intellectual history for a literary text's future reception.[11] This history of ideas furnishes us with resonant models, from Søren Kierkegaard and Friedrich Nietzsche, for appreciating Romantic negotiations of authorial posterity. These intellectual connections do not reverse Harold Bloom's 'anxiety of influence' to establish Kierkegaard and Nietzsche as formative sources for Romanticism.[12] Instead the fragmented mediations of Keats and Shelley on subjectivity, history and poetic form are considered below as, firstly, anticipating developments in the philosophy of Nietzsche and Kierkegaard and, secondly, performing rather than articulating the concerns of these post-Romantic philosophies.[13] The formal incompletion of these fragments both exacerbates the inherent instability present in teleological-driven understandings of human agency, memory and meaning, and revises the parameters of posthumous influence.

II

Reading authors: Keats and Kierkegaard

Keats's *The Eve of St Mark* is a poetic meditation on literary posterity. *The Eve of St Mark* resurrects the world of ritual and romance to confront the reader with a series of oblique figures, which stand in for the inscrutable event of death itself. Rhetorical exchanges of this kind enable Keats to defend *The Eve of St Mark* against those prospective readers who might reduce his narrative to a single critical reading. As the poem's central figure, Bertha, substitutes the martyred figure of Saint Mark for her own imagined martyrdom, so Keats as deceased author enters his text as the sole imaginative cohesion behind the eremite's footnotes, the 'Auctour['s]' legend and the performing 'queens of spades' (86).[14] Bertha's perplexing and perplexed figure is rapt by the 'legend page / Of holy Mark' (89–90) just as Keats's readers are by the poetic fragment which contains her. Keats challenges his audience to extract meaning from 'holy Mark['s]' unfinished 'legend', the cryptically revealed rite of St Mark's Eve, and the incomplete story of Bertha. *The Eve of St Mark* voices Keats's anxiety over the delicate symbiotic relationship that exists between a writer's work and its reader. This authorial concern manifests itself as a spectral shadow-play staged behind the unsuspecting, relentlessly reading Bertha:

> Untired she read; her shadow still
> Glower'd about as it would fill
> The room with wildest forms and shades,
> As though some ghostly queens of spades
> Had come to mock behind her back. (83–7)

The enigmatic phrase, 'queens of spades', dramatises Keats's own misgivings about the narrative's posthumous existence and those future readers who will claim his text for their own. Keats's diabolical scene of reading resonates with Kierkegaard's haunting speculation that it

> was as if the seducer moved like a shadow over my floor, as if he threw a glance at the papers, as if he had fastened his demonic eye on me.[15]

These 'ghostly' forms (86), for Keats and Kierkegaard, usher in the inevitable closure of life with death and yet still resist, through generating conjecture amongst future readers about their significance, their formal closure. Keats's shadowy 'queens of spades' (86) figuratively displace the actual event of death, recognising that formal control is a shared endeavour between author and reader whether deceased or living. By avoiding detection and thereby interpretation, those 'queens of spades' mock Bertha's earnest efforts to interpret the figures of her legend and pre-empt the formal difficulties encountered by modern readers. Keats's heroine represents a contemporary reader of his own time engaged in reading a literary work from an earlier historical period. Bertha's 'legend page' (89) is a canonical account of a saint's life as well as a source for the apocryphal – superstitious – practices associated with its martyr. Bertha's interpretation and identification with Saint Mark's 'many pains' (92) is vital to an imaginative resuscitation of his many 'holy' deeds (90–2), but in itself also constitutes part of her own pagan vigil on St Mark's Eve. Her solitary act is one of seemingly pious devotion, but is perpetrated in isolation from the crowd's communal prayer. Bertha's solitude is only possible, and all the more striking, when viewed in relation to the collective activity of the 'pious companies' and 'patient folk' (15, 20). Bertha's 'fireside' (41) reflections echo those 'fireside oratories' (16) abandoned by the gathering congregation, reinforcing, simultaneously, her ties to the community she withdraws from and her solitary, alienated, state. Bertha's ability to inhabit these contradictory 'uncertainties, Mysteries, doubts, without any irritable reaching after fact & reason' encapsulates the malleability of the Keatsian poetical character that is vital to the authorial self's posthumous reputation and survival.[16]

Paradoxically, the relationship Keats perceives in *The Eve of St Mark* between the creative process of writing and the creation of an authorial self guarantees Keats's continued authority over his narrative poem through the dispersal of his identity as author. Keats derives poetic strength from the prospect of his own self-dissolution. Keats calls into question with Kierkegaard – who enigmatically claims that 'I regard myself rather as a *reader* of books, not as the *author*' (12)[17] – the distinction between those who read and write to suggest shared imaginative experience is an essential prerequisite for reader and author to comprehend one another. As Keats writes elsewhere, 'nothing ever becomes real till it is experienced':

> Axioms in philosophy are not axioms until they are proved upon our pulses. We read fine things but never feel them until we have gone the same steps as the author.[18]

Keats holds with Kierkegaard that interpretative choices are not mere abstractions and that any refusal to make such choices is a denial of life and existence itself. Similar to Kierkegaard, Keats is acutely aware that as an author he cannot be certain of readers making the right interpretative choice, but that he can make his audience more aware of the necessity of choice by presenting a multiplicity of interpretative points of view. In a late work entitled *The Point of View for My Work as an Author*, Kierkegaard reflects on this authorial dilemma:

> Compel a person to an opinion, a conviction, a belief – in all eternity, that I cannot do. But one thing I can do [...] [is] compel him to become aware. By compelling him to become aware, I succeed in compelling him to judge. Now he judges. But what he judges is not in my power. Perhaps he judges the very opposite of what I desire. (50)

Keats's apparent lack of formal control compels those reading *The Eve of St Mark* to make interpretative choices about the indeterminate oppositions that exist in the poem between reading and writing, public and private, action and inaction, aesthetic and religious, life and death. These alternatives are mediated through Bertha's observance of a religious vigil and engagement in the aesthetic process of reading. She desires to re-write what she reads as she tirelessly studies her book and paces around her chamber. Keats's election of Bertha for heroine recalls Thomas Chatterton's pseudonymous production of the Rowley poems (alleged to be of fifteenth-century provenance) and signals the extent to which Keats had issues of literary production and consumption in mind.

Imbued with this distinctive medieval English flavour of Chaucer, Gower and Chatterton's imitations, Keats's narrative portrays reading as a secretive, and often frustrated, enterprise of unlocking the clandestine meaning of a text's 'many mysteries' (37).[19] In its fragmented, incomplete form *The Eve of St Mark* defies its audience's desire to uncover the secret at the heart of Keats's narrative, forecasting that its reader, like Bertha, will become a 'poor cheated soul' (69) unable to decipher its 'legend' (28, 89). Anticipated by the 'lamp' (70) that illuminates her book, Bertha's realisation of intellectual or spiritual enlightenment is literally engulfed by unknown 'wildest forms and shades' (85). *The Eve of St Mark*'s 'queens of spades' represent the impossibility of accurately comprehending figures and remain beyond Bertha's comprehension as a figural representation. Her interpretative faculties are confounded by the narrative's 'learned eremite' (93) who is, on one hand, the original author of St Mark's legend and, on the other, only a later editor who supplies those 'crow quill size' (96) footnotes to the main body of text scribed by Keats's implied 'Auctour' (113). Keats's formal dissolution of his authorial presence into the multiple perspectives and figures of eremite, Auctour and Bertha, protects his sovereign claim over formal meaning as the reader's capacity to settle on any one interpretation is disrupted by the narrative's inherent formal indeterminacy. Keats's *The Eve of St Mark* obliges its readers to judge between previously established oppositions and frames within the narrative. Kierkegaard's own work, *Either/Or*, itself appeared under the three pseudonyms of Victor Eremita the editor, an anonymous aesthete author of *Either* and Judge Vilhelm, the ethical writer of *Or*. These authorial deceptions are, for Kierkegaard, the presentation of 'one author as lying inside the other, as in a Chinese-box puzzle' (32).

Keats presents Bertha, in *The Eve of St Mark*, as a symbol that conflates reader and author, complicating the reader's ability to make an interpretative choice as she represents a coalescence of those binary oppositions held in contradistinction throughout Keats's opening scene.[20] Future readers of *The Eve of St Mark* will find their critical attitudes towards the fragment's 'many mysteries' (37) foreshadowed by those fictional perspectives formally embedded and explicitly elaborated within the very narrative they seek to elucidate, certifying the prophylactic element of Keats's poetics and subjectivity.

Keats's negatively capable poetics resist the singular authorial presence of a Wordsworthian 'egotistic sublime',[21] as well as classical theories of authorial impersonality, in anticipation of Kierkegaard's conception of the aesthetic self in *Either/Or* as comprised of 'a multiple concretion inwardly determined in many ways' (525).[22] Both author and reader as fictional constructs must take up a vital interpretative choice in relation to literature as, in Kierkegaard's verdict, their very being-in-the-text is mediated through their commitment to a critical perspective which determines their stance on textual existence and living itself. Keats's anxiety over his own cultural influence from beyond the grave provided the substance for and impetus behind his speculative poetics. Keats and Kierkegaard posthumously confer a prominence on those authors who, as ideal readers, choose an active and authentic critical judgement in relation to their life and work.

III

Writing readers: Shelley and Nietzsche

The Triumph of Life's fragmentary formal state has become a prolepsis of Shelley's incomplete and ill-fated voyage and broken body. On 8 July 1822, *The Triumph of Life* was rendered a fragment poem by accidental tragedy rather than lack of artistic vision. The interrupted ending heightens a reader's sense of self-conscious and responsible participation in a fictional exchange with the author and implicates that reader as protagonist in the unfolding poetic drama. Prefiguring Nietzsche's response to Enlightenment thought, Shelley conceives of rational metaphysics as only one interpretation of the universe out of an infinite series of possible fictions. Nietzsche writes:

> Every word immediately becomes a concept, inasmuch as it is intended to serve as a reminder of the unique and wholly individualized original experience. Every concept originates through our equating what is unequal. No leaf ever wholly equals another, and the concept 'leaf' is formed through an arbitrary abstraction from these individual differences, through forgetting the distinctions; and now it gives rise to the idea that in nature there might be something besides the leaves

which would be 'leaf' – some kind of original form after which all
other leaves are woven, marked, copied, coloured, curled and painted,
but by unskilled hands, so that no copy turned out to be a correct,
reliable, and faithful image of the original form.[23]

For Nietzsche, at least, our interaction with observable phenomenon
is constituted from an intricate series of fictions, which, in this case,
mistakenly project geometric equality where there is none to be found
and so falsifies the actual state of affairs in the world. Nietzsche's passage,
partly, caricatures those aspects of the Kantian project that furnished
Shelley with a basis upon which to oppose Enlightenment faith in a rigid
metaphysics of absolute categories and values. Such a view incorpor-
ates metaphysics into the metaphorical mode, regarding Enlightenment
philosophy as merely another fiction, rather than a given absolute. In
The Triumph of Life, Shelley's poet-figure, as narrator (spectator, author
and reader) of Rousseau's presence, questions, as does Nietzsche, the
founding assumptions of Enlightenment thought:

> And suddenly my brain become as sand
>
> Where the first wave had more than half erased
> The track of deer on desert Labrador,
> Whilst the fierce wolf from which they fled amazed
>
> Leaves his stamp visibly upon the shore
> Until the second bursts – so on my sight
> Burst a new Vision never seen before. (405–10)[24]

For Paul de Man in *The Rhetoric of Romanticism*, Shelley's simile represents a 'failure to satisfy a desire for self-knowledge' (99),[25] because of the
eventual impossibility of accurately recording such knowledge on the
sandy surface of Rousseau's transformed 'brain' (405). De Man registers
these lines as recording a nihilistic erasure of the figural 'I' at the exact
moment of its own positing. To go against the tide of de Manian opinion
is to interpret these lines as a tragic attempt at self-invention for both
author and reader alike. De Man's deconstructive reading suggests that
vital to all attempts at self-knowledge is a subscription to the illusion of
idealism. For de Man, Rousseau asking to be shown 'whence I came, and
where I am, and why' (398) is a request posited with a naive expectation
that he will be answered by a revelatory metaphysical insight into life.
Yet it is precisely the idealism of Rousseau's question that permits scepticism about the possibility of metaphysical absolutes. Idealistic illusions
are stripped away to divulge a mode of epistemological and ontological

uncertainty, as the self is perpetually erased by the constant action of shifting sands and incessant sea-change. Nevertheless, the questioning speaker's character, in *The Triumph of Life*, is never entirely erased, for as one identity fades the creation of another modified one begins. De Man's critical effort to erase the self leads only to a re-emergence of its importance and responsiveness to its own elusive fictional status. De Man's sense of disfiguration in *The Triumph of Life* does not testify to the impossibility of reading, as he claims, but instead to the scholarly endeavour to extract a readable, formally complete text from Shelley's fragment.[26] That editorial task was occasioned by the random occurrence of Shelley's death, as this single event rendered the manuscript of the poem forever fragmented, displaced, incomplete and, for precisely these reasons, forever readable. De Man's obliterating 'madness of words' (122) is avoidable, however, if what emerges is a countless series of writings and readings through which author and reader participate in a relentless succession of self-revision and self-fashioning. Shelley's posterity is shaped by countless readers who re-mould his poetic identity for a future time.

The unease about posthumous reputation in *The Triumph of Life* finds expression in Shelley's treatment of Rousseau, which fluctuates between his rehabilitation and rejection as a thinker of the Enlightenment. Shelley's irresolute attitude to the Enlightenment is reflected by Rousseau's 'last' look (546), marking his separation from the 'sad pageantry' (176), which still consists of 'those spoilers spoiled, Voltaire [...] and Kant' (235–6). *The Triumph of Life*'s interpenetrating patterns of light and dark point to Shelley's fixation with intellectual reputation, enlightenment and ignorance.[27] His exploration of what it means to be enlightened or ignorant is sketched out in the myriad questions asked by the younger Rousseau and the dreaming narrator: 'Half to myself I said, "And what is this? / Whose shape is that within the car? & why?"' (176–8). The narrator's questions are cut short by Rousseau's interjection of 'Life' (180) in response to them. Rousseau's 'strange distortion' diagnoses in the narrator a 'thirst of knowledge' (194), which once may have been like his own, but Rousseau, having already 'feared, loved, hated, suffered [...] and died' (200), has become 'weary' (196) of seeking out knowledge. Rousseau's affliction extends beyond weariness to an incapacity to know, as he is unable to answer the narrator's question, 'who art thou?' (199), replying only that his present form is a 'disguise' and that there 'was once Rousseau' (204). Rousseau's credibility as an enlightened guide is shrouded in a shadow of doubt even before he has began to 'relate / The progress of the pageant' (193). The narrator's constant questioning represents a human desire, which achieved its fullest expression in the Enlightenment, to wrest order, purpose and meaning from the indifferent, ceaseless, 'mighty torrent' of life which randomly buffets an individual 'through the sky [as] / One of million leaves of summer's bier' (53, 50–1).[28] This craving leads to the belief that beyond the chaos of existence there is a metaphysical realm that lends life a purpose or what Shelley, echoing *Adonais*, identifies as a 'native noon' for 'the sacred few' (131, 128).

Shelley's narrator and the young Rousseau believe that an absolute, unquestionable and transcendental meaning can be imposed upon life, and they strive to establish its definitive significance. By implication, Rousseau belongs with those feigners of the 'morn of truth' (214) and the supposedly enlightened company of Voltaire and Kant, who remain chained to the car of Life. If Rousseau is enlightened, his insight is derived not from philosophical abstraction, but (with a Keatsian emphasis on experience) through his confessional response to the question, 'whence camest thou and whither goest thou?' (296). Seminal to Rousseau's own autobiographical search for knowledge is his encounter with 'a shape all light' in the 'orient cavern' (344, 352):

> which with one hand did fling
> Dew on the earth, as if she were the Dawn
> Whose invisible rain forever seemed to sing
>
> 'A silver music on the mossy lawn,
> And still before her on the dusky grass
> Iris her many coloured scarf had drawn. –' (352–6)

Significantly, Rousseau's 'shape all light' is a product of 'the bright omnipresence / Of morning' which 'burned on the waters of the well' (344, 346). Recalling Wordsworth's regret for the passing of 'a glory from the earth' ('Ode: Intimations of Immortality', 18), Rousseau's vision becomes symbolic of those ideals he sought to extract from a chaotic universe. The sensual 'shape all light' is a momentary coalescence of invisible vision, material insubstantiality and 'many coloured' white brilliance (356, 351–2) occasioned by Rousseau's own imaginative fiction. Reminiscent of Manfred's Astarte, Shelley's 'shape all light' is born of the youthful Rousseau's will to knowledge, which insists that the transcendental 'realm without a name' (396) can be known and expressed.

The older Rousseau's confession voices a scepticism about the 'shape all light' that was absent from his original experience of her, acknowledging that to contemplate such ideal unity and beauty risks 'the gazer's mind' being 'strewn beneath / Her feet like embers' (386–7).

Contemplation of an ideal metaphysical realm turns out not to be valuable in itself, but for exposing a human world of contingencies and transience. Rousseau's 'shape all light' does not enlighten him through her revelatory brilliance, for she is 'a Day upon the threshold of the east' (389), but by a 'darkness' which 'reillumines even the least / Of heaven's living eyes' (391–2). Rousseau's pursuit of the 'shape all light' embodies Nietzsche's estimation that the Apollonian world of light, order, reason and harmony must itself be overreached by a Dionysian tragic acceptance of reality's transient chaos.[29]

What, if anything, the 'shape all light' reveals to Rousseau is that pursuing an ideal leads only to an existential acceptance of this 'harsh world' (334). After all, her 'fair shape waned in the coming light' of 'the new Vision' with 'its cold bright car' of Life (412, 434) and, having drugged Rousseau with 'Nepenthe' (299), she abandons him to 'the sick day in which we wake to weep' (430). Rousseau's quest for enlightenment ends with the realisation that aspirations to ideals are only 'forever sought' and 'forever lost' (431). More importantly, Rousseau acknowledges the 'shape all light' as an illuminating darkness, which teaches an acceptance of life's procession and a certain responsibility for his words that 'were seeds of misery' (279). Shelley's Rousseau, if he is to avoid condemnation, has to come to terms with 'a world of agony' (295) in which his mind's 'fires' will be extinguished in 'the dust of death' (388). First-hand knowledge of the 'harsh world' (334) is evident in Shelley's distinction between Classical 'great bards of old who inly quelled' and recent poets of tragic feeling (274–9). Those 'great bards of old' – who had previously attained sanctuary in the abode of the 'sacred few' (*Adonais*, 128, 131) – are purged by being infected with human existence's 'contagion' (277) in order that their words become a future balm to the world. Life cannot be substituted with esoteric ponderings, and all writers, including Rousseau, should learn to suffer the 'viler pain' of human existence with the rest of the multitude (279). These 'great bards of old', Rousseau, the dreaming narrator and *The Triumph of Life*'s audience are urged through their acute awareness of suffering to participate in self-revision:

> Figures ever new
> Rise on the bubble, paint them how you may;
> We have but thrown, as those before us threw. (248–50)

These emerging 'New figures' (247) constantly risk becoming 'faded' (248) and threaten to disclose the falsity of their supposed truths and their own fictionality. The validity of any one of these self-revisions or self-creations will always be in doubt and open to question, capable only of a momentary self-affirmation which is constantly revised and replaced by 'Figures ever new'. Readers must, as Shelley urges in *The Triumph of Life*, 'from spectator turn / Actor or victim in this wretchedness' so that they actively engage with life and literature teaching the deceased author's text, in Rousseau's words, 'what thou wouldst be taught' (305–7). Once again poetic self-identity and self-knowledge are products of both assemblage and disclosure: a procedure worked out for the author through composing a literary work and for the reader through the construction – or reading – of that writing. Nietzsche accurately gauges the extent to which a reader's restorative imagination revives a departed author's words on the page when he, prophetically, sketches the afterlife of his own work and others:

> Every writer is surprised anew how, once a book has detached himself from him, it goes on to live a life of its own; it is to him as though part of an insect had come free and was now going its own way. Perhaps he almost forgets it, perhaps he raises himself above the views he set down in it, perhaps he no longer even understands it and has lost those wings upon which he flew when he thought out that book: during which time it seeks out its readers, enkindles life, makes happy, terrifies, engenders new works.[30]

A reader's response is governed by these formal difficulties of knowing and interpretation, but Shelley's fragment demands that a reader loyal to their meaning will, eventually, pass beyond its broken poetic form to an active life of living, knowing and suffering. The Nietzschean duality of Shelley's vision of tragic consciousness is evident in the 'icy cold' (77) anticipation of the car of Life's approach, driven relentlessly on by the 'Janus-visaged Shadow' whose 'four faces [...] had their eyes banded' (99–100):

> So came a chariot on the silent storm
> Of its own rushing splendour, and a Shape
> So sate within as one whom years deform
>
> Beneath a dusky hood and double cape
> Crouching within the shadow of a tomb,
> And o'er what seemed the head a cloud like crape
>
> Was bent, a dun and faint ætherial gloom
> Tempering the light. (86–93)

Heralded by a 'cold glare [...] intenser than the noon' (77) and borne 'on the silent storm / Of its own splendour', Shelley's chariot recalls how the 'shape all light' tramples Rousseau's mind 'thought by thought' (387) with its 'light's severe excess' (424). The 'Shape' concealed 'beneath a dusky hood [...] crouching within the shadow of a tomb' (89) is the inevitable dark other to Rousseau's idealised vision of the 'shape all light' and a reminder that unity, fixed meaning and transcendent ideals lead only to a realisation of reality's relentless indifference and random chaos. Such chaotic indifference is reinforced by the charioteer's 'banded eyes' (103), and the 'wonder-winged team['s]' obscurity, whose 'shapes' are lost in apocalyptic and self-destructive 'thick lightnings' (95–6). The chariot's 'rushing splendour' points to, as the 'shape all light' instructs Rousseau, the destruction of idealised vision and the acceptance of negation and self-annihilation which is itself an impetus for poetic fictions; the 'car's creative ray' (533) is the obliterating 'cold glare' (77). Exquisitely dramatising Nietzsche's symbiosis of Apollonian and Dionysian, light and darkness, creation and destruction, life and death coalesce as the 'shape all light' fades into the shadowy unknown form of the 'Shape'.[31] In *The Triumph of Life*, neither of these visions is final and the car of Life might at any moment dissolve into a new vision as the chariot succeeds the 'Shape all light'. This implied succession of visions play out Rousseau's understanding of how 'figures ever new / Rise on the bubble' (247–8) and his later observation that 'mask after mask fell from countenance / And form of all' (536–7).[32]

If Shelley's own fragmented 'form' is to leave 'his stamp visibly upon the shore' (536, 408) as an enduring posthumous influence, then his poetic meaning and subjectivity must be numerously recast in those subsequent interpretative 'visions' of future readers. Signposts to these Nietzschean self-revisions are scattered everywhere amongst the ruins of Shelley's *The Triumph of Life*; waiting to be read in and written on the hidden countenance of the 'Shape' within the car of Life (89). The lessons written and read in this concealed face promote an overcoming of life and literary text. Yet Shelley's *The Triumph of Life* refuses to be prescriptive about the lessons that are written or read into this undetermined visage. Its lasting authority and meaning rests not with Shelley, or Nietzsche, but with their readers' countersignatures.[33] Shelley and Nietzsche ensure, through an infinite indeterminacy of meaning and signification, that the responsibility of reconstituting their texts is firmly placed with the reader. Actual ruins and literary fragmentary forms belong neither strictly to history's past or present moment, as their very incompletion heightens a consciousness of historicity and the impossibility of possessing a total historical knowledge. Through their incomplete formal state, these literary fragments become both temporal and ahistorical grounds of their own absence and presence, knowing and unknowing, being and non-being.

Read through Nietzsche and Kierkegaard, these self-reflexive Romantic meditations on poetic reputation, posthumous authority and future reception are intensified. Byron's *Manfred*, Keats's *The Eve of St Mark* and Shelley's *The Triumph of Life* (re-)inscribe their deceased, once living, authorial presences into the future historical present of reading. In each poem, ruinous forms obscure these 'ghostlier demarcations',[34] resisting temporal restrictions to safeguard themselves as enduring ahistorical monuments of authorial posterity.

Notes

1. See Marjorie Levinson, *The Romantic Fragment: A Critique of Form* (Chapel Hill: North Carolina University Press, 1986), p. ix.
2. Discussed in Andrew Bennett, *Romantic Poets and the Culture of Posterity* (Cambridge: Cambridge University Press, 1999) and Lucy Newlyn, *Reading, Writing, and Romanticism* (Oxford: Oxford University Press, 2000).
3. Balachandra Rajan, *The Form of the Unfinished: English Poetics from Spenser to Pound* (Princeton: Princeton University Press, 1985).
4. Daniel P. Watkins regards Byron's drama as inextricable from social and historical processes. See *A Materialist Critique of English Romantic Drama* (Gainsville: University Press of Florida, 1993), pp. 149–62.
5. All quotations from *Manfred* are taken from *Lord Byron: The Complete Poetical Works*, ed. by Jerome J. McGann, 7 vols (Oxford: Oxford University Press, 1980–93), IV. Act, scene and line references follow quotations in the text.
6. Vincent Newey similarly detects private and public 'levels of response' in the Coliseum episode of *Childe Harold's Pilgrimage* IV ('Authoring the Self', in Beatty and Vincent Newey (eds), *Byron and the Limits of Fiction* (Liverpool: Liverpool University Press, 1988), pp. 148–90 (p. 172)).
7. Jane Stabler offers this reading and surveys key critical readings of *Manfred*. See Stabler, *Burke to Byron, Barbauld to Baillie 1790–1830* (Basingstoke: Palgrave, 2002), pp. 73–4. Elsewhere, Stabler's 'historically rooted' examination of Byron's digressive poetics avoids issues of posterity (see *Byron, Poetics and History* (Cambridge: Cambridge University Press, 2002), p. 9).
8. Alternatively, Peter Manning emphasises historical remembrance over forgetfulness in *Manfred* in *Byron and His Fictions* (Detroit: Wayne State University Press, 1978), pp. 73–4.

9. Such studies of personal and political history include: Jerome J. McGann, *The Romantic Ideology: A Critical Investigation* (Chicago: Chicago University Press, 1983); Malcolm Kelsall, *Byron's Politics* (Brighton: Harvester, 1987); Richard Lansdown, *Byron's Historical Dramas* (Oxford: Clarendon Press, 1992); Watkins, *A Materialist Critique of English Romantic Drama*; Moyra Haslett, *Don Juan and the Don Juan Legend* (Oxford: Clarendon Press, 1997); Stabler, *Byron, Poetics and History*.

10. Philip W. Martin notes that *Manfred* 'bears everywhere the stamp of its period' while nevertheless insisting that 'it could not have been written by anyone but Byron' (*Byron: A Poet Before His Public* (Cambridge: Cambridge University Press, 1982), p. 108).

11. Susan Wolfson has re-opened the debate between critical conceptions of intrinsic textual form and its relation to extrinsic historical forces: see *Formal Charges: The Shaping of Poetry in British Romanticism* (Stanford: Stanford University Press, 1997), p. 30.

12. Such a move would approximate Harold Bloom's idea of *apophrades*. See Bloom, *The Anxiety of Influence: A Theory of Poetry* (London: Oxford University Press, 1975), pp. 19–45, 139–55.

13. For Nietzsche's complex relationship with Romanticism see my *Poetics of Self and Form in Keats and Shelley: Nietzschean Subjectivity and Genre* (Aldershot: Ashgate, 2005), pp. 1–12.

14. Quotations from Keats are taken from *The Poems of John Keats*, ed. by Jack Stillinger (London: Heinemann, 1978). Line references follow quotations in the text.

15. Søren Kierkegaard, *Either/Or: A Fragment of Life*, trans. by Alastair Hannay (Harmondsworth: Penguin, 1992), p. 33.

16. Keats's letter to his brothers of December 1817, in *The Letters of John Keats*, ed. by Hyder Rollins, 2 vols (Cambridge, Mass.: Harvard University Press, 1958), I, p. 193.

17. Søren Kierkegaard, *The Point of View for My Work as an Author*, ed. and trans. by Howard V. Hong and Edna H. Hong (Princeton: Princeton University Press, 1998). Page references follow quotations in the text.

18. Letter to George and Georgiana Keats of 19 March 1819; letter to John Hamilton Reynolds of 3 May 1818 (*The Letters of John Keats*, II, p. 81; I, p. 279).

19. This issue is further vexed by Keats's inclusion of the poem in a September 1819 letter (omitting lines 133–7), which separates his mock-medieval lines from the main body of the narrative (see *Letters of John Keats*, II, p. 204). For a discussion of this see Mary Rebecca Thayer, 'Keats: *The Eve of St Mark*', *Modern Language Notes*, 34 (1919), pp. 149–55, and David Luke, '*The Eve of St Mark*': Keats's "ghostly Queen of Spades" and the Textual Superstition', *Studies in Romanticism*, 9 (1970), pp. 168–71 (pp. 162–7). For a more recent account, see David B. Pirie, 'Old Saints and Young Lovers: Keats's *The Eve of St Mark* and Popular Culture', in Michael O'Neill (ed.), *Keats: Bicentenary Readings* (Edinburgh: Edinburgh University Press, 1997), pp. 48–70 (pp. 58–9).

20. Newlyn notes that this 'system of defence [...] turns on a dialectic, in which writers and readers figure each other as reflexes of themselves' (*Reading, Writing, and Romanticism*, p. 48).

21. Letter to Richard Woodhouse, 27 October 1818, in *The Letters of John Keats*, I, p. 387.
22. Tilottama Rajan explores Kierkegaard's ironic position in relation to these Romantic concepts. See Rajan, *The Supplement of Reading: Figures of Understanding in Romantic Theory and Practice* (Ithaca: Cornell University Press, 1991), pp. 78–9.
23. Friedrich Nietzsche, 'On Truth and Lie in the Extra-Moral Sense', in *The Portable Nietzsche*, ed. by Walter Kaufmann (Harmondsworth: Viking-Penguin, 1982), p. 46.
24. All quotations from Shelley are taken from *Shelley's Poetry and Prose*, ed. by Donald H. Reiman and Neil Fraistat (New York: Norton, 2002). Line references follow quotations in the text.
25. Paul de Man, *The Rhetoric of Romanticism* (New York: Columbia University Press, 1984). Page references follow quotations in the text.
26. For de Man's account of Shelley's disfiguration see *The Rhetoric of Romanticism*, p. 123.
27. For further discussions of these patterns of light and dark in *The Triumph of Life*, see: Tilottama Rajan, *Dark Interpreter: The Discourse of Romanticism*. (Ithaca: Cornell University Press, 1980), p. 66; Balachandra Rajan, *The Form of the Unfinished*, p. 192; Edward E. Bostetter, *The Romantic Ventriloquists: Wordsworth, Coleridge, Keats, Shelley, Byron* (Seattle: Washington University Press, 1963), p. 187.
28. Ronald Tetreault explores this esoteric image further: see *The Poetry of Life: Shelley and Literary Form* (Toronto: University of Toronto Press, 1987), pp. 250–1.
29. See *The Birth of Tragedy*, trans. by Walter Kaufmann (New York: Random House, 1967), p. 113.
30. Friedrich Nietzsche, *Human All Too Human: A Book for Free Spirits*, trans. by R. J. Hollingdale, introduction. by Richard Schact (Cambridge: Cambridge University Press, 1996), pp. 96–7.
31. Tilottama Rajan and Harold Bloom connect the 'Shape' and the 'shape all light'. See Rajan, *Dark Interpreter*, pp. 68–9 and Bloom, *Shelley's Mythmaking* (New Haven: Yale University Press, 1959; repr. Ithaca: Cornell University Press, 1969), pp. 265–7.
32. Paul de Man's definition of prosopopeia is anticipated by Nietzsche and Shelley (see *The Rhetoric of Romanticism*, p. 80). Neither Shelley nor Nietzsche employs the 'mask' as a deceptive device to conceal or veil the nature of the self, but as an 'organising principle that explains things' and indicates the 'enigma and dissemblance of phenomena' (Charles E. Scott, 'The Mask of Nietzsche's Self-Overcoming', in Clayton Koelb (ed.), *Nietzsche as Postmodernist: Essays Pro and Contra* (New York: University of New York Press, 1990)), pp. 217–19.
33. Daniel W. Conway discusses how Nietzsche uses the prophet-figure of Zarathustra to ensure a reader's active participation in reading *Thus Spoke Zarathustra* ('Nietzsche contra Nietzsche: The Deconstruction of Zarathustra', in Koelb (ed.), *Nietzsche as Postmodernist*, pp. 91–110 (pp. 109–10)). Nietzsche encourages his readers to be active participants in life and literature as opposed to passive receivers of a text and its wisdom. Shelley's *The Triumph of Life* endorses this sense of reader-responsibility. More recently, Clifford J.

Marks has read the poem as exhibiting a 'human need for an other [that] relies on our incomplete subjectivity in the face of an unknowable whole' ('Fragments and Fragility: Permeable Foundations in "The Triumph of Life"', *European Romantic Review*, 10 (1999), pp. 515–41 (p. 535)).

34. 'The Idea of Order at Key West', line 55, in Wallace Stevens, *Complete Poems* (London: Faber, 1984).

5
Combinatoric Form in Nineteenth-century Satiric Prints

Steven E. Jones

Forms of composite art that combined words and images, spectacle and music, proliferated in the Romantic period in a diverse array of popular expressions. Take the Boydell Shakespeare Gallery (1789–1805), for example, which gathered for viewing and purchase a collection of paintings and prints based on the Bard's plays. This kind of thematic experience of pictures, as illustrating and interpreting well-known texts, was actually extremely common in the era of history painting. Or, to take an example from the 1820s, consider the popular gift-book annuals. Their editors commissioned poetry or fiction in direct response to pre-selected images, then juxtaposed text and image in the final publication. Authors and readers alike often read both text and image as if in arranged dialogue with one another. In the realm of live-action multimedia, there were famous theatrical spectacles of the day, as well as quasi-theatrical immersive experiences such as the panorama, which sometimes depended on accompanying texts or performed music. Gillen Wood has rightly situated the production and reception of such visually orientated multimedia works at the heart of Romantic-period culture, the era of immense spectacles and exotic galleries of many kinds.[1] In particular, the Romantic period is rich in examples of the material interrelation of verbal and visual form, text and image, and this richness stands as a caution against limiting our thinking about such matters to a single prominent model, such as William Blake's handmade books, much less the more limited concept of mere textual 'illustration'.

The most widely experienced form of verbal-visual art in the Romantic period was probably the satiric print. Whether as an individual object to be bought or viewed in a shop window, or as images integrated into chapbook-like pamphlets such as William Hone's, for example, this form of popular art and entertainment was everywhere at the time. Though we think of prints and cartoons as manifestations of visual culture, in fact they almost always work by combining an allegorical or symbolic visual language with actual words, engraved in or around the image, language literally represented as a material visual feature of the print, as another part of the image. In the hands of artists such as Gillray or Cruikshank prints combined image and text in a variety of ways: titles, mottoes, word bubbles, captions, inscriptions and object-labels, a complex collage of vernacular meanings. This chapter will focus on the combined verbal-visual form of satiric prints in the Romantic period, the formative but permeable boundary between image and text in this extremely popular form of composite art. Its thesis is that the relation of verbal to visual representation in prints is 'modular' – that the words and images in satiric prints are separable units opportunistically combined, and that the dominant aesthetic of such prints calls attention to these possibilities for combining and recombining words and images. The form of satiric prints, I suggest, and this extends to the verbal texts that were almost always included in such works, is best understood as 'combinatoric'. This is an aesthetic conceptually opposed to the 'organic' form usually celebrated in Romanticism.

In his *Picture Theory*, W. J. T. Mitchell proposes that we study the relation of verbal and visual art not through the conventional protocols of inter-art comparisons, by juxtaposing a poem with a painting, say, but by attending to the internal interrelations, the 'actual conjunctions of words and images in illustrated texts, or mixed media such as film, television, and theatrical performance'. In such forms, Mitchell argues, we encounter 'an image-text structure responsive to prevailing conventions (or resistance to conventions) governing the relation of visual and verbal experience'. As a first move in the direction of a method, Mitchell tries out a set of experimental terms – his own visual/verbal signs based on marks of punctuation – through which to express the complex particulars of heterogeneous relationships between verbal and visual forms of representation. He uses the slashed 'image/text' to stand for the 'problematic gap, cleavage, or rupture in representation', the compounded 'imagetext' to designate 'composite, synthetic works', and the hyphenated 'image-text' to indicate specific 'relations of the visual and verbal'. In practice these terms are to be understood as describing not entirely separate instances of representation but separate facets or differential factors in all representation, as different ways of talking about what goes on in any instance of composite media. As Mitchell argues, 'all media are mixed media, and all representations are heterogeneous; there are no "purely" visual or verbal arts'.[2]

There are a number of difficulties with Mitchell's differential terms, beginning with the presumptive use of typographical conventions to represent pictorial effects. I think the terms remain useful, however, mostly because they pose the right kind of questions. Mitchell's theoretical gesture, his effort to make these kinds of subtle distinctions in the first place, represents an attempt to do justice to the complex array of possibilities that open up to view once we begin to take seriously the *interrelation* of text and image *as* form. Mitchell is a Blake scholar who has worked extensively in the Romantic period and his first example in the chapter I have just cited, which he adduces just after proposing his differential terms, is the illuminated books of William Blake. But the second example Mitchell introduces, significantly enough, is modern comics. The obvious nineteenth-century precursor to the newspaper comic strips and comic books Mitchell discusses, and for that matter the popular form most in evidence when Blake was developing his own composite art in the late eighteenth and early nineteenth centuries, was the satiric print.

Writing about the Romantic- and Victorian-era printmaker George Cruikshank, Richard Vogler observes that the artist

> became the nineteenth-century exponent of a visual tradition in European religious and secular art which relates symbols and language in a unique way. Pictorial traditions tend to survive more pervasively in popular art forms like caricature than in almost any other kind of art. Emblem books as well as the hieroglyph and the heraldic device became a standard part of the visual vocabulary of an artist steeped in the tradition of caricature.

This tradition, Vogler points out, amounts to 'a very complex visual language that has steadily lost its power over the modern world. Furthermore, as an artist working in a tradition going back to Hogarth, Cruikshank produced art inextricably linked with language and literary tradition.'[3]

Indeed, all of these earlier forms (and more) flow into the grotesque vernacular language of prints, as just a brief session reading through the descriptions in the incomparable *Catalogue of Prints and Drawings in the British Museum* will establish.[4] Consider the emblem book, a Renaissance form of verbal-visual art that was putatively based on the idea of the hieroglyph, the notion of a picture language (what Mitchell might call 'imagetext'), and which pursued a closely interwoven relation between word and image. Each emblem consisted of a motto (for example, 'A fickle woman, wanton grown, prefers a crowd before a crown'), an allegorical or parabolic image and a set of epigrammatic verses to expound on the relations thus opened up. Ronald Paulson has suggested that the emblems came self-consciously into caricature with its first British practitioner, George Townshend, in the 1750s, and that emblems were particularly ripe for (we might say) repurposing by the print satirists:

> Because the emblem itself began as a verbal concept the added visual image carried enough of the irrelevant and irrational to allow for a remythologizing when removed from its verses and mottoes and placed in a jarringly different context, as it is in a Gillray cartoon.

What Paulson means by 'irrational' here is something like 'arbitrarily combined'. That is, the original emblem began as a bit of text to which an image was more or less forcibly yoked. But what if this arbitrariness were in fact one of the desired and pleasurable formal effects – essentially satiric effects, part and parcel of the *saturae* of satire – of both emblems and cartoons? Indeed, as Paulson suggests in general, this kind of image/text relationship is part of the aesthetic of the grotesque in which both emblem and print participate, the aesthetic of diabolic excess, of what 'fills in the empty spaces, the areas beyond the composition of the heroic image', the combination of 'whatever inhabits the empty spaces of rational, charted life – associated with both visual images and notions, words, and thoughts'.[5]

Consider for a moment another well-known example from the Romantic period: George Cruikshank's woodcuts for William Hone's *Political House that Jack Built* (1820).[6] On any given plate in the book there is something like a motto ('THIS IS THE HOUSE THAT JACK BUILT') and a visual emblem (a classical temple surmounted with a figure of Liberty or Britannia holding a staff [or pike?] topped with a Phrygian cap). In this case the verse expounding the relation of the two fills out the motto, as it were, with the parody of the children's rhyme running from plate to plate through the pamphlet according to its own cumulative logic. The satire arises from the relations between, say, the 'HOUSE' (in context a surprisingly revolutionary emblem) and, on the next plate, the 'WEALTH that lay in the House' – which turns out to be an overflowing treasure chest containing the 'Magna Charta', 'Habeas Corpus' and the 'Bill of Rights', as the images of scrolls and documents in the chest are clearly labelled. The associations accumulate as the chain of interlinked emblems follow on successive plates. Along the way we discover some surprising juxtapositions among the parts, at least some of which appear to be improvised or partly the result of chance. And there is one more layer in the emblematic construction of the cartoon images I have failed to mention. Every plate also contains an inscription of a brief passage from Cowper's famous long poem, *The Task*. These quotations are usually wrenched entirely out of context, sometimes with comic/parodic effects, sometimes with the sense of the author's ingenuity in re-using the lines apart from Cowper's original. On the first plate, for example, a passage from book five of *The Task* reads, 'A distant age asks where the fabric stood', as if to prophesy the future fall of the 'House' in the wake of the Six Acts and other reactionary legislation of the moment. The 'fabric' here is completely redefined after being appropriated from Cowper, but in a way that suggests Gnostic strategies of revelatory rereading. At other times, frankly, the Cowper passages produce only the jarring effect of the absolute arbitrariness of the combination.

This kind of textual insertion is not unusual in satiric prints. Bits of Shakespeare or Pope were frequently added, sometimes serving as *de facto* mottoes or inscriptions, sometimes providing commentary on the image or altering the tone of what was visibly represented. Sometimes such fragmentary quotations simply added another open-ended representational layer to the images, but the point is that the combinations of text and image were an important feature of the form, that the combinations went far beyond the mere images that most people think of when they think of 'cartoons'. We might adapt Mitchell's general observation here and say that there were no 'purely' visual cartoons in the early nineteenth century. Satiric prints are always already a complex and multilayered composite form of art. Even the temple on the first plate of *The Political House that Jack Built*, which I have just discussed as an image, on second glance also contains in its verbal-visual excess labelled garlands twined around its columns: text in the image and images of text.

A Cruikshank cartoon typically included a title engraved in its border or frame, sometimes incorporating a bit of a quotation within it, but this is of course only the beginning of its textuality. All sorts of objects and persons depicted in the image may be labelled, either to identify them or to comment on them. Like Hogarth before him, Cruikshank sometimes makes opportunistic use of represented shop signs and other 'found' texts in his images, but he also frequently uses word bubbles, pretty much like those we are familiar with in modern comic books, for representing direct speech. And he often indulges in an excessive or 'grotesque' labelling of the landscape and its objects themselves, sometimes with a rough and ready allegorical purpose: a giant trough is labelled 'PUBLIC MONEY', for example, or a pump is labelled 'Royal GAS' and stands ready to fill the hot-air balloons symbolising speculative stock investments.

That last example, from an 1825 print, *A Scene in the Farce of 'Lofty Projects as performed with great success for the Benefit & amusement of John Bull'*,[7] is a useful case study in how complex Cruikshank's image and text combinations can be. It is based on a familiar trope of speculative balloon flight, going back at least to the satires about the South Sea Bubble in the 1720s and to Hogarth in particular. It appropriates the emblem and reapplies it a century later to the new situation of market speculation. The title suggests that we are witnessing a theatrical farce, or, rather, that we are seeing an etching that commemorates a theatrical production previously performed (in this case for the English citizen, for 'John Bull', who presumably laughs at the wealthy speculators). The 'stage' is a wide London street with the open sky above. In the fore-ground a line of balloons with passenger gondolas resemble hackney coaches waiting for fares. Some drivers relax and smoke, others ask for gas for their balloons or loiter in the gondolas. At one end of the line a well-dressed couple are procuring a balloon; at the other end, passengers are just taking flight, shaking hands to bid a friend on the ground farewell. Everywhere word bubbles contain what amounts to a kind of omnisciently overheard dialogue, both in the foreground, in the line, and far aloft, from the tops of buildings and from distant airborne balloons. The print as a whole is heavily marked up, we might observe – is in fact a busy near-palimpsest of marks, images and texts, lettering and cross-hatching, at first a confusing scene for the modern viewer. The sky is littered with balloons, some with wings and other contraptions attached, some going down in flames, and the street scene is dominated by a row of buildings with their façades virtually tattooed with wordy 'signage'.

The words and images here may appear at first in the busy compos-ition to add up to an integrated whole, but that appearance is based on what would be in this case a misplaced Romantic assumption, the privilege accorded to Coleridge's famous definitions of artistic form as 'organic'. As opposed to 'mechanical form', Coleridge proposed (borrowing the idea from German theorists) that 'organic form' is not externally impressed on arbitrarily selected material but 'is innate, it shapes as it developes itself from within, and the fullness of its devel-opment is one & the same with the perfection of its outward Form'.[8] It remains an open question, one that I will not take up here, as to whether Coleridge's own work or that of other Romantic poets is best described by his own Romantic theory of organic form. It could easily be argued that 'Kubla Khan', for example, along with any number of 'fragment poems' produced by Romanticism, owes something to the kind of cartoon aesthetic I am outlining. Suffice it to say that the composition of a satiric print such as those I have been discussing produces an effect precisely the opposite from that of Coleridge's organic form: *its* form is the result of a decidedly material, and in this case literally 'mechanical', process of accretion, appropriation and combination (mixed and combined with a degree of original invention, to be sure). A satiric print typically displays not the wholeness of innate identity but a grotesque excess in which anything and everything can be inscribed, is to some degree already multiply inscribed, whether literally or not, and is merely being recombined in arbitrary and improvised relationships – self-consciously and wittily repurposed by the artist. Few prints, even among Cruikshank's works, have quite as much literal text in them as the *Scene in the Farce of 'Lofty Projects'*, but the form in general opens up the possibility of similar verbal-visual excess. In literature we are familiar with a version of this general aesthetic in Byron's 'Epic Satire' (or massive *satura*), *Don Juan*, say, a poem that arguably takes its cue for generic mixture from the form of popular works such as Cruikshank's. Byron's poem, however, works hard (though the labour is concealed in its stylistic *sprezzatura*) to convince us that it ultimately transcends its motley, to argue implicitly that it is in fact more a 'versified Aurora Borealis' (VII, st. 2), a prodigy of the poet's own strong voice and natural abilities rather than an artificial and arbitrary, pantomimic display of effects. For the most part, the cartoons make no such claims. The success of their kind of verbal-visual satire depends not on exhibiting its achieved Romantic organic wholeness but on flaunting the grotesque promiscuity of its text and image combinations. The desired result is to display the dense and arbitrary layerings that are potentially possible, even beyond the actual instantiation of the print, using the same or similar verbal and visual components to self-consciously display these possibilities, the combinatoric process itself, *as* satiric effect.

The combinatoric aesthetics of satiric prints, in terms of both image and text, can be made clearer (perhaps surprisingly) by a formal comparison with modern comics. Although there are undoubtedly certain historical and generic family connections between the two forms, a Cruikshank or Hogarth cartoon is of course not simply the same thing as a modern comic. But they can be said to descend, historically and generically, from common ancestors, at least, and both combine images and graphically represented text in multilayered combinations. Indeed, this is one of the key aesthetic pleasures that both prints and comics offer. As I have already noted, the convention of the word bubble survives in modern comics, more or less as it was used in nineteenth-century prints. In fact, a variety of kinds of framing or 'voice-over' narrative or metanarrative commentary texts, as well as designations of settings or dates and times, even reported speech overheard from someplace not directly depicted in the comic frame, can be incorporated in the frame of a modern comic along with its images.[9] The form encourages layerings of text as well as image – and the text is often still represented either as hand-lettered calligraphy or, even when the comic is digitally produced, in a font (such as **Comic Sans**) that imitates calligraphy. Such text, serving a variety of representational or narrative functions, can be incorporated into the comic in addition to direct speech (or even silent thoughts, in puffier-looking bubbles). The most skilful artists or artist–writer collaborative teams know how to exploit these kinds of visual-verbal combinations in the service of narrative or to enhance the atmosphere of a panel. But there is something about the form itself, the history and the conventions of comics as composite image/texts, which produces recognisable or potentially 'meaningful' formal effects quite apart from any explicit semantic intention.

We see this dramatised in a recent experimental artwork on the World Wide Web, *Grafik Dynamo*, by Kate Armstrong and Michael Tippett.[10] In a Web browser it looks like three panels of a conventional comic, with word bubbles and a layer of narrative text running along the bottom of the frames. As one watches the screen, however, the page changes and reloads its images and text, and the result of several such changes is a sense of dislocation, a sense of finding oneself in an oddly surrealistic fragmentary narrative. The work is actually making use of computer scripts to load 'live' images randomly taken (via automatic 'feeds') from Weblogs and news sites. These are automatically combined with texts, short passages selected from a master file written by one of the artists and randomly loaded into word bubbles, represented within both speech and thought bubbles ('Odd! Isn't it?'), as well as in narrative or commentary panes along the foot of each frame ('I could see that he was drawing nearer and nearer to collapse'). Streams of text and streams of images are mixed at the interface to produce a modular, combinatoric comic.

Grafik Dynamo owes as much to the aleatory or chance-based art experiments of the Surrealists' *Exquisite Corpse*, the poetry generators of OULIPO and William Burroughs' 'cut-ups', as it does to Cruikshank or Gillray or Hogarth. I do not mean to imply any simple analogy or formal equivalence between these otherwise extremely disparate forms of cartoon. And yet, despite the artists' claims that their experiment is a 'dynamically' built and 'animated' comic, 'a new hybrid' based on randomness, what is perhaps most interesting about *Grafik Dynamo* is how *utterly conventional* its effects feel to anyone familiar with paper-based comics. I believe that this is because the designers have hit upon (and have algorithmically amplified) something inherent in the 'cartoon' form itself, something already present in Cruikshank's balloon satire or *Political House* and potentially present throughout the broad history of graphic satire in general (and thus in its descendant form, modern comics): its conventional exploitation of multilayered verbal-visual combinatorics, and the accompanying potential for disjunction and surprise recombination. In good postmodern fashion, *Grafik Dynamo* makes highly self-conscious and thematises structures that have been historically significant in numerous forms of verbal-visual cartooning. Like the emblematic mottoes, verses, labels and (often) repurposed images of nineteenth-century cartoons, the computer-generated dynamic Web comic uses algorithmic scripts to find and paste together word and image in order to achieve its own effects – one of which is inevitably the formal effect of calling attention to its own modular process of combinatoric image/text representations. Whereas *Grafik Dynamo* uses javascript, HTML pages and XML feeds of JPEG images from the Internet, Cruikshank and Hone used chapbooks, children's nursery rhymes and woodcut images combined and printed cheaply as a pamphlet, all to a surprisingly similar formal effect.

The modularity of nineteenth-century graphic satires is not a technique so much as it is an attitude towards form, an attitude eventually encoded within the form itself. Artists such as Cruikshank or, before him, Hogarth treat various sources of text as 'streams' from which to 'feed' their own new compositions. And they treat sources of visual signs or emblems, including popular lore, in the same way. Satiric effect for the viewer depends in part on recognition of the sources and in part on appreciation for the sometimes rough and ready combinations of these verbal and visual elements as achieved by the artist. The combinatoric nature of the process itself is particularly emphasised in cases where these elements retain some degree of aesthetic autonomy and thus reveal their separability as modular components, their potential use in further combinations.

Take a famous pair of satiric prints by William Hogarth, *The Invasion: France* and *England* (1756).[11] Though they come just before the conventional Romantic period, they remained popular well into the nineteenth century, as we shall see, and it is the Romantic afterlife as it were of these prints that interests me here. Etched in March at the commencement of the Seven Years' War, these satires form a diptych of jingoistic nationalism, emblems of 'them' and 'us' that turn on images of gastronomy and bodily well-being as a kind of metonymy for political liberty or the health of the body politic.

France depicts preparations for a planned invasion of England in front of a tavern (Figure 5.1). The sign above the door is a peasant's wooden shoe (*sabot*) and it reads 'Soup Meagre a la Sabot Royal'. We see skinny beef ribs hanging from a hook in the window. Off to the right an officer beside a campfire uses his sword as a spit to roast the stereotypic French fare – frogs. On this meagre fuel the soldiers gather to march to the ships and the invasion (we see one such ship being loaded in the middle distance). They look confused and disorganised, as well as unhealthy. Far off in the distance women struggle to guide the plough over barren soil, a sexual

Figure 5.1 William Hogarth, *The Invasion*, Plate I, *France* (8 March 1756), BM#3446. Used by permission of R. Russell Maylone, Curator, McCormick Library of Special Collections, Northwestern University Library

emblem wrapped in an agricultural insult within a nationalistic boast. A flag behind the frog-barbecue reads, 'Vengeance et le Bon Bier et Bon Beuf de Angletere'. In the foreground a tonsured monk prepares instruments of torture for forced conversions to Catholicism, a perennial threat in the English imagination (a document reveals plans for a monastery at Black-friars). But Hogarth typically suggests that the real motives are much more basic, more bodily and material than any religious controversy.

The matching bookend print, *England* (Figure 5.2), depicts the opposing scene in a parallel universe across the channel. Recruits drill in close order, and a would-be soldier stands on tiptoe to be sure he measures up for the fighting to come. A happy cluster of soldiers, a sailor and their companions relax on a laden table in front of *their* kind of inn, the 'Duke of Cumberland' (shown nobly on horseback), where the sign reads 'Roast & Boil'd every Day'. The military men, tellingly surrounded by relaxed women, enjoy a feast of drink and music – and, oddly enough, a bit of verbal-visual satire.

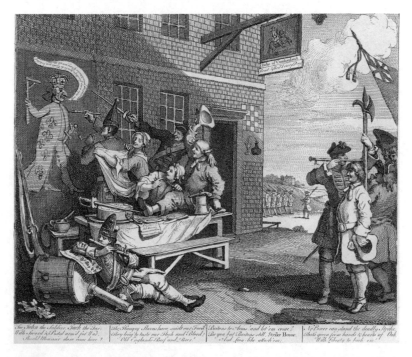

Figure 5.2 William Hogarth, *The Invasion*, Plate II, *England* (8 March 1756), BM#3454. Used by permission of R. Russell Maylone, Curator, McCormick Library of Special Collections, Northwestern University Library

A standing grenadier smoking a pipe is depicted in the act of painting a life-sized caricature of the King of France on the exterior wall of the inn. The king's robes are decorated with the *fleur-de-lis* and he holds a gibbet in one hand and the pommel of his sword in the other. A cartoon word bubble extends from his mouth and curves up over his head, reading: 'You take a my fine Ships, you be de pirate, you be de Teef, me send my grand Armies, & hang you all, Marblu.' Meanwhile the macho cartoonist's broad shoulders are measured admiringly by one of the tavern women using her apron; her friend, in the lap of another man, suggestively touches the sharp tines of a fork as the sailor brandishes his sword. The group has plenty of beef and porter and is clearly in a celebratory mood going into the hostilities. The caricature on the wall is of course a cartoon within the cartoon, a meta-pictorial self-reference. But it is also a propaganda image that represents caricature as just one more activity falling under the heading of the pleasures of British liberty. The ability to produce caricature, it is suggested, is essentially English. More than freedom of speech, this particular emblem celebrates the generally confident and sardonic tone of the figures depicted in the whole print, *England*. They are pointedly at ease, healthy, sexually intermingled (unlike the French in every case), their very postures and facial expressions conveying the association of satire with national identity, right along with good tavern provisions, an ideal of bodily as well as cultural robustness.

Besides the cartoon word bubble, there are other examples of verbal text incorporated into this print. In the foreground a piper plays from sheet music 'God save great George our King' and another sheet on the table contains the lyrics to 'Rule Britannia' ('Britons never will be Slaves'). Finally, both Hogarth plates are literally framed at the foot with stanzas of verse for the occasion written by David Garrick, the famous actor.[12] Unremarkable as poetry, they more or less describe each scene with an added exhortation or two:

> See John the Soldier, Jack the Tar,
> With Sword & Pistol arm'd for War,
>   Should Mounsir dare come here!

> The Hungry Slaves have smelt our food
> They long to taste our Flesh and Blood,
>   Old England's Beef and Beer!

> Britons to Arms! And let 'em come,
> Be you but Britons still, Strike Home,
>   And Lion-like attack 'em.

> No Power can stand the deadly stroke,
> That's given from hands & hearts of Oak,
>   With Liberty to back 'em.

The verses also contain verbalised images taken from the same 'streams' of popular emblems that Hogarth draws upon (for example, 'Lion-like'). If flesh and blood is beef and beer then the cannibalistic enemy is starved for both; and liberty becomes the power enabling the enjoyments of the free flesh and the power behind the ability to strike down would-be invaders. The French language, like French food and religion and sexuality, just does not fully translate, the cartoon insists. The verses for the *France* plate are even more blatantly chauvinistic, more in the way of directly verbalised caricature and a direct curse sending the invaders to the devil:

> With lanthern jaws, and croaking Gut,
> See how the half-starv'd Frenchmen strut,
>   And call us English Dogs!
>
> But soon we'll teach these bragging Foes,
> That Beef & Beer give heavier Blows,
>   Than Soup & Roasted Frogs.
>
> The Priests inflam'd with righteous hopes,
> Prepare their Axes, Wheels & Ropes
>   To bend the Stiff neck'd Sinner;
>
> But should they sink in coming over,
> Old Nick may fish 'twixt France & Dover
>   And catch a glorious Dinner.

Inevitably, it is possible to deconstruct the emblematic jingoism of these lines and images. The Britons are apparently free to satirise the French king but only to revere their own, a fairly safe form of free expression, after all; and the relative lack of any religious interference in the tavern scene on the English side can be taken as an absence of church power, even perhaps a strain of irreligion, as well as a sign of freedom. Moreover, if you are what you eat, in terms of national identity, what does that say about the *essential* differences on which such satire seems to depend? Is the British national character really *dependent* on supplies of beer and beef, on something as arbitrary and as culturally constructed as cuisine, the choice of beef over frog?

But for the present I am more interested in the verbal and visual form of these prints, which I find remarkably instructive, especially when we attend to the specific combinations of text and image that Hogarth employs. The first thing to realise is that such formal consideration cannot limit itself to some imagined unitary or self-identical aesthetic object. The whole widely dispersed textual and pictorial *history* of these prints must be the focus of any real formal analysis. Just to point to one important detail: in their original edition the prints exist in two states, a first without the labels 'France' and 'England' and a second with these keywords added! Presumably very early in the publication process the tableaux were deemed in need of this additional verbal disambiguation. Clearly any reading of the verbal dimension of these image/texts must take into account both states.

In terms of their format and mode of distribution, the original pair of prints were essentially broadsides, advertised as 'Proper to be stuck up in publick Places' (*Catalogue of Prints and Drawings in the British Museum*), but Hogarth's popularity and growing fame ensured that they were reproduced many times over the course of the century that followed. As I mentioned earlier, they had a powerful afterlife during the Romantic period. The *Catalogue of Prints and Drawings in the British Museum* contains almost two pages of entries listing reproductions of Plate I, different versions in different formats and sizes, mostly for publication in book form under the sign of the artist's well-known name, to illustrate, for example, *Hogarth Moralized* by the Reverend J. Trusler in 1768 and *Hogarth Illustrated* by John Ireland in 1791.[13] We can trace in these entries the arc of Hogarth's fame, leading eventually to books collecting his 'works' in the nineteenth century and including books containing reproductions of the images by other etchers, even a woodcut 'after' Hogarth for a book published in 1831.

The possible variations introduced by new versions of these prints, reformatted or published in different material and historical contexts, are an important part of the history of these cartoons. It gets even more complicated when we consider the varying audiences and socio-historical contexts within which such a work would have been read and interpreted. The life of a popular print in the culture at large was not limited to the specific reproductions listed in the *Catalogue of Prints and Drawings in the British Museum*. It is a truism based in truth that such graphical satires had an audience or viewership that is finally impossible to quantify or even accurately characterise in terms of social class. Since such prints would have been 'stuck up in publick Places' and viewed (as several prints themselves depicted) in shop windows, say, by a mixed street audience, they were in this sense a truly popular form. It is appropriate therefore that the images of sheet music and David Garrick's verses are combined with the visual emblems in *France* and *England*, rendering them even more clearly as scripts for public performance, broadside ballads to be sung or verses to be recited. *England* contains within it meta-representations of not only music but, as we have seen, visual caricature as well, both a cartoon within the cartoon and songs within the song, as it were.

The literary text, the verses running along the foot of the prints, which we might think of as comparable to the narrative texts fed into the footers of *Grafik Dynamo*, are part of the original artworks – or are at least part of their borders or frames. In the nineteenth century, having text alongside an exhibited image, and sometimes actually on the frame itself, was conventional. I mentioned above the Boydell Shakespeare Gallery and gift-book annuals, with their dependence on image–text juxtapositions. But even an Academy painter such as J. M. W. Turner not only painted narrative subjects or landscape settings taken from literature, he actually used excerpts from well-known literary texts as parts of his exhibits. Turner also composed his own long (unfinished) poem, 'Fallacies of Hope', early in the nineteenth century and incorporated fragmentary passages from that work in exhibitions of paintings for many years. Or think of Pre-Raphaelite painter-poet Dante Gabriel Rossetti, who later in the century designed his own frames and sometimes incorporated his own poetry into their design. In the world of satiric prints, the framing space just outside the image itself was frequently the space used for a hand-lettered, motto-like title. Cruikshank's balloon satire, *A Scene in the Farce of 'Lofty Projects'* (like most of his prints) situates the title in this space, along with the signatures and publication information.

Garrick's verses for *France* and *England* are squeezed into precisely this space, outside the primary picture frame but still part of the print as an object. They clearly represent a modular textual component in the print as a whole, working as a sign of the constitutive gap implied in Mitchell's term, 'image/text'. The poetry not only offers metadescriptive verbalisations of the emblems, but by doing so also calls attention to the basic disjunction between word and image, a disjunction across which the print forges its text and image alliances. At the same time, this partic-ular text gestures outside the frame to the reception and performance of the print by an audience who might actually sing its songs and recite its verses.

This interpretation of the literary text, the verses, as a separately performable component of the prints is vividly dramatised in this case by the facts of their publishing history in the Romantic period. It turns out that 37 years later, on 2 December 1793, at the commencement of yet another war with France, these verses were detached from Hogarth's two prints and republished – in effect repurposed – in *The Star*. A headnote reminded readers of the Hogarths, though most may not have needed to be reminded of them, given that the prints themselves less than two years prior to this date had been republished in Ireland's *Hogarth Illustrated*:

> When, during the late war, there was a rumour of an intended invasion by the French, Hogarth engraved two prints, entitled France and England, to ridicule the idea. Beneath the prints are two inscriptions, written by the late David Garrick, but not inserted in the volume of his poems. The first is FRANCE.

The two disentangled and reprinted textual 'inscriptions' then follow, word for word (though with a few minor editorial changes in orthography). But of course their material embodiment has in the process changed utterly, from Hogarth's handwritten script to being set in type, from the print frame to the newspaper page. It is interesting that readers can so easily be reminded of the images and be expected to call them up in imagination, find them in a recent reprint, or simply make do with the verses alone; in this case, the verbalisations are so literal that the words might be expected to produce eidetic images in the minds of new readers who might never have seen the Hogarths. Either way, the 'images' or nationalistic and satiric emblems are clearly 'portable': across two different wars with the perennial enemy of England, the stereotypes are presumably still effective with a new audience (even if we might have thought that, say, the Revolution should take centre stage over Catholicism by 1793).

But the bigger story, here, once we look at the histories of the prints and their verses across the latter half of the eighteenth century, is about the pragmatic modularity of text and image components in this form. This is an aesthetic very different indeed from Coleridgean idealisations of innate organic unity, a whole from which no part can be removed without doing violence to the composition. In this case, the components of the prints simply go their separate ways and make themselves available for new occasions (which include the repetition of yet another war with France). Hogarth is repeatedly 'illustrated' with reprints and reproductions and Garrick is reprinted in a newspaper; the original satiric composite medley is broken up and recombined in new forms.

The point of this chapter has been to call attention to how those forms were always already implicit in the original work, by which I mean not the mystified aesthetic object but the conventional, opportunistic and combinatoric procedures by which the satiric image/text got produced in the first place.

Notes

1. Gillen D'Arcy Wood, *The Shock of the Real: Romanticism and Visual Culture, 1760–1860* (New York: Palgrave, 2001).
2. W. J. T. Mitchell, *Picture Theory: Essays on Verbal and Visual Representation* (Chicago and London: University of Chicago Press, 1994), pp. 90, 89n. 9, 5.
3. Richard A. Vogler, *Graphic Works of George Cruikshank* (New York: Dover, 1979), p. xvi.
4. *Catalogue of Prints and Drawings in the British Museum*, 11 vols (London: Trustees of the British Museum, 1870–1954), III:2, ed. by Frederic George Stephens and Edward Hawkins (1877).
5. Ronald Paulson, *Representations of Revolution, 1789–1820* (New Haven: Yale University Press, 1983), pp. 178, 180, 202, 203.
6. William Hone and George Cruikshank, *The Political House That Jack Built, Romantic Circles* <http://www.rc.umd.edu/editions/hone/coverp.htm> [accessed 8 March 2005].
7. Volger, *Graphic Works of George Cruikshank*, p. 20.
8. *Lectures on Literature 1808–1819*, ed. by R. A. Foakes, 2 vols (London: Routledge & Kegan Paul; Princeton: Princeton University Press, 1987), I, p. 495.
9. See Scott McCloud, *Understanding Comics: The Invisible Art* (New York: Harper Perennial, 1993), pp. 138–61.
10. Kate Armstrong and Michael Tippett, *Grafik Dynamo* <http://turbulence.org /Works/dynamo/> [accessed 8 March 2005].
11. William Hogarth, *The Invasion: France and England* (1756) (BM nos. 3446, 3454. Accessed March 2005, Deering Library, Northwestern University).
12. David Garrick, 'France and England' (1793), in *British War Poetry in the Age of Romanticism, 1793–1815*, ed. by Betty T. Bennett, with digital text ed. by Orianne Smith, *Romantic Circles* <http://www.rc.umd.edu/ editions/warpoetry/> [accessed 8 March 2005].
13. *Hogarth Moralized* (London: S. Hooper, 1768), p. 100; *Hogarth Illustrated*, 3 vols (London: J. E. J. Boydell, 1791–98), I, p. 391.

6
Romantic Form and New Historicism: Wordsworth's 'Lines Written a Few Miles above Tintern Abbey'

Alan Rawes

I

The idea that poetry, or even consciousness, can set one free of the ruins of history and culture is the grand illusion of every Romantic poet.

The grand illusion of Romantic *ideology* is that one may escape [the] world through imagination and poetry.

These are some of the big claims with which Jerome McGann famously inaugurated the new historicist transformation of Romantic Studies. From the start, Wordsworth's 'Tintern Abbey' was one of new historicism's exemplary texts. For McGann himself, 'Tintern Abbey' perfectly demonstrates the kind of 'poetic conceptualization' that for him characterises Romantic literature, 'whereby the actual human issues with which the poetry is concerned are resituated in a variety of idealized locations'.[1]

Similarly, according to Marjorie Levinson, 'the primary poetic action' of 'Tintern Abbey' is

the suppression of the social. 'Tintern Abbey' achieves its fiercely private vision by directing a continuous energy toward the nonrepresentation of objects and points of view expressive of a public [...] dimension [...]. Wordsworth cancels the social less by explicit denial and/or misrepresentation than by allowing no scope for its operation.[2]

For Kenneth Johnston, to give one final example, 'Tintern Abbey' dramatises Wordsworth's political 'retrenchment', creating space for its

95

'meditation and explanation about the source and meaning of human appreciation of natural beauty' by 'downplay[ing]' the 'social implications' of the 'unpleasant aspects of the landscape around Tintern Abbey'.[3]

Key to each of these readings, and to new historicist readings of Romanticism more generally, is the idea of reading silences about social and political realities and issues, and reading into those silences deliberate acts of ideologically motivated exclusion – or, to use McGann's now famous word, 'displacement'.[4] Each of the critics I have mentioned offers key examples of this displacement – silence about – the social and political in 'Tintern Abbey', and, since it will be useful to have these examples in mind later – I will be re-examining them in this chapter – it is worth pausing to briefly review them.

For McGann, 'no passage in Wordsworth better conveys the actual moment when a spiritual displacement [of the social and political] occurs' than the following:

> And now, with gleams of half-extinguished thought,
> With many recognitions dim and faint,
> And somewhat of a sad perplexity,
> The picture of the mind revives again. (59–62)[5]

For McGann, by this point the poem has 'replaced what might have been a picture *in* the mind (of a ruined abbey) with a picture *of* the mind': the 'abbey associated with 1793 fades, as in a palimpsest, and in its disappearing outlines we begin to discern not a material reality but a process, or power' by which 'the light and appearances of sense fade into an immaterial plane of reality, the landscape of Wordsworth's emotional needs'.[6]

Levinson's example is rather longer – what she calls the poem's 'second strophe' (lines 49–111) – but the following lines are key to her case:

> here I stand, not only with the sense
> Of present pleasure, but with pleasing thoughts
> That in this moment there is life and food
> For future years. And so I dare to hope
> Though changed, no doubt, from what I was, when first
> I came among these hills
> [...]

I [am] still
A lover of the meadows and the woods,
And mountains; and of all that we behold
From this green earth; of all the mighty world
Of eye and ear, both what they half-create,
And what perceive; well pleased to recognize
In nature and the language of the sense,
The anchor of my purest thoughts, the nurse,
The guide, the guardian of my heart, and soul
Of all my moral being. (63–8, 103–12)

Here, according to Levinson,

> we see that the self has replaced the landscape as the poetic subject
> [...] an achievement produced by the rejection of present place and
> occasion [...]. The social world in its actual and compelling character is
> [...] annihilated by this celebratory representation [...] of private life.[7]

Finally, for Johnston, 'the entire poem may be said to turn upon the
fulcrum of Wordsworth's assertion that he has'

learned
To look on nature, not as in the hour
Of thoughtless youth, but hearing oftentimes
The still, sad music of humanity. (89–92)

Johnston's focus is here on 'how "the still, sad music of humanity" is
represented *in the poem*', and, for him, it is represented by means of
'elision, mutation, or restriction'. The key word here is 'sad': as Johnston reads it, the word restricts the reference to a rather 'narrow [...]
range' of human experience and elides – leaves out – the rather more
than 'sad' experiences of 'poverty, famine, disease, war' and 'all the irre-
vocable losses of love and life, irreversible, unmerited, and uncontrolled
suffering which are inescapable in the human condition'.[8]

The consistency of approach and interpretation here is striking, and
both have been criticised before. Thomas McFarland, for example, has
pointed out that the new historicist emphasis on historical 'absence' – or
the history that is absent from texts – tends to 'compromise relevance'
as it sends the critic out into the potentially endless 'ocean of historical
context'.[9] A suspicion that relevance has been compromised certainly
hovers around Levinson's imaginative reconstruction of the personal,
historical and ideological significance for Wordsworth of the abbey that

'is not of course and to belabor a point *in* the poem',[10] as well as around the biographical speculations that inform Johnston's reading of the poem, but what contexts can we safely say are relevant? One – a formal one – is signalled by the famous note that Wordsworth attached to the poem in the 1800 edition of *Lyrical Ballads*:

> I have not ventured to call this Poem an Ode; but it was written with a hope that in the transitions, and the impassioned music of the versification would be found the principal requisites of that species of composition.[11]

For Paul Fry, the poem is in fact 'nothing like an ode': in this note, Wordsworth may well have been simply assuring 'his readers that the poem had all the virtues of an ode' but 'none of the absurdities' found in the kind of public ode produced annually by the Laureate Henry Pye. Stuart Curran, on the other hand, argues that the poem 'lies fully within the grounds of the Horatian ode, and, in respect to its immediate traditions, shares the meditative structure of loco-descriptive poetry with the heightened language and moral issues of that species of ode called by Nathan Drake "the *Descriptive*" '.[12]

If we take the note seriously and read the poem in the light of it, we certainly do not find any obvious or straightforward triadic structure of strophes, antistrophes and epodes – though critics have seen these in the poem – or a sequence of irregular stanzas.[13] To this extent, Fry is right. But we do find other essential features of the form. As we do so, a very different poem from the one offered by new historicist analyses comes into focus – but not quite the poem offered by critics who have already taken issue with the new historicists.

II

Commentators on the ode over the last five decades all agree that the key features of the canonical odes of the English tradition from, say, Jonson through to Dryden and the Romantic odes of Wordsworth, Coleridge and Shelley are that they are determinedly dialectic, fundamentally ambivalent in their attitude towards their subject matter, built on and around incompatible/opposing points of view and resistant to any sort of intellectual closure or resolution.[14] Poets across centuries have used the ode as a form to hold together, in sustained and generative tension, opposing ideas and attitudes. Obvious examples are Marvell's 'Cromwell Ode', famously ambivalent about its subject, Milton's 'Nativity Ode', which celebrates the Nativity while lamenting the passing of the classical gods the Nativity displaces, and Coleridge's 'Dejection Ode', where Coleridge is blaming dejection for the loss of his poetic powers precisely as it supplies him with the inspiration for great poetry.

It is to the presence in 'Tintern Abbey' of the determinedly dialectic quality of the ode, a sustained resistance to closure or resolution, that Wordsworth's note points us. And it is this quality that complicates both new historicist readings of 'Tintern Abbey' and later alternatives and rejoinders. A comment in 'Essay, Supplementary' (1815) makes clear the value of this kind of sustained dialectic contradiction to Wordsworth as a poet generally: the Muse's 'liveliest excitements', says Wordsworth, 'are raised by transient shocks of conflicting feeling and successive assemblages of contradictory thoughts'.[15] It is Wordsworth's emphasis on 'transitions' in his 1800 note to 'Tintern Abbey' that signals his awareness of the essentially dialectical nature of the ode as a form and his adoption of this formal quality in this particular poem. Let us look at an example of the poem's dialecticism:

> If this
> Be but a vain belief, yet, oh! how oft,
> In darkness, and amid the many shapes
> Of joyless day-light; when the fretful stir
> Unprofitable, and the fever of the world,
> Have hung upon the beatings of my heart,
> How oft, in spirit, have I turned to thee
> O sylvan Wye! Thou wanderer through the woods,
> How often has my spirit turned to thee!
>
> And now, with gleams of half-extinguished thought,
> With many recognitions dim and faint,
> And somewhat of a sad perplexity,
> The picture of the mind revives again. (50–62)

This passage immediately follows some of the poem's largest claims, which climax in the idea that, in the mood the poem celebrates, 'We see into the life of things' (50). The first thing we notice here, then, is an obvious retreat from these grand statements of faith in 'If this / Be but a vain belief'. As Curran puts it, even the poem's 'great statements of belief' can be followed up by 'nagging doubts',[16] and 'critics have repeatedly pointed out the doubts and hesitations that define the poem's language' throughout.[17] The best and most detailed analysis of the ways in which the poem's 'impassioned testimonies are limited and sometimes subverted' is Susan Wolfson's in *The Questioning Presence*,[18] but readers from David Simpson to Philip Cox and Susan Zimmerman have stressed the 'conditionals' that give the poem 'an impression of tentative or partial conviction', the 'strong counterimpulse to the poem's [visionary] introspective pull' or the poem's 'urgent self-questioning' and 'productive uncertainty'.[19] These readings already challenge new historicist accounts of the poem by pointing out the repeated surfacing of what Zimmerman calls a 'lingering involvement' with Wordsworth's 'radical past'.[20] For these readers, the poem does not, because in the end it cannot, 'displace' or 'annihilate' the social and political. But these readers still assume that it wants to, and that the driving force of the poem is towards the visionary. The poet is simply held back by 'nagging doubts', 'uncertainties' and 'lingering involvements'. For Wolfson, the poem is a 'declaration under stress', but a declaration nonetheless, with 'an argument that proceeds by fits and starts'.[21] For Simpson, the poem is a 'poem of aspiration' though not of 'achievement'. For M. H. Abrams, 'qualifications' about the poem's explicit visionary 'proposals' are introduced 'in order to reassert the [visionary] experience itself'. For Zimmerman, 50 lines before the poem ends, a 'rhetoric of closure is operative in the poet's assertions of confidence in his lasting relationship to nature', while the final turn to Dorothy is an attempt to 'ratify' his 'lyrical reflections' with a 'social exchange'.[22]

The idea that the poem possesses 'the principal requisites' of the ode form pushes us further than this. In particular, the idea that it has a dialectic structure within which 'conflicting feeling[s]' are deliberately – determinedly – juxtaposed suggests that 'doubts', 'hesitations', 'counter-impulses', 'conditionals', 'self-questioning', 'uncertainty' and 'lingering involvements' do not find their way into the poem despite Wordsworth's best efforts to exclude them, but are actively inserted into the poem to produce an 'assemblage' of 'contradictory thoughts'. In particular, we might agree with Helen Vendler that the poem describes (at least) 'two new aspects of personal growth' – a sense of 'the presence of something accompanied by elevated thoughts and a sense of sublimity', certainly, but also an 'awareness of the still, sad music of humanity' that works against it – and that Wordsworth's poem is interested in both, as equally 'disturbing and yet compensatory interruptions to the continuity of the ego'.[23] More importantly for our purposes here, however, they function in the poem as contradictory, irreconcilable interruptions to the continuity of each other.

The movement we see in the lines above, from faith to doubt let us say, is only the first instance of the poet's 'voice and vision' being 'troubled, hesitant and conditional', even in this short extract.[24] The next is less overt but no less powerful, moving from the solitary experience of integration and enlightenment to the memory of a social world of restless, alienating 'darkness': 'the fretful stir / Unprofitable, and the fever of the world'. McGann's best example of 'spiritual displacement' of 'the ruins of history and culture', then, is immediately preceded by a pointed reminder of those 'ruins'.[25] But McGann's passage does not then 'displace' the recollection of these 'ruins' from the poem. It is, in fact, quickly followed up by more reminders of them. Within three lines, Wordsworth is already talking about a future return to the 'fever' and 'fret' of 'the world' as he consoles himself with the idea that 'in this moment there is life and food / For future years' (65–6). Six lines further on, the memory of 'the world' and Wordsworth's experience in it surface again as he describes himself 'more like a man / Flying from something that he dreads, than one / Who sought the thing he loved' (71–3). Then, before long, there is the claim to 'have learned / To look on nature, not as in the hour / Of thoughtless youth, but hearing oftentimes / The still, sad music of humanity' (89–92). In the light of Wordsworth's note to the poem, all this begins to look very much like a determined refusal to give the poem over to the impulse to retreat into the solitary and visionary. The last reminder of society here is Johnston's best example of political retrenchment, but it now looks more like a stubborn insistence on the social world that the poem's vision of private communion with nature pulls away from.

While the very mention of 'sad humanity' at this point in the poem is a movement away from private spiritual vision and back towards social realities, what of the word 'sad' and its undeniable muffling of the social suffering it glances at? As Johnston suggests, 'fretful stir', 'fever of the world', 'still, sad music' hardly scream social deprivation, urban squalor and political oppression. We can begin to re-assess the significance of this word and the muffling it does, however, by noting that the 'elevated thoughts and a sense of sublimity' that have, by line 112, temporarily drowned out the 'still, sad music of humanity', are themselves muffled, and held in check, by the recollection of that music. The lines that immediately follow Johnston's quotation – 'Nor harsh nor grating, though of ample power / To chasten and subdue' (93–4) – describe a force that can be repeatedly seen at work throughout the poem. Its influence can be clearly heard in lines 50–5, where the celebration of visionary experience is checked by doubt and then by recollections of the 'fretful stir' and 'fever' of 'the world'. It is also active in the shift from the 'we' in line 49 to 'I' in line 56, where a universalising impulse retreats back into recounting personal experience. It can be heard in the deliberate, almost wilful, calming of the poem's celebration of nature enacted by the mid-line full stop and return to a language of measured, logical connection ('Therefore') in the line 103 ('And rolls through all things. Therefore am I still'), in the self-conscious imagining of the possibility of being 'not thus taught' in line 113 that redirects the poem away from nature and towards Dorothy and in the 'startlingly misanthropic' intrusion[26] – the account of 'evil tongues', 'sneers of selfish men', 'greeting where no kindness is' in 'the dreary intercourse of daily life' (129–32) – into the 'prayer' (122) asking for a 'chearful faith that all which we behold / Is full of blessings' (134–5) in the poem's final section. If the poem muffles the social to give voice to 'elevated thoughts', those thoughts are themselves repeatedly chastened and subdued, and usually by the recollection of social actualities, as the poem oscillates back and forth between 'great statements of belief' in Nature and memories of the 'joyless day-light' (53) of the city.

An attention to the odal form of 'Tintern Abbey' adds weight to those challenges to new historicist readings of 'Tintern Abbey' that have pointed out that the poem *does not* displace the social. It suggests, in fact, that the poem goes to considerable lengths to keep the social in view. Read as an ode, the poem does not look like a poem seeking but failing to leave the social behind but like a poem that sets out to dramatise a tension between an interest in private visionary experience and an ongoing concern with – anxiety about, perhaps – social actualities and that brings these into dialogue and confrontation with each other, allowing each to clash, modify and counter the other. As Stuart Curran has it, the poem offers an 'irrevocably dialectical vision',[27] and, viewed from this perspective, the poem seems to be about the collision of two irreconcilable priorities and what it is like to live in that irreconcilability. Wordsworth depicts himself as both tied to the social and drawn to the solitary. He uses the dialectic form of the ode – and signals that he is doing so – to lyrically dramatise precisely this fundamental and irreducible doubleness.

III

The implications of this formal reading of 'Tintern Abbey' are not simply biographical or psychological. It is, in fact, in the relation of Wordsworth's poem to the tradition of ode writing that led up to it that we uncover the most powerful formal challenge to new historicist readings of the poem – a challenge that turns that reading on its head.

In the eighteenth-century renaissance of the ode, Wordsworth would have repeatedly seen an ethos of retreat from social realities coupled with a depoliticisation of the Horation ode model whereby the rural/rustic becomes entirely detached from contemporary society and politics.

William Collins wrote overtly political odes, but again and again in Collins's odes we see images of retreat from politics into rustic retirement. Even in a poem such as 'Ode to Simplicity', in which Collins suggests the possibility of some direct relation between poetry and politics by recalling the relationship between Augustus, Virgil and Horace (31–5), the speaker asks only to find Simplicity's 'temp'rate vale: / Where oft my Reed might sound / To maids and Shepherds round' (51–3). In Collins's odes, we often see poetry valued for 'its remoteness from external reality'.[28] The poet figure frequently dwells in an 'imagined world', a 'world beyond the ordinary',[29] and 'can invent, decorate, imagine, create' – in short, 'distance [...] painful reality'.[30] The imagined location for this poetic activity is, as often as not, a rustic retreat detached from political and social realities that instead looks out, for instance, 'from the Mountain's Side' and 'Views Wilds, and swelling Floods, / And Hamlets brown, and dim-discover'd Spires' ('Ode to Evening', 35–7).

In Thomas Gray's 'Horatian' odes we see Gray's 'crippling but addictive distance from the madding crowd'.[31] Rarely is there any direct engagement with the social or political here, which are normally given no quarter at all: in the Eton College Ode, the 'happy hills' and 'fields' are sites for 'careless childhood' (11–13) not adult cares – or even childhood's own power struggles, which are kept at arm's length by both the distance imposed by a 'prospect' and the speaker's idealistic memory of his own childhood.[32] Adult experience – and especially anything like adult politics – is held off by both the emphasis on childhood ignorance and the language of universal, humanist generalisation.[33]

In 'Ode to Spring', 'the Crowd' (18) is viewed by the speaker 'At ease reclin'd in rustic state' (17), a 'rustic state' that forms an essential part of the most powerful poetic image of the famous writer of great Pindaric odes for both contemporaries and later readers – that offered by the 'Elegy Written in a Country Church Yard'. Here the poet is imaged as solitary, wrapped up in an imaginary world of his own, 'Mutt'ring his wayward fancies' (106) to himself and, of course, sequestered away 'Far from the madding crowd's ignoble strife' (73) in rural retirement.[34] A self-reflexive 'uncertainty about the value' of such sequestration does surface in Gray's poetry, in the 'Elegy' but also, of course, in 'Ode to

Spring', but this does not lead into any kind of engagement with a wider social world or politicisation of Gray's poetic 'rustic state'. It leads into 'a kind of ontological paralysis' in which Gray remains hidden away from society and politics in his rustic retreat as a 'self-absorbed melancholic'.[35] Even in the odes of Mark Akenside, perhaps the most political ode writer of the mid-eighteenth century,[36] we repeatedly encounter an ethos of retreat and a depoliticisation of rural retirement.[37] In Akenside's Ode I, 'Preface', for example, it is in 'lowly, sylvan scenes, / On river-banks and flowery greens', says the poem, that the poet's 'Muse delighted plays' (25–7). Even a 'political poet' can dream of escaping politics,[38] and it is escape, into a rural retreat where 'No more would noisy courts ingage; / In vain would lying faction's rage / Thy sacred leisure claim' (10–13), that is offered to the addressee of Ode XIV, 'Ode to the Honourable Charles Townsend: From the Country'. Indeed, in Ode XIII, 'On Lyric Poetry', Akenside's celebration of his 'lonely bower', a place of 'retirement' that 'emphasizes [...] seclusion from the external world', 'becomes the statement of a poetic manifesto': 'Akenside suggests that, though the outside world may be harsh and hostile, it can be negated' by the poet, and we see him 'create a poetic refuge' in his 'bower' to which he can 'withdraw from the real world' altogether.[39]

Such are the immediate precursors of Wordsworth's odes, and examples of the tradition out of which his odes come and against which they are written. We know much about Wordsworth's debts to, and antagonism towards, the model of Gray, not least from the Preface to *Lyrical Ballads*: that he was one of the models of ode writing that Wordsworth drew on is made clear by the note to 'Ode to Duty' in which he states that his own poem was 'on the model of Gray's Ode to Adversity'.[40] In relation to Collins, Wordsworth had already paid 'tribute' to the older poet in the early ode, 'Remembrance of Collins', while offering 'a revision of Collins's practices' as an ode writer – depicting 'with respect' those 'practices' while clearly 'separat[ing] his own poetic aims from them'.[41] The influence of Akenside on Wordsworth, as well as Wordsworth's obvious knowledge of his work, is evidenced in a variety of ways: in Wordsworth's use of the inscription; in the fact that the stanza form Akenside used in odes such as Ode I, 'Preface', and helped to make 'increasingly popular as a serious lyric form', became 'a favourite stanza of Wordsworth's'; in Wordsworth's use of 'some favorite verses' from *Pleasures of the Imagination* as the epigraph to his 1835 *Yarrow Revisited* collection.[42] But it is the repeated retreat from social realities into a depoliticised rural idyll found in the work of all of these ode writers that

'Tintern Abbey' seems to be worrying about and worrying at. To put this another way, Wordsworth, by repeatedly dragging the memory of social realities into his account of a trip to the Wye Valley, is critically engaging with a long-standing 'displacement' of political and social contexts and 'resituation' of 'human issues' to 'idealised' rural 'locations' that are strikingly close to the displacements and resituations that McGann sees as characteristic of both Romantic poetry and Wordsworth's poem. Reading 'Tintern Abbey' as an ode in the context of the eighteenth-century ode tradition suggests that the poem actively problematises the very ideology McGann attributes to it.[43]

'Tintern Abbey' haunts and invades rustic retreat with the recollection of the world such retreats wish to leave behind. It does not explode the notion of rural retreat by any means, but it certainly problematises it – without ever resolving the contradictions it exposes. Wordsworth wants both to claim great things for communing with nature and to explore the limits of those claims. 'Tintern Abbey', we might say, is a poem that subjects the ideal of rustic retreat that it inherits from odal tradition to doubts and misgivings even as it adds its own, greater idealisation of the rural to that tradition. 'Tintern Abbey' is deeply ambivalent – double-minded – in a way that more straightforward, narrative politicisations of the pastoral such as 'Michael, A Pastoral Poem' are not.

The poem's problematising of – worrying at and worrying about – retreat into communion with nature, its keeping social and political realities in view, begins with its title, which imports into a conventional picturesque title form, as Levinson was the first to point out,[44] a range of political references, the kind of references usually suppressed by the genre the title announces: the reference to 'Tintern Abbey' itself (not even visible 'a few miles' upriver) and, implicitly, the vagrancy associated with it; references to the date of the fall of Bastille and the murder of Marat. For Levinson, the poem then 'effectively muffle[s] the social and political resonance[s] [...] inscribed in the title', but, while the particular references she uncovers in the title are not carried forward into the poem, the 'social world in its actual and compelling character' is by no means 'annihilated'. In the 'details and activities' within the landscape that are 'actually noticed' in the poem,[45] we can trace a subtly sustained awareness of the political and social almost from the outset:

> These hedge-rows, hardly hedge-rows, little lines
> Of sportive wood run wild; these pastoral farms

> Green to the very door; and wreathes of smoke
> Sent up, in silence, from among the trees,
> With some uncertain notice, as might seem,
> Of vagrant dwellers in the houseless woods,
> Or of some hermit's cave, where by his fire
> The hermit sits alone. (16–23)

Plenty of details here suggest an idealised rural retreat from, and an erasure of, the social and the political: 'sportive wood', 'pastoral farms', 'hermit's cave'. But, equally, we can suggest that numerous details keep the social and political in view and resist their erasure: hedgerows are 'run wild', neglected, and the 'green' is allowed to creep to 'the very door'. We might want to argue that here the poem 'modifies human presence as picturesque theory required', moving towards the notion 'that nature and man might be "melted together" to recover Paradise'.[46] But is this what is going on? These details can just as easily be read as signs of a rural society more like that of Gold-smith's *Deserted Village* than that of picturesque tradition – hinting at the eighteenth-century exodus from and decline of traditional rural communities, suggesting a decline that has reached a point where the activity and evidence of those communities 'lose themselves' in, and no longer 'disturb', the 'wild green landscape' (13–15). Other 'details in this prospect' certainly seem inserted to 'awaken precisely the associations that picturesque vision sought to camouflage or suppress: human suffering and history'.[47] We are given clear indications of the encroachment of industry on the landscape, for example. Humanity, absent from 'cottage grounds' and orchards, is to be found in the (as yet) 'houseless' woods, where 'wreathes of smoke' sent up 'from among the trees' (21,18,19) give notice of the 'industrial activity at Tintern', especially 'charcoal burning in the woods that lined the valley'.[48] Such 'notices' immediately lead to the idea of 'vagrants' (20–1), and, as Nicholas Roe has pointed out, the reference to 'vagrant dwellers in the houseless woods' 'keys "Tintern Abbey" to the most impassioned attack on social injustice in English literature, *King Lear*' – an allusion that announces 'a knowledge of humanity at odds with the picturesque attempt to subdue such an awareness'.[49] This picturesque impulse is immediately heard in the rapid shift from 'vagrants' to 'hermit' (22), but the idea of vagrancy is not 'displaced' by the idea of hermitage: the smoke gives 'uncertain' notice, the word keeping both vagrants and hermits in view as possibilities and 'alternative readings of the landscape' that are left to compete with each other in the reader's mind.[50] These lines, so easily read by new historicists as enacting a displacement of the social are in fact packed with references to it, and they end on a clear note of pathos: the hermit may choose isolation, but he nevertheless 'sits alone' (23). The poem's idea of the solitude of a hermit remains haunted by the idea of loneliness of the vagrant, and it is the final word 'alone' and these alternative 'figures of isolation' that 'yield the transition to the next verse paragraph, in which Wordsworth remembers himself withdrawn from the world [...] in London's "lonely rooms" ':[51]

> Though absent long,
> These forms of beauty have not been to me,
> As is a landscape to a blind man's eye:
> But oft, in lonely rooms, and mid the din
> Of towns and cities, I have owed to them,
> In hours of weariness, sensations sweet,
> Felt in the blood, and felt along the heart,
> And passing even into my purer mind
> With tranquil restoration. (23–31)

If Wordsworth's rustic retreat is disturbed by rural realities, it is also invaded by the fact of the urban and urbanisation. Already we have seen that while the poem is located in and talks about the countryside, social and political realities are allowed to intrude into its idyll. The largest intrusion of the social into the poem's rustic location is the recollection of the city. And here the idea that the visionary might offer something to the social is implicitly brought into play: the poem's dialectic brings the private and the social into direct confrontation, as, in the lines above, the speaking 'I' gains tranquil restoration but the poem rhetorically builds up to 'we' and to universalising claims: the personal experience described here is implicitly offered as available to all 'mid the din / Of towns and cities'. Wordsworth is, in other words, tentatively and implicitly offering the private and visionary as consolation and spiritual succour to urban alienation. The very fact that Wordsworth must build up to a universal-ising position – from 'I' to 'we' – rather than offer it from the outset, reminds us of the dialectical nature of the poem: all assertions are subject to, and subdued by, doubts; all positions are aware of others that oppose them. Nevertheless, Wordsworth turns from rural retreat and to urban suffering, seeking to bring personal visionary experience to bear on the social. Once again, the social is not erased. Indeed, in this confrontation between the visionary and the social, the visionary is subordinated to the social – brought to bear on its problems. The visionary offers

> feelings too
> Of unremembered pleasure; such, perhaps,
> As may have had no trivial influence
> On that best portion of a good man's life;
> His little, nameless, unremembered acts
> Of kindness and of love. (31–6)

As the passage builds, so Wordsworth tentatively and testingly inches towards universality – we are no longer hearing about the experience of 'I' but of any 'good man'. And here Wordsworth offers the visionary as the root of an undeniably social attitude: a relation to others based on 'kindness and love'. Small beer, we might say, considering the actualities of late eighteenth-century urban living, but this is nevertheless offered as a mood in which 'the affections' are dominant and in which affection 'gently lead[s] us on' (43) to social 'acts'.

The poem's dialectic nature holds these ideas in check and allows doubts – that we might share – to modify them and their expression. We hear this is in 'perhaps', 'no trivial influence', 'little'. Nevertheless, Wordsworth is clearly addressing his personal visionary understanding at the social here. Far from displacing the social, Wordsworth uses the ode precisely to bring two distinct and seemingly contradictory modes of understanding – the political/social and the private/visionary – together in such a way as to tentatively suggest some potentially fruitful results while acknowledging doubts about that potential. The poem offers implicit claims about the visionary's value to the social, while its form allows 'the still, sad music of humanity' in its social reality to 'chasten and subdue' those claims even as they are being made.

'Tintern Abbey' problematises the eighteenth-century odal tradition of retreat from the social into a depoliticised rustic idyll. It places its own encounter with the rustic in the context of some of the largest political events of recent years. It exposes the social ills that mark its rural location, hinting at social processes going on across the nation's rural economy. It recalls and thinks about the problems of urban life. It tentatively attempts to relate the solitary experience of nature to social realities. To insist that the poem displaces or annihilates the social and political seems rather perverse – we might say instead that, far from eliding the political, the poem offers a politicisation of the literary tradition to which it claims to belong.

We might still want to argue that Wordsworth deflects the visionary impetus of this passage away from the social and into the wholly private experience of the visionary, as the poem describes a mood in which

> we are laid asleep
> In body, and become a living soul:
> While with an eye made quiet by the power
> Of harmony, and the deep power of joy,
> We see into the life of things. (46–50)

Fair enough, though there is a universalising impulse here too. But we have already seen the way in which this headlong leap into the visionary is itself dialectically followed in the next section of the poem by first doubt and then the recollection of 'the fretful stir' and 'fever' of 'the world'. If Wordsworth breaks free of the social at times in 'Tintern Abbey', he is always sure to return to it, sustaining and wilfully renewing the dialectic that is one of 'the principal requisites' of the ode form.

IV

The ultimate test of these claims is the poem's closing section. For the new historicist readers we have looked at as well as for a large number of other readers, the turn to Dorothy aims at a resolution of – or at least a moment of respite from – the tensions that drive the earlier sections of the poem. For Levinson the 'address' to Dorothy 'represents a genuine effort to escape the binary problematic through which the poem gets written'.[52] For McGann, in the turn to Dorothy, 'the mind has triumphed over its times' and Dorothy, 'the reader's surrogate', receives, on the reader's behalf, Wordsworth's visionary consolation.[53] Just as famously, perhaps, and certainly very powerfully, John Barrell argues that the poem's concluding section in fact effects a double resolution of the poem's internal tensions. On the one hand, 'the suddenly unproblematic account of Dorothy's future development, from wildness to depth [...] from the realm of the wild, the savage, the primitive, the undifferentiated, to the realm of the cultivated, the autonomous, the transcendent', validates Wordsworth's claims about his own relationship to nature by 'recapitulat[ing] and historicis[ing]' the progress of that relationship and making it appear an 'entirely natural' and normal 'process' – 'a matter of growing up'. On the other hand, Dorothy's maturation is imaginatively held off 'for the moment' so that her immature, child-like response to nature, repeating his own, can provide Wordsworth 'with the private reassurance that his own articulate and artificial language is still securely tethered' to 'nature' and 'the language of the sense'.[54]

Foregrounding the poem's odal structure highlights a number of problems with such notions of resolution. First, the continuation of the poem's 'binary problematic', rather than its resolution, is clearly signalled at the outset of the Dorothy section with 'If I were not thus taught' (113) and its pulling back from the rhetoric of celebration. Secondly, as we read forwards dialectically, we quickly see that Dorothy is not positioned on the visionary side of this dialectic, either as a validation or as a recipient of Wordsworth's visionary consolation, but on the side of doubt. She is described as an alternative source of consolation should the visionary fail: if he were not taught that nature is the 'soul' of all his 'moral being', the speaker would not 'suffer' his 'genial spirits to decay' because she is with him (111, 112, 114).

As the poem moves forward, it remains determinedly, dialectically resistant to closure or resolution. On the one hand, it articulates a need to underpin Nature's power to console with a second source of sustenance – friendship (Dorothy is 'my dearest Friend / My dear, dear Friend (116–17)) and the shared experience of nature in friendship. On the other hand, however, it does not seek a final resolution of the poem's social and private impulses and allegiances in a third term, 'friendship', that combines the visionary and the social. The poem makes it very clear that Dorothy, even as a 'worshipper of Nature' (153), will have to face exactly the same challenges and dilemmas as the speaker – and, 'perchance' (147), do so without him ('If I should be, where I can no more hear / Thy voice' (148–9)). All he can offer is the 'prayer' (122) that

> neither evil tongues,
> Rash judgements, nor the sneers of selfish men,
> Nor greetings where no kindness is, nor all
> The dreary intercourse of daily life,
> Shall e'er prevail against us, or disturb
> Our chearful faith that all which we behold
> Is full of blessings. (129–35)

That this is all cast as a 'prayer' is absolutely key: it signals the fact that the poem has not detached itself from one half of its dialectic. The poet's earlier celebratory rhetoric is here 'chastened and subdued' to a prayer by exactly the same recollections of the social that chasten and subdue the poem throughout – by the knowledge that the power of nature to inform the mind with this sense of blessings will, in Dorothy's case as in his own, have to contend with encounters with humanity in its social actuality that will directly challenge that power: not simply private encounters with personal 'solitude', 'fear', 'pain' and 'grief', but encounters with human society at large – 'evil tongues', 'Rash judgements', 'the sneers of selfish men', 'greetings where no kindness', 'all / The dreary intercourse of daily life'.

This is not an attempt to escape the 'binary problematic through which the poem gets written', then. What we see is a resignation to the inescapability of that binary and a projection of it into the future. Nor is Dorothy the 'recipient' of Wordsworthian consolation. At best, she is the object of his hopes – his prayers. Equally, Dorothy's future development is not presented as 'unproblematic'. She is very clearly not going to move happily 'from the realm of the wild, the savage, the primitive, the undifferentiated, to the realm of the cultivated, the autonomous, the transcendent' and her imagined future is not a valida-tion of Wordsworth's claims about his own relationship to nature. Her future will be as much of a challenge to those claims as his past, and her movement forward is not held off 'for the moment' so that her present state can reassure Wordsworth about his past state: it is held off 'for a moment' because it will lead her into pain and suffering – from which there is no certain escape. As Vendler has it, Wordsworth

> announces that her present experience as a passionate but socially inexperienced young person corresponds *exactly* to his own past experience when he was a passionate but socially inexperienced young person. He announces further that her future experience, when she has passed through the crucible of social sorrow, will correspond to his own present state.[55]

That state, I have suggested, is one of fundamental and irreducible doubleness, in which an attraction to the solitary communion with nature contends with and competes with an emotional entanglement in social and political realities. The turn to Dorothy offers no escape from this but an extension of it, unresolved and inescapable, into some indeterminate future. The poem never does displace or annihilate the social, but rather insists upon it to the end.

Highlighting this aspect of 'Tintern Abbey' by reading the poem as an ode does not just add weight to the growing challenge to new histor-icism's reading of this particular poem. It suggests, on the one hand, that we might do well to pay less attention to what texts do not say and more to what they do say, and, on the other hand, that we might need to pay rather more attention than new historicists have tended to pay to *how* texts say what they say. That 'how' is a matter of form, and this chapter has had in its sights a cornerstone of the new historicist understanding of form: the assumption, as Wolfson puts it, quoting Terry Eagleton, that 'literary form' is 'typically in the business' of 'recasting "historical contradictions into ideologically resolvable form" '.[56] To approach poetry with the assumption that it always, or 'typically', seeks what McGann calls 'imaginative resolutions', or seeks, in Levinson's words, to 'resolve [...] issues' by creating what she calls aesthetic 'contexts' in which 'resolution' can be 'imagined and implemented' or 'mythic resolutions to logically insoluble problems' can be offered is, it seems to me, to risk misreading a great deal of Romantic poetry from the very outset – and not only those poems written in forms that resist resolution, such as the ode.[57] As we have seen, Romantic-period writers such as Wordsworth could save their highest praise for poetry of any kind that, far from offering solutions to or resolutions of problems, holds together, without reconciling, 'conflicting feeling[s]' and 'contradictory thoughts'. Form here is not a means of resolving so much as a way of giving voice to irresolution and the irresolvable. To reach any kind of understanding of this Romantic (aesthetic) ideology, I suggest, we need to spend less time reading Romantic silences and more time reading Romantic form.

Notes

1. Jerome J. McGann, *The Romantic Ideology: A Critical Investigation* (Chicago: University of Chicago Press, 1983), pp. 91, 131, 1.
2. Marjorie Levinson, *Wordsworth's Great Period Poems: Four Essays* (Cambridge: Cambridge University Press, 1986), pp. 37–8.
3. Kenneth R. Johnston, 'The Politics of "Tintern Abbey" ', in *The Wordsworth Circle*, 14 (1983), pp. 6–14 (pp. 12, 9, 8).
4. McGann, *The Romantic Ideology*, p. 87.
5. Ibid. Quotations from 'Tintern Abbey' are taken from Stephen Gill (ed.), *The Oxford Authors: William Wordsworth* (Oxford: Oxford University Press, 1984). Line references follow quotations in the text.
6. McGann, *The Romantic Ideology*, p. 87.
7. *Wordsworth's Great Period Poems*, pp. 47–8.
8. Johnston, 'The Politics of "Tintern Abbey" ', pp. 6, 7.
9. Thomas McFarland, *Romanticism and the Heritage of Rousseau* (Oxford: Clarendon Press, 1995), pp. 32, 46, 33.
10. *Wordsworth's Great Period Poems*, p. 25.
11. Quoted in *The Oxford Authors: William Wordsworth*, p. 692.

12. Paul Fry, *The Poet's Calling in the English Ode* (New Haven and London: Yale University Press, 1980), p. 179; Stuart Curran, *Poetic Form and British Romanticism* (Oxford and New York: Oxford University Press, 1986), p. 76.
13. Levinson has suggested a strophe, antistrophe, second strophe and epode structure (*Wordsworth's Great Period Poems*, pp. 47–8), while Vendler, arguing that the poem 'breaks into three equal pieces, not four as Levinson says', suggests the poem has a 'triadic' structure (' "Tintern Abbey": Two Assaults', in Pauline Fletcher and John Murphy (eds), *Wordsworth in Context* (Lewisburg: Bucknell University Press, 1992), pp. 173–90 (p. 179)).
14. In addition to Fry and Curran, see, for example: Norman Maclean, 'From Action to Image: Theories of the Lyric in the Eighteenth-Century', in R. S. Crane (ed.), *Critics and Criticism: Ancient and Modern* (Chicago: University of Chicago Press, 1952), pp. 408–60; Irene H. Chayes, 'Rhetoric as Drama: An Approach to the Romantic Ode', in *PMLA*, 79 (1964), pp. 67–79; Cyrus Hamlin, 'The Hermenuetics of Form: Reading the Romantic Ode', in *Boundary 2*, 7:3 (1979), pp. 1–30; Susan Conley, 'Odes', in Iain McCalman (ed.), *An Oxford Companion to the Romantic Age* (Oxford: Oxford University Press, 1999), pp. 625–6.
15. *The Oxford Authors: William Wordsworth*, p. 641.
16. *Poetic Form and British Romanticism*, p. 77.
17. Sarah Zimmerman, *Romanticism, Lyricism and History* (New York: State University of New York Press, 1999), p. 100.
18. Susan Wolfson, *The Questioning Presence: Wordsworth, Keats and the Interrogative Mode in Romantic Poetry* (Ithaca and London: Cornell University Press, 1986), p. 61.
19. David Simpson, *Wordsworth's Historical Imagination: the Poetry of Displacement* (New York and London: Methuen, 1987), p. 110; Zimmerman, *Romanticism, Lyricism and History*, p. 75; Philip Cox, *Gender, Genre and the Romantic Poets* (Manchester: Manchester University Press, 1996), p. 39.
20. *Romanticism, Lyricism and History*, p. 107.
21. Wolfson, *The Questioning Presence*, p. 61. Wolfson's view of the poem seems to have shifted slightly by 1990. In an essay of that year, she argues that 'McGann reads the poetics of displacement all in one direction, from the social to the ostensibly natural, but Wordsworth's poem tests both directions: the ideal of "Nature" is vulnerable to the sensations of the world in which such ideas cannot be sustained. The deepest work of the poem is its interrogation of this double economy.' However, the essay argues that this is part of an 'utterly Wordsworthian' 'interrogative poetics' rather than a feature of the poem rooted in the ode tradition ('Questioning "The Romantic Ideology": Wordsworth', *Revue Internationale de Philosophie*, 44 (1990), pp. 429–47 (pp. 438, 436, 433)).
22. Simpson, *Wordsworth's Historical Imagination*, p. 113; M. H. Abrams, 'Political Readings of *Lyrical Ballads*', in Michael Fischer (ed.), *Doing Things with Texts* (New York and London: Norton, 1991), p. 378; Zimmerman, *Romanticism, Lyricism and History*, p. 97.
23. Helen Vendler, ' "Tintern Abbey": Two Assaults', p. 185.
24. Nicholas Roe, *The Politics of Nature: William Wordsworth and Some Contemporaries*, 2nd edn (Basingstoke: Palgrave, 2002), p. 169.
25. McGann, *The Romantic Ideology*, p. 91.

26. Mary Jacobus, *Tradition and Experiment in Wordsworth's Lyrical Ballads* (Oxford: Clarendon Press, 1976), p. 113.
27. Curran, *Poetic Form and British Romanticism*, p. 77.
28. Patricia Meyer Spacks, 'The Eighteenth-Century Collins', in Thomas Woodman (ed.), *Early Romantics: Perspectives in British Poetry from Pope to Wordsworth* (Basingstoke: Macmillan, 1998), pp. 70–92 (p. 86).
29. Ralph Cohen, 'The Return to the Ode', in John Sitter (ed.), *The Cambridge Companion to Eighteenth-Century Poetry* (Cambridge: Cambridge University Press, 2001), pp. 203–24 (p. 210).
30. Spacks, 'The Eighteenth-Century Collins', p. 86.
31. Fry, *The Poet's Calling in the English Ode*, p. 78.
32. Quotations from Gray's poetry are taken from David Fairier and Christine Gerrard (eds), *Eighteenth-Century Poetry: An Annotated Anthology* (Oxford: Blackwell, 1999). Line references follow quotations in the text.
33. As Vincent Newey has pointed out, there are 'buried ideological assumptions' about 'School and State' as 'bastions of established rule' in the poem ('The Selving of Thomas Gray', in *Centring the Self: Subjectivity, Society and Reading from Thomas Gray to Thomas Hardy* (Aldershot: Ashgate, 1995), pp. 1–18 (p. 11)), but such assumptions are buried beneath precisely the emphasis on childhood and universal, subjective experience.
34. This is not to say that Gray's poetry generally, or the 'Elegy' in particular, are free of politics. See, for example, William Empson on the 'Latent Bourgeois Ideology' in the 'Elegy' in *Some Versions of the Pastoral* (London: Chatto & Windus, 1935; repr. Harmondsworth: Penguin, 1995), pp. 11–13, or see W. M. Newman, 'When Curfew Tolled the Knell', in *National Review*, 127 (1946), pp. 244–8, for a reading of the 'Elegy' as a response to contemporary political events. Nevertheless, as Newey argues, if 'the poem has a message about politics [...] it is to keep out of them' (*Centring the Self*, p. 242, n38).
35. Newey, 'The Selving of Thomas Gray', pp. 5, 9, 6.
36. See Dustin Griffin, 'Akenside's Political Muse', in Robin Dix (ed.), *Mark Akenside: A Reassessment* (Madison: Fairleigh Dickinson University Press, 2000), pp. 19–51, for a 'fresh look at Akenside's two books of odes' that 'prompts the rediscovery of what was once a commonplace – that he is a vigorous political poet' (p. 19).
37. There are also examples of the opposite in Akenside's odes, most notably, perhaps, in Ode XVIII, 'To the Right Honourable Francis Earl of Huntingdon. MDCCXLVII' (lines 189–96), though such overt politicisations of the rural are the exception rather than the rule even in Akenside's poetry. Quotations from Akenside's odes are taken from *The Poetical Works of Mark Akenside*, ed. by Robin Dix (Madison: Fairleigh Dickinson University Press; London: Associated University Presses, 1996). Line references follow quotations in the text.
38. Griffin, 'Akenside's Political Muse', p. 27.
39. Paul Whiteley, 'Gray, Akenside and the Ode', in W. B. Hutchings and William Ruddick (eds), *Thomas Gray: Contemporary Essays* (Liverpool: Liverpool University Press, 1993), pp. 171–88 (pp. 178, 179, 185).
40. Quoted in *The Oxford Authors: William Wordsworth*, p. 713.
41. Ralph Cohen, 'The Return to the Ode', p. 220.

42. Brennen O'Donnell, *The Passion of Meter: a Study of Wordsworth's Metrical Art* (Kent, Ohio and London: Kent State University Press, 1995), p. 155; John Heath Stubbs, *The Ode* (Oxford: Oxford University Press, 1969), p. 61; O'Donnell, *The Passion of Meter*, p. 170. For an account of Akenside's importance for Wordsworth as an inscription writer, see Geoffrey Hartman, *The Unremarkable Wordsworth* (Minneapolis: University of Minnesota Press, 1987), pp. 37–9.
43. We might agree here with those commentators who have suggested that McGann's 'Romantic Ideology' was in fact already evident as early as the 1740s. See, for example, Robert Griffin, *Wordsworth's Pope: A Study in Literary Historiography* (Cambridge University Press, 1995), p. 7, or Newey, 'The Selving of Thomas Gray', p. 11.
44. See *Wordsworth's Great Period Poems*, p. 16.
45. Ibid., p. 2; Roe, *The Politics of Nature*, p. 166.
46. Roe, *The Politics of Nature*, pp. 169, 165.
47. Ibid., p. 165.
48. Ibid., p. 169.
49. Ibid., p. 170.
50. Ibid.
51. Wolfson, *The Questioning Presence*, p. 66.
52. *Wordsworth's Great Period Poems*, p. 49.
53. *The Romantic Ideology*, p. 88.
54. John Barrell, *Poetry, Language and Politics* (Manchester: Manchester University Press, 1988), pp. 160, 162, 166.
55. ' "Tintern Abbey": Two Assaults', p. 186.
56. Susan Wolfson, *Formal Charges: the Shaping of Poetry in British Romanticism* (Stanford: Stanford University Press, 1997), pp. 2–3, quoting Terry Eagleton, 'Ideology and Literary Form', in *Criticism and Ideology: a Study in Marxist Literary Theory* (London: Verso, 1978), pp. 102–62 (p. 112).
57. *The Romantic Ideology*, p. 103; *Wordsworth's Great Period Poems*, pp. 5, 6, 4.

7
Southey's Forms of Experiment

Nicola Trott

A good part of Chapter 3 of *Biographia Literaria* is spent defending, and analysing, the works of Robert Southey. Apart from the intrinsic interest of the case, the subject of Southey also enables Coleridge to pursue his wider argument with the periodical reviewers, who had been severe on Southey's minor works especially, and had used the publication of *Thalaba* to launch an attack on the 'new school' of poetry, in which Coleridge was himself enrolled, with what he considered to have been lastingly detrimental effects on the reception of his own writings. In addition, the appearance of Southey acts as a dress-rehearsal for the much weightier drama that is to be played out, in later chapters of the *Biographia*, with Wordsworth and on questions of poetic diction and common language. Altogether, then, Chapter 3 is a nice exercise in owning a friend and keeping him at a distance. In the course of the discussion, Coleridge excuses the 'careless lines' and 'inequality' in Southey's early output as the 'faults' of 'a young and rapid writer', while accusing his 'critics' of 'a party spirit to aggravate' those faults, as the by-products of a poet who was zealous 'for a cause, which he deemed that of liberty' (I, 55–6).[1] Whatever his 'defects', Southey hardly meant them to carry any new theoretical baggage, says Coleridge:

> it was as little objected by others, as dreamt of by the poet himself, that he *preferred* careless and prosaic lines on rule and of forethought, or indeed that he pretended to any other art or theory of poetic diction, besides that which we may all learn from Horace, Quintilian, the admirable dialogue of Causis Corruptæ Eloquentiæ, or Strada's Prolusions; if indeed natural good sense and the early study of the best models in his own language had not infused the same maxims

more securely, and, if I may venture the expression, more vitally. All that could have been fairly deduced was that in his taste and estimation of writers Mr. Southey agreed far more with Warton, than with Johnson. Nor do I mean to deny, that at all times Mr. Southey was of the same mind with Sir Philip Sidney in preferring an excellent ballad in the *humblest* style of poetry to twenty indifferent poems that strutted in the *highest*. (I, 56)

In spite of his concession to the ballad, Coleridge's purpose is to separate Southey from his early style. He insists that later works have shown a marked improvement, by which he means 'a more sustained dignity of language and of metre' (I, 57). For the purposes of *Biographia Literaria*, Southey is a sort of reformed Wordsworth, a poet who has learnt the error of even occasional lapses and inequalities, and who (unlike Wordsworth) has never had to unlearn a 'theory of poetic diction' which might seek to justify them. Insofar as theory *is* involved, it is that of Warton *versus* Dr Johnson: 'All that could have been fairly deduced', Coleridge informs the critics, 'was that [...] Mr. Southey agreed far more with Warton, than with Johnson'.[2] Coleridge is arguing for himself here: it was he, along with Wordsworth, who liked to hold Johnson's *Lives of the Poets* responsible for 'the bad taste in writing which now prevails';[3] whereas Southey, on occasion at any rate, took the opposite view, siding with Johnson *against* Warton. Christopher Smith, for instance, has drawn attention to the 'burlesque voice in poetry' with which Southey treated 'the kind of magazine poems which sprang up from Joseph Warton's *The Enthusiast or the Lover of Nature* of 1740'. Southey achieved his burlesque manner by crossing the nature-led meanderings and meditations of Warton with some frankly animal and domestic comforts, typically so that all that the convention of lone contemplation leads up to is a hearty appetite and a big dinner. In this, Christopher Smith remarks, 'one cannot fail to be reminded of Dr Johnson's burlesques of Thomas Wharton's [*sic*.] poetry'.[4] Perhaps one can, just for a moment, fail to recall the verses in question, so here is a Johnson parody of this kind:

> Hermit hoar, in solemn cell,
>   Wearing out life's evening gray;
> Smite thy bosom, sage, and tell,
>   Where is bliss? and which the way?
>
> Thus I spoke; and speaking sigh'd;
>   Scarce repress'd the starting tear; –

>   When the smiling sage reply'd –
>   Come, my lad, and drink some beer.[5]

Here, for comparison, is Southey's rendition of the same 'burlesque voice', in a sonnet of 15 April 1799:

>   That gooseberry-bush attracts my wandering eyes,
>   Whose vivid leaves, so beautifully green,
>   First opening in the early spring are seen:
>   I sit and gaze, and cheerful thoughts arise
>   Of that delightful season drawing near,
>   When those grey woods shall don their summer dress,
>   And ring with warbled love and happiness.
>   I sit and think that soon the advancing year
>   With golden flowers shall star the verdant vale:
>   Then may the enthusiast youth at eve's lone hour,
>   Led by mild Melancholy's placid power,
>   Go listen to the soothing nightingale,
>   And feed on meditation; while that I
>   Remain at home, and feed on gooseberry-pie.[6]

The effect is not quite bathos, since good humour and healthy hunger play such an evident part in the process, and the senses are satisfied even if the spirit is undermined. While Johnson's quatrains extract comic deflation from a dialogue of youth and age, Southey's sonneteer does not use a mature voice to bring the immature up short, but rather shows both cheerful and contemplative types relishing – 'feed[ing] on' – different aspects of the same nature.[7] For all that, though, a Wartonian melancholia is being laughingly rebuffed, his own included: 'the enthusiast youth' is at least partly Southey himself in other 'moods of mind'.

Evidently, then, Southey happily joined in some Johnsonian debunkings of Wartonian fine feelings and poetic ardours. But this is not the way that Coleridge wants to paint him in *Biographia*; and it is not the way he is generally pictured in modern criticism either: to cite two influential examples, we find Kenneth Curry sidelining the satirical in Southey as a doubtful rarity that is 'not his customary mode',[8] and Mary Jacobus marking him down as an enfeeblingly conventional picker and stealer from Wordsworth and Coleridge's volume of lyrical ballads.[9] Refutations of the critical tradition that views Southey as a derivative poet have been made recently (though chiefly on grounds I do not intend to take up here), arguing that his work contests a prevailing (sometimes described as a 'Wordsworthian') understanding of Romanticism as a retreat from history.[10] With the new edition of Southey out from Pickering & Chatto, under the General Editorship of Lynda Pratt, now seems a good moment to have another look, and to see what can be said for Southey as an experimental poet, of a different sort from Wordsworth, and as a surreptitious satirist of Coleridge as well as of himself.

Let us take the satirical aspect first. Southey appears to have practised a few reversals of the Johnsonian kind on Coleridge himself – or at least on Coleridgean modes of thinking. Southey's fondness for gooseberry-pie was such that he dedicated 'A Pindaric Ode' to the theme. That in itself burlesqued a poetic form in which Coleridge had attempted to write seriously; but his light treatment did not prevent Southey from including the subject of human suffering, and in an identifiably Coleridgean manner. 'Gooseberry-Pie' chooses to source the ingredients of the pie it makes, prominent among them the sugar by which it will be sweetened. However, this is a sweetener laced 'with the Blood of the Murdered'.[11] Southey knows that 'sugar and slave trade' (199) are practically synonymous in radical-abolitionist circles;[12] and his ode deliberately includes the spectacle of humanity being sacrificed to supply Western markets, which had informed the 'Lecture on the Slave-Trade' that Coleridge delivered when both men were collaborators in Bristol: 'For this on Gambia's arid side / The Vulture's feet are scaled with blood, / And Beelzebub beholds with pride, / His darling planter brood' (37–40).[13] Coleridge had made the much more direct accusation that 'the first and constantly acting cause of the Slave-Trade' is 'self-evidently the consumption of its Products! and does not then the Guilt rest on the Consumers?'.[14] So the question in which Southey's ode deliberately implicates itself is whether it is going to give up sugar in response. On the contrary, as the poem comes to its conclusion, so does the pie, and, with almost complete insouciance, the poet-consumer declares,

> The flour, the sugar, and the fruit,
> Commingled well, how well they suit. (52–3)

A still brusquer version of Johnsonian upending takes place in 'The Pig'.[15] This poem has as its point of departure the kind of fellow-feeling with the victims of hierarchical distinctions that is exhibited in Coleridge's poem 'To a Young Ass': 'Poor little Foal of an oppressed Race! [...] Innocent Foal! thou poor despis'd Forlorn! / I hail thee BROTHER – spite of the fool's scorn' (1, 25–6). Likewise, Southey's speaker ostensibly protests that 'A democratic beast', such as the pig, should be 'born to be brawn'd / And baconized' (11, 15–16). He does so by offering to act as the 'Pig's Counsel' in an imaginary refutation of the charges which his keeper, Jacob, is supposed to have brought against the creature – that 'he is obstinate [...] ugly; and the filthiest beast / That banquets upon offal' (6–8, 9). A contemporary audience might have been expected to be immediately alert to allegorical possibilities: to the 'swinish multitude' of the Revolution Debate and a low-bred Jacob's 'Burkean' prejudices, but also to the possible casuistries of 'Jacobin' reason. For the whole poem is apparently dedicated to a quasi-legal defence, aimed at saving the pig from species-ist 'scorn' and inevitable butchery – that is, up until the very last lines. Having eloquently pleaded the pig's cause on all counts, the speaker turns casually to catch the breeze, as 'O'er yon blossom'd field / Of beans it came, and thoughts of bacon rise' (61–2).[16] This beast is 'born to be brawn'd / And baconized' after all.

The scent of beanfield in Southey's poem has unquestionably drifted across from 'The Eolian Harp' (9–10). That Coleridge's innocent flowers should have acquired this porcine association certainly looks like a satirical gesture: the spiritualising ascent of the effusion is put into reverse by reflex animal appetites. In its limited way, this is a rather telling exposure of a logical weakness in Coleridge's Hartleian-associationist method: what goes up, Southey implies, can also come down; and his counter-method is a *reductio ad absurdam*. If there is a formal aspect to the legalistic case he brings, it is to present the 'colloquial' *versus* the 'conversation' poem. 'The Pig' undoubtedly has the Coleridge form in view, but it has been cross-bred, as it were, with a vigorous and vernacular stock: subtitled 'A Colloquial Poem', 'The Pig' announces its anti-aesthetic or anti-poetic intentions from the start; and the effect is to pit a 'Wordsworthian' 'real language' experiment – of a fairly rudimentary sort, admittedly – against a 'Coleridgean' blank verse philosophy.

The poetic weakness which Coleridge detected in Southey's inability 'to plan *a Whole*' becomes a kind of poetic strength when it acts to prize apart the contradictory impulses that are contained within the Wordsworth–Coleridge partnership.[17] That these tensions play to Southey's strong suit is interestingly of a piece with Coleridge's admission that 'in character, & *dramatic* dialogue, Southey is unrivalled'.[18] In his 'colloquial' riposte to Coleridgean 'conversation', not only is the higher purpose of the argument undone by the simple and habitual sensory link between pork and beans, but the pig itself, by virtue of 'A dirty life' (44), offers a sardonic commentary on the aspirant spirituality of the conversational model: Southey's note for the poem in his *Common-Place Book* reads, 'What is dirt? Berkleian hypothesis sublimely introduced' (197). It was to Southey, of course, that Coleridge had in July 1797 sent his 'Lime-Tree Bower my Prison' with the explanatory note, 'You remember, I am a *Berkleian*', appended to the poem's *exaltatio*, in which the landscape, having been gazed at 'till all doth seem / Less gross than bodily', reveals 'such hues / As cloathe the Almighty Spirit, when he makes / Spirits perceive His presence!'.[19] But from a piggish perspective, philosophical idealism equals bestial filth: 'If matter be not, but as Sages say, / Spirit is all, and all things visible / Are one, the infinitely modified, / Think, Jacob, what that Pig is, and the mire / In which he stands knee-deep?' (55–9).

The sceptic or satirist in Southey seems to enjoy confronting a theology of universal spiritual unity and harmony with some hard cases. The pig is one such; another, still more taxing, is found in 'The Filbert':

> Nay gather not that Filbert, Nicholas,
> There is a maggot there, – it is his house –
> His castle – oh commit not burglary!
> Strip him not naked, 'tis his cloaths, his shell,
> His bones, the very armour of his life,
> And thou shalt do no murder Nicholas! (1–6)[20]

The principle of the sanctity of all life forms may be extended to water-snakes, conceivably. But to maggots?[21] Southey's crude but effective manner of taking a premise literally and to its logical conclusion is again given exhibitionist rhetorical display in 'Inscription under an Oak':

> All around
> Is good and lovely: hard by yonder wall
> The kennel stands; the horse-flesh hanging near
> Perchance with scent unsavoury may offend
> Thy delicate nostrils, but remember thou
> How sweet a perfume to the hound it yields,
> And sure its useful odours will regale
> More gratefully thy philosophic nose. (4–11)[22]

Southey owned his 'Inscription under an Oak' an 'imitation'[23] – modern scholarship calls it a parody – of 'Lines Left upon a Seat in a Yew-Tree'.[24] The closing injunction of Wordsworth's poem, 'that he, who feels contempt / For any living thing, hath faculties / Which he has never used' (48–50), is answered by an inscription which moves to assert the axiom that 'All [...] Is good and lovely' while in fact putting it to a stiff test from the faculty of smell. This is rubbing Wordsworth's philosophic nose in it, as it were. And Coleridge's also; for the dialogue with Wordsworth is mediated by the same letter in which Coleridge had transcribed for Southey 'This Lime-Tree Bower my Prison', itself a counter- or mirror-poem to the 'Yew-Tree' Lines. In writing to Southey, Coleridge cast himself as one beneficiary of the Wordsworthian speaker's exhortation – 'I am as much a Pangloss as ever – only less *contemptuous*, than I used to be, when I argue how unwise it is to feel contempt for any thing' – before moving on to tell of his 'visit to Wordsworth's at Racedown' and his unbounded confidence that 'Wordsworth is a very great man – the only man, to whom *at all times* & in *all modes of excellence* I feel myself inferior'.[25]

To Southey, Coleridge's quondam friend and collaborator, such a confession was presumably less than complimentary. But while personal animosity – the fallout from the falling out with Coleridge over Pantisocracy and marriage – must play a part in his poetic response, so also does something more like genuine bemusement. Southey reads for the letter rather than the spirit, taking as his scripture the morals of *The Ancient Mariner* and 'Yew-Tree' Lines, and pushing them to the limit-points that are logically entailed by their brother-ass Jacobinism. Hazel-maggots and horse-flesh, pig-muck and beans-and-bacon are Johnsonian practical jokes played upon those who enthusiastically endorse 'the one Life within us and abroad' ('The Eolian Harp', 26). The three poems, 'The Pig', 'The Filbert' and the 'Inscription', were all included by Southey in his *Annual Anthology* under the signature 'Theoderit', which, in addition to being an anagram of his editorial role, has been (loosely) translated as 'God he will be'[26] – a codename that offers to label these pieces as reflections upon religious pretensions of some sort, and which seems also to imply or impute 'derision'. 'Theoderit' may stand for a Southey who is materialistically obtuse to the pantheistic aspirations and inspirations of Coleridge, and who places the grand vision of a God 'diffused through all' in a tight corner or two. It is interesting that Southey's satirising of Coleridge sits alongside the Coleridge being satirised: 'This Lime-Tree Bower my Prison. – A Poem addressed to Charles Lamb, of the India-House' is printed in the second and last *Annual Anthology*, of 1800 (pp. 140–4). Yet the formal response is less secure, or less thoroughgoing, than satire as such. The poet who 'wants' – that is, lacks – 'totality' tends to combine parody with imitation in unstable and finally undecidable configurations.[27]

Even so, more is to be claimed for Southey's forms of experiment than his reductive or absurdist pranks might lead us to expect. This claim involves him in a rather more distanced mode of reflection upon the Wordsworth–Coleridge partnership. And it raises again the question of poetic language which emerges in the passage from Chapter 3 of *Biographia Literaria* quoted at the start – a question Coleridge posed above all of Wordsworth and which by the time of the Laureate's death had come to be known as 'the Wordsworth question', but which for this once may be regarded as 'the Southey question' also.

When in November 1798 Charles Lamb got back to Southey after reading a draft of his latest Eclogue, 'The Last of the Family',[28] he found it 'plain', almost *too* plain: 'Servants speak', he wrote,

> and their language ought to be plain, and not much raised above the common, else I should find fault with the bathos of this passage:

> And when I heard the bell strike out, / I thought (what?) that I had never heard it toll / So dismally before.[29]

Lamb has picked up on the vacuity of the 'thought' that does no more than reiterate that a tolling bell has been heard. He, along with others, had been taught to recognise Southey's limitations by Coleridge: Lamb, Wordsworth and later De Quincey all agreed that Southey was 'best suited to' a 'humbler choice of themes'.[30] 'Leave the lowlands unenvied in possession of Such men as Cowper & Southey', Lamb told Coleridge, in what was a flattering way of saying that his revisions to the 'Maid of Orleans' were not exalted enough. The corollary of what Lamb expected from Coleridge was also clear: 'Southey certainly has no pretensions to vie with you in the Sublime of poetry, but he tells a plain tale better than you.'[31] Plainness and Southey were, he found, the same.

Southey himself begged to disagree. While he was prepared ostentatiously to subtitle 'The Pig' a 'Colloquial Poem', this was a strictly limited occasion – directed chiefly, perhaps, to burlesquing Coleridgean revelations of spiritualised matter. In the single page of prefatory remarks he added to his 'English Eclogues', on collecting them for publication in his *Poems* of 1799, he expressed his reservations about the Wordsworth–Coleridge experiment in poetry: 'How far poems requiring almost a colloquial plainness of language may accord with the public taste I am doubtful.'[32] It is not hard to hear in Southey's doubts as to the public's lack of readiness for such poems a check upon the ambitions recently announced by the Advertisement to *Lyrical Ballads* (1798). Certainly, Southey had shown himself to be that unready reader in his hostile review of the volume (*Critical Review*, October 1798); and in 1799 appeared to offer his own Eclogues by way of a generic reply.[33] Their anti-lyrical balladry casts another sort of light on Southey's jibe about *The Ancient Mariner* as a 'Dutch attempt at German sublimity':[34] the criticism, too, suggests a semi-satirical method;[35] the reviewer, like the poet, is deliberately or instinctively blind to the 'Sublime of poetry' as Coleridge represents it.

Lamb, as we have seen, assigns the lowlands to Southey so as to leave the 'loftier walks' to Coleridge. But this involves a flattening out on both sides. After all, some of Coleridge's extraordinary achievement comes of his locating 'the Sublime of poetry' in idiomatic, if not plain, surroundings. Equally, much of what is innovative in Southey's early work has nothing to do with his undoubted ability to tell 'a plain tale'. His remarks on the eclogue, for instance, apparently refuse one kind of poetic experiment (in 'colloquial plainness of language', as newly conducted by Wordsworth and Coleridge), while embracing another, that of form. Southey is bold enough to assert that his own eclogues 'bear no resemblance to any poems in our language';[36] and explains their power to strike out of the common way by reference, first, to 'German Idylls' he knows of only by hearsay,[37] and, second, to English models which slyly circumvent a worn-out mode: 'Pastoral writers "more silly than their sheep" have like their sheep gone on in the same track one after another. Gay stumbled into a new path. His eclogues were the only ones that interested me when I was a boy, and did not know they were burlesque'[38] – an admission that says a good deal about the insecure tone and uncertain satire of Southey himself.

Gay's originality consisted in both the town eclogue, which redeployed for wry urban uses the classical literary form of rural life, and the *Shepherd's Week*, which proceeded bucolically but mockingly from 'Monday or The Squabble', to 'Wednesday or The Dumps', to 'Friday or The Dirge'. Either way, Southey ignores the spirit of irony which allows for comedy or comment,[39] and concentrates instead on the potential for renewing, or evading, a Theocritan tradition. Formal experimentation, not tonal control, is uppermost. This can be generic,[40] or metrical,[41] or, indeed, linguistic. For all Southey's distrust of its Wordsworthian and Coleridgean manifestations, this last is a distinctive, and relatively neglected, aspect of his contribution to the poetic revolution of the 1790s. A contemporary reviewer of his *Metrical Tales*, the volume in which he gathered his shorter pieces for republication in 1805, could readily stereotype him as 'an egregious poetical coxcomb' of the Lakist variety:

> It seems to be his aim to strike out a new model for English poetry; to be as it were the founder of a new sect. [...] In his 'Songs of the American Indians,' as well as on several other occasions, he treats us with that newfangled and non-descript species of poetry, that prose-like verse or verse-like prose, which it is not possible sufficiently to reprobate.[42]

So far, so conventional, in that Southey is given a role defined on the one hand by Wordsworth's 1800 Preface to *Lyrical Ballads* and on the other by Francis Jeffrey's attack upon the 'new sect' of Lake poets in his review of *Thalaba* in the opening number of the *Edinburgh Review* (October 1802). However, the main complaint *this* reviewer has about Southey's language is not with his 'prose-like verse', but something else altogether:

> We must also decidedly express our disapprobation of the system of coining new words, which is too common in the present public-ation; such as, for instance, 'unharming,' 'unfatiguable,' 'unre-callable,' 'disbranches,' 'quintessential,' 'brooklet,' and many others too numerous to mention. [...] It is not only for making words of his own that he has a partiality: he is equally fond of compounding *ad libitum*. But this also he had better let alone; he is invariably unsuc-cessful. He gives us 'heart-sincerity,' 'heart-delight,' 'blood-banner,' 'death-day,' &c. &c. It would be difficult to discover any beauty in them.[43]

Alongside 'plain' Southey, then, we find a Southey who is anything but plain, a coiner and compounder of words. These, and not his tame borrowings and divergences from *Lyrical Ballads*, are his contri-bution to the ordinary language debate being promoted by Coleridge and Wordsworth. It is indicative that, while his 'Metrical Letter, Written from London' consciously defends the use of 'the homely and familiar phrase', it does so with a parallel awareness that such language sits awkwardly 'amid the measured line' and that an epistolary poet has various rhetorical flourishes at his command – a verbalised or adjectival noun, a vernacularised classical formula.[44] An exception-ally florid example of Southey neologising is provided by his 'Cool

Reflections during a Midsummer Walk' – the walk in question being from Warminster to Shaftesbury – which appeared in the 1800 *Annual Anthology* (pp. 29–31). Given that its verbal innovations are also linked, directly or indirectly, to various forms of experiment, it may be worth quoting in full:

> O spare me – spare me, Phoebus! if indeed
> Thou hast not let another Phaeton
> Drive earthward thy fierce steeds and fiery car;
> Mercy! I melt! I melt! no tree – no bush,
> No shelter! not a breath of stirring air
> East, West, or North, or South! Dear God of day,
> Put on thy nightcap! – crop thy locks of light,
> And be in the fashion; turn thy back upon us,
> And let thy beams flow upward! make it night
> Instead of noon! one little miracle,
> In pity, gentle Phoebus!
>   What a joy,
> Oh what a joy to be a Seal and flounder
> On an ice-island! or to have a den
> With the white bear, cavern'd in polar snow!
> It were a comfort to shake hands with Death –
> He has a rare cold hand! to wrap one's self
> In the gift shirt Deianeira sent,
> Dipt in the blood of Nessus, just to keep
> The sun off, – toast cheese for Beelzebub,
> That were a cool employment to this journey
> Along a road whose white intensity
> Would now make platina uncongelable
> Like quicksilver.
>   Were it midnight, I should walk
> Self-lanthorn'd, saturate with sunbeams. Jove!
> O gentle Jove! have mercy, and once more
> Kick that obdurate Phoebus out of heaven.
> Give Boreas the wind-cholic, till he roars
> For cardimum, and drinks down peppermint,
> Making what's left as precious as Tokay.
> Send Mercury to salivate the sky
> Till it dissolves in rain. O gentle Jove!
> But some such little kindness to a wretch
> Who feels his marrow spoiling his best coat –

Who swells with calorique as if a Prester
Had leavened every limb with poison-yeast –
Lend me thine eagle just to flap his wings,
And fan me, and I will build temples to thee,
And turn true Pagan.
                    Not a cloud nor breeze –
O you most heathen Deities! if ever
My bones reach home (for, for the flesh upon them
That hath resolved itself into a dew),
I shall have learnt owl-wisdom. Most vile Phoebus,
Set me a Persian sun-idolater
Upon this turnpike road, and I'll convert him
With no inquisitorial argument
But thy own fires. Now woe be to me wretch,
That I was in a heretic country born!
Else might some mass for the poor souls that bleach,
And burn away the calx of their offences
In that great Purgatory crucible,
Help me. O Jupiter! my poor complexion!
I am made a copper-Indian of already,
And if no kindly cloud will parasol me,
My very cellular membrane will be changed –
I shall be negrofied.
                    A brook! a brook!
Oh what a sweet cool sound!
                                    'Tis very nectar!
It runs like life thro' every strengthen'd limb –
Nymph of the stream, now take a grateful prayer.

The poem may be called 'Cool Reflections', but it is not a cool work. Nor, at first glance, is it very reflective. Its rhetoric is as overheated as the midsummer sun it addresses. Even the little sub-fantasy of cool in the second paragraph, the ice-floundering seal, is pretty frisky; and the grotesque idea which follows, of shaking the 'rare cold hand' of Death, merely sends the poet back to the theme of heat, in the thought that he would go so far as to wear the shirt poisoned with the blood of the centaur Nessus, the shirt which sent Hercules to his death by fire, 'just to keep / The sun off' (a casual dress classicism of a sort Southey's lighter verse enjoys). And Hercules' fate and fiery shirt lead by association to a burlesque vision of the job from hell, 'toast[ing] cheese for Beelzebub' – and even 'That were a cool employment to this journey'.

The poem is a series of variations on one idea: it is hot. And all it has to rely on as a way of sustaining itself, apparently, is a raft of rhetorical devices, figures of hyperbole and amplification, together with some neologisms:

> my poor complexion!
> I am made a copper-Indian of already,
> And if no kindly cloud will parasol me,
> My very cellular membrane will be changed –
> I shall be negrofied.

The race-terms will stand out as inescapably and uncomfortably racial to readers today; and may also serve to identify Southey as a Bristolian at a time when Bristol was a centre of the British slave-trade. That much was a given, in 1799, when the poem was written; but the word 'negrofied' was not: this is Southey's invention and, we might say, he is making new linguistic coin out of some very dark historical materials.[45] However, Charlotte Smith's nearly contemporaneous use of 'simple negro face' ('The hedge-hog seen in a frequented path', 18) to describe a hedgehog is probably more offensive – as well as less inventive. And modern readers for their part may have to acknowledge that they no longer see past the race-term to the word-root beneath, which makes the verb 'negrofy' mean 'to blacken', or cause to appear black. Of greater interest, perhaps, is that Southey's white speaker is fantasising about becoming a black one; and that, worries about his 'complexion' apart, no particular horror attaches to the prospect. It is understood to be a matter of pigmentation, due to the skin's exposure to sunlight. It is also understood to be a progressive change, from white, to red, to black: the first race-term is found three lines earlier, in 'copper-Indian'. This too is Southey's coinage, a compound noun prompted by an existing association of the red colour of copper with the Indians (now native Americans) of North America.[46] Copper also, of course, conducts heat and, it follows, the theme of 'Cool Reflections'. The link here is with the sun of Coleridge's *Ancient Mariner*, 'All in a hot and copper sky' (107); but the heat conducted in Southey's poem is imagined to cause racial change, as a hyperbolic way of talking about sunburn.

Before moving on to the poem's other innovations, it may be worth pausing on Southey's use of a word he did not invent, 'crucible'. This is a vessel in which substances may be heated to high temperatures so as to produce new compounds, and as such is an apt metaphor for the kind of language experiment which the poem undertakes – as, for example, in the quasi-compound form it takes here, 'Purgatory crucible'. Southey's 'crucible' turns his verse into a site of both poetic and scientific experimentation. Once these experimental links are made, others reveal themselves: the poem is scattered with references to chemical substances and elements, processes and theories. Take, for instance, 'calx', in the preceding lines, 'the poor souls that bleach, / And burn away the calx of their offences / In that great Purgatory crucible'. Southey has imagined Purgatory as a vast scientific lab in which souls purge their sins by fire, just as early chemists thought of 'burning or roasting ("calcining") a mineral or metal, so as to consume or drive off all its volatile parts, as lime is burned in a kiln' (*'calx* 1; L. *calx, calc-em* lime', *OED*). This process was written about, scientifically, by Humphry Davy, but Southey's is the only figurative application cited in the *OED* (and seems to be a slight misapplication, signifying that which is purged away – 'offences' – rather than the purged substance that remains).

The effect of temperature on different elements is also registered in another of the poem's hyperbolic heat-experiments: at the end of the second paragraph we come upon 'a road whose white intensity / Would now make platina uncongelable / Like quicksilver'.[47] Copper, we have met with already; here we find two more metals. Platina was the name given to what we call platinum,[48] and that we do so is due to Davy, who had adopted this Latin form (in conformity with the names of other metals ending in -um) from Bergman by 1812. In 1799, the year Southey was writing, platinum was a discovery barely 50 years old, and still went by the name of platina (from the Spanish for silver, *plata*, because it had been sourced only in South America). Its relevance for 'Cool Reflections', however, is the property it has under the conditions the poem experiments with: the word 'platina' is homologous with 'quicksilver' in the next line; but Southey knows that the metal is *opposite* to quicksilver in being extremely heavy, and fusible only at extremely high temperatures (whereas quicksilver, as its name implies, is liquid even at room temperature, and would have to be cooled if it were to solidify). It is so hot, the poem asserts, that under these conditions platina would be in a quicksilver or liquid state. That is, the 'white intensity' of the road the poet travels by subjects him to the kind of heat that would fuse even the least fusible of metals.

Southey's outrageous Davy-inspired hyperbole is linked to two further keywords in the poem, both in the third paragraph. Quicksilver takes us, by association, to Mercury, and to the somewhat unsavoury prospect of Jove sending his son 'to salivate the sky / Till it dissolves in rain'. This eccentric prayer for rain, incidentally, makes a poeticism of a sort out of the fact that mercury was used medicinally to make patients spit. But, all of a sudden, a metal has become a god, as a lower case 'q' shifts to an upper case 'M'. The change depends on the metal having properties akin to the swift and volatile Roman god for whom it was named. The liveliness of mercury – its figuratively quicksilver or mercurial qualities – seems naturally allied to the poem's own poetic. Messenger of the gods, Mercury is also the messenger-boy for the poem as a whole, and works as a link-figure in various ways. One of his messages leads, by yet another association with heat – the metal mercury is if course used for measuring temperature – to the word 'calorique', in lines towards the end of the third paragraph, 'a wretch [...] Who swells with calorique as if a Prester / Had leavened every limb with poison-yeast'. A prester is a venomous snake,[49] the bite of which was fabled to cause death by swelling – hence the yeasty leavening of limbs – and, by association with mercury-poisoning, presents another facet of the many-sided figure of Mercury.

The more interesting and experimental word, though, is 'calorique', which simply means 'heat', but which draws attention to itself by its spelling, and by its substitution of specialised jargon for ordinary language – just as, towards the end of the poem, the phrase 'cellular membrane' is preferred to the much more usual word 'skin' (Southey's is only the second use of that collocation given in the *OED*, and the first outside its origins in eighteenth-century physiology). These cant terms are drawn, playfully and self-consciously, from new scientific disciplines and theories. 'Calorique' was the 'name given to a supposed elastic fluid, to which the phenomena of heat were formerly attributed' (*OED*). Southey's usage is especially notable because it follows the spelling of its inventor, Lavoisier, perhaps following on from Erasmus Darwin, who noted the 'elastic matter of heat' as something 'termed Calorique in the new nomenclature of the French Academicians'.[50] Such terminology makes Southey's poem rather grander in scope than its deliberately fanciful spirit might suggest. It becomes possible to see it as a work touching, however tangentially, on the projects and knowledges of the Enlightenment. Perhaps Southey's 'Cool Reflections' are cool after all.

The name of Davy has cropped up a number of times, and with good reason. At the time of writing, the author of 'Cool Reflections' was living at Westbury, near Bristol, and enjoying what he later remembered as 'one of the happiest portions of [his] life'.[51] He was 'then also in habits of the most frequent and intimate intercourse with Davy'; and, just to complete the picture, was very happily experimenting with a new drug, nitrous oxide or laughing gas, Davy's discovery, and the treat with which, Southey recalled, 'he generally regaled me upon my visits to him', but which was not, he added, 'required for raising my spirits to the degree of settled fair, and keeping them at that elevation'.[52] 'Cool Reflections' pays testimony to the relation of chemical experiment, based in the empirical method, to personal experience. No sooner has this been said, however, but the experiment reveals itself as the work of old science as well as of new. As in the much more famous literary experiment of *Frankenstein*, new chemistry is merged with old alchemy. In the latter context, Southey's 'crucible' takes on a different function, as does the race-change experiment from white to red to black. These colours represent three main phases of alchemical transformation also – though in its sequence black is the first and least refined, and red the phase which heralds the work's completion, out of which gold, or the elusive philosopher's stone, might arise. The switch from quicksilver to mercury is another alchemical change, in that the latter was the term used by alchemists when matching the names of their seven metals to the seven planets of the ancients.

On reflection, Southey's 'Reflections' venture yet further away from modern categories of knowledge. In its linguistic inventiveness, the verse is in line with a tradition of wit, visible in Southey's seventeenth-century favourites, Quarles and Wither,[53] and – given the alchemical theme – traceable to the Jacobean arcana (if not the chicanery) of Ben Jonson's *Alchemist*. The poem is also littered with old gods. Mercury, obviously (a presider over roads, so the poet asks for protection from the right deity), but also Jove and Boreas and, set against these, the sun-god Phoebus, followed by the sun-worship of Persia and purgatorial fires of Catholicism. From first to last, the ostensible structure of the poem is one of petition and prayer; and, considering the range of divinities it nominates, some sort of salvation might seem to be in order – except that its prayerfulness is entirely in vain. Having run through a gamut of heathen gods, and even offered to 'turn true Pagan' in the search for cool, the poet alludes to the Catholic doctrine that souls suffering in Purgatory are benefitted by the prayers of the faithful.[54] To no avail: relief from this quarter is merely a fantasy, since Roman masses can help neither the poet nor his Protestant and therefore 'heretic country'. The last in the litany of deities who fail to 'spare' him the heat of the sun is the God of the Israelites Himself, who, in the last neologism I shall mention, and the last ineffectual petition of the poem, provides 'no kindly cloud' to 'parasol' the midsummer walker.[55] The miracle of God's protection in the wilderness of *Exodus* (40: 34–8) is mentioned by

Southey himself, in a note to *Thalaba*,[56] and the line in 'Cool Reflections' is clearly alluding to the same biblical verse.

Insofar as they represent more than an overheated speaker's self-dramatising rhetoric, there may be two ways of thinking about these religious references: either the poet is abandoned of God, or the poem is an undoing of gods altogether. Given what we know of Southey's own attitudes at this time, the latter appears more likely. Still more so, if we consider that this is another of the poems signed Theoderit in the *Annual Anthology* – a byline that we have already seen functioning satirically elsewhere – and also the tone of the poem itself, which allows for the gods to be treated with burlesque irreverence: 'Kick [...] Phoebus out of Heaven'; 'Dear God of day, / Put on thy nightcap' (where 'Dear God of day' functions momentarily as an oath); 'O you most heathen Deities!'. (Alongside the classical and scientific resources, then, room *is* found for a colloquial plainness of language, if only of the literary vernacular.)

If mercury is the figure in which all three of the poem's frames of reference – chemical, alchemical and classical – intersect, it is also the point at which they may be seen to clash or contradict one another. As it happens, the date of 'Cool Reflections' coincides roughly with the thorough discrediting, by chemical experiment, of the spiritualised mercury of the philosophers, not the ordinary metal but the long-held theory of an elemental principle, thought to be present in all metals.[57] Similarly, where Southey's poem is not merely flippant or jocular, it does seem rather calculatedly to pitch new science and old religion against one another. They are shown to be historically and culturally linked, even at times fused, in the 'crucible' of the poem; but they are also kept apart, separated by a light-heartedly enlightened-ecumenical understanding of different world faiths as forms of superstition aimed at warding off or appeasing a hostile environment. Not only does the poem invoke, and turn its back on, the gods of Greece and Rome – the whole tribe of 'Godkin and Goddessling' that Coleridge, too, magisterially dismisses[58] – but it does the same to the Judeo-Christian tradition also: God does not send the miracle of the cloud. Instead, in the very last lines, nature sends a material and inspirational stream: 'A brook! a brook! / O what a sweet cool sound!' Here at last the poet finds welcome refreshment, and for this a purely fanciful and fictitious 'Nymph' is called upon to receive 'a grateful prayer'. Nymph and natural world appear to converge in an empirical and material understanding of the universe.

A tentative reading of the poem might go as follows: Southey is tormented into religious fantasy, but also purged of religious error, by extreme heat; and is then saved or redeemed by the waters of material nature. By implication, then, Southey's 'Cool Reflections' are counter-Coleridgean, and themselves reflect upon the enthusiasm for signs of 'Omnipresence' (38) which had dominated Coleridge's own, earlier 'Reflections', his 'Reflections on Having Left a Place of Retirement'. In that case, the entire landscape of the Bristol Channel became, in the poet's eyes, a place of religious worship: 'God, methought, / Had built him there a Temple' (38–9). Southey's poem playfully sets Davy against Coleridge, chemistry against theology, and physical against theist explanations of the natural world. It posits universal experiment rather than universal Godhead; including in that experiment a poetic language that is reinvigorated by virtue of its contact with the concepts and loanwords of new disciplines rather than with the anti-poetic or the plain. Southey's 'Reflections' testify to an experimentation with form and diction that is contemporaneous with, but of a quite different order from, that being practised and advocated by Wordsworth and Coleridge.

Notes

An early version of this chapter was delivered as a lecture to the Coleridge International Summer Conference at Cannington, Somerset, 2004: I am most grateful to both the Director and the Secretary, Nicholas Roe and Graham Davidson, for the opportunity to speak and to the audience for the discussion which followed.

1. *Biographia Literaria*, ed. by James Engell and W. Jackson Bate, 2 vols (London: Routledge & Kegan Paul, 1983). All quotations are taken from this edition and page references follow quotations in the text.
2. See *Biographia Literaria*, I, p. 56n. on the tangle of possible references involved here.
3. As reported by Lady Beaumont, in *The Diary of Joseph Farington*, 17 vols (New Haven and London: Yale University Press, 1978–98), IX, p. 3426 (entry dated 28 March 1809), though similar opinions can be found in remarks as far apart as the 1800 Preface to *Lyrical Ballads*, Coleridge's 1811–12 Lectures and Wordsworth in conversation in 1846.
4. Christopher J. P. Smith, *A Quest for Home: Reading Robert Southey* (Liverpool: Liverpool University Press, 1997), pp. 258, 260.
5. 'Parody of Thomas Warton', in *The Oxford Authors: Samuel Johnson*, ed. by Donald Greene (Oxford: Oxford University Press, 1984), p. 32, and see p. 798 n.
6. *The Contributions of Robert Southey to the 'Morning Post'*, ed. by Kenneth Curry (Alabama: University of Alabama Press, 1984), pp. 145–6.

7. Southey's nightingale-seeking youth combines Gray's 'Elegy' with the set of conventions about the melancholy night-bird he had used in *Poems* (1795) ('To the Nightingale', but see also 'To Lycon') and which Coleridge had recently worked to overturn in his 'Conversation Poem'. The sonnet's adjective of choice, 'soothing nightingale', recurs in one of the poems selected by Southey for his *Annual Anthology* (*The Annual Anthology: 1799, 1800*, facs., by Jonathan Wordsworth (Poole and Washington: Woodstock Books, 1997)); see also George Dyer, 'To the Nightingale' (*Annual Anthology* (1800), pp. 217–18), line 6.

8. Curry, Introduction to *The Contributions of Robert Southey to the 'Morning Post'*, p. 206. Curry also states that attributions are most difficult for the 'satirical poems, because this mode, although sometimes used by Southey, was not a favourite with him' (p. 7).

9. Mary Jacobus, 'Southey's Debt to *Lyrical Ballads* (1798)', *Review of English Studies*, 22 (February 1971), pp. 20–36 (pp. 35–6), quoting from Southey's letter to C. W. W. Wynn of 9 April 1799.

10. See Simon Bainbridge on 'The Poetic Histories of Southey and Wordsworth' in *British Poetry and the Revolutionary and Napoleonic Wars: Visions of Conflict* (Oxford and New York: Oxford University Press, 2003).

11. 'Lecture on the Slave-Trade', in Coleridge, *Lectures 1795 On Politics and Religion*, ed. by Lewis Patton and Peter Mann (London: Routledge & Kegan Paul, 1971), p. 248.

12. *Southey's Common-Place Book. Fourth Series. Original Memoranda, Etc.*, ed. by John Wood Warter (London: Longman, Brown, Green, and Longmans, 1851). Page references follow quotations in the text.

13. Unless otherwise stated, texts of Southey poems are taken from the *Annual Anthology*. Line references are given after quotations in the text. For 'Gooseberry-Pie', see *Annual Anthology* (1800), pp. 53–5.

14. 'Lecture on the Slave-Trade', p. 247.

15. *Annual Anthology* (1799), pp. 237–9.

16. These lines did not appear in the first printing (*Morning Post*, 24 May 1799), but were added in *Annual Anthology* and retained thereafter. However, similar thoughts occur in two other *Morning Post* poems, 'Elegy upon Eggs and Bacon' (28 August 1799) and 'To a Pigeon' (4 October 1799).

17. Letter to John Thelwall, 31 December 1796, in *Collected Letters of Samuel Taylor Coleridge*, ed. by E. L. Griggs, 6 vols (Oxford: Clarendon Press, 1956–71), I, p. 294.

18. Ibid., I, p. 293.

19. Letter to Southey, c. 17 July 1797, *Collected Letters of Samuel Taylor Coleridge*, I, p. 335.

20. *Annual Anthology* (1799), p. 129.

21. See Coleridge's use of the same analogy, when writing to his Unitarian friend John Prior Estlin on 18 February 1798 to reprove the 'definition of Deity' – 'a being whose power is equal to his will' – given in 'a Sermon in defence of Deity' annexed to Paine's *Letter to Erskine*, as one which 'in all probability applies equally to a Maggot' (*Collected Letters of Samuel Taylor Coleridge*, I, p. 386).

22. *Annual Anthology* (1799), p. 181.

23. Southey to Taylor, 12 March 1799, in *A Memoir of the Life and Writings of the late William Taylor of Norwich*, compiled and ed. by J. W. Robberds, 2 vols (London: John Murray, 1843), I, p. 262.

24. For example: Donald G. Priestman, 'An Early Imitation and a Parody of Wordsworth', *Notes and Queries*, 26 (1979), pp. 229–31; *Romantic Parodies, 1797–1831*, ed. by David A. Kent and D. R. Ewan (London and Toronto: Associated University Presses, 1992), p. 35. Lines in the *Morning Post* version, cut from *Annual Anthology*, show that Wordsworth's 'Yew-Tree' Lines are a target of 'The Pig' also (see *Robert Southey: Poetical Works 1793–1810*, gen. ed. Lynda Pratt, 5 vols (London: Pickering & Chatto, 2004), V, p. 348).

25. *Collected Letters of Samuel Taylor Coleridge*, I, p. 334.

26. *Romantic Parodies*, p. 35. To translate thus the name would have to lose the 'd': 'Theo erit' as a Greco-Latin compound sentence can be rendered 'God he will be' (whereas the Germanic 'theod' means 'people'). It is possible that Southey merely intended Theoderit to resemble the name Theodoric ('people ruler') or Theodore ('God's gift').

27. Letter to Southey postmarked 11 December 1795, in *Collected Letters of Samuel Taylor Coleridge*, I, p. 133.

28. See *Robert Southey: Poetical Works 1793–1810*, V, pp. 380–4.

29. *The Letters of Charles and Mary Anne Lamb*, 3 vols to date, ed. by Edwin W. Marrs (Ithaca and London: Cornell University Press, 1975–), I, p. 142 (quoting a version of the text printed in *Robert Southey: Poetical Works 1793–1810*, V, p. 380, lines 8–10). It is in this letter, of 8 November 1798, that Lamb remonstrates with Southey over his negative review of *Lyrical Ballads*.

30. De Quincey, 'Lake Reminiscences, From 1807 To 1830. By the English Opium-Eater. No. V. – Southey, Wordsworth, and Coleridge', *Tait's Edinburgh Magazine*, 6 (1839), pp. 513–17 (p. 517). For Coleridge's influence on Lamb's view of Southey, see *Letters of Charles and Mary Anne Lamb*, I, p. 28; for his influence on Wordsworth's, see *Collected Letters of Samuel Taylor Coleridge*, I, p. 320.

31. Letter of 5–6 February 1797 (in *Letters of Charles and Mary Anne Lamb*, I, pp. 94–5).

32. Robert Southey, *Poems (1799)* (facs., by Jonathan Wordsworth (Poole and Washington: Woodstock Books, 1997), p. 183).

33. See Smith, *A Quest for Home*, pp. 282, 293–4.

34. Review of *Lyrical Ballads*, *Critical Review*, 24 (October 1798), pp. 197–204, quoted in *Coleridge: The Critical Heritage*, ed. by J. R. de J. Jackson (London: Routledge & Kegan Paul, 1970), pp. 53–4 (p. 53).

35. See my 'Wordsworth and the Parodic School of Criticism', in Steven E. Jones (ed.), *The Satiric Eye: Forms of Satire in the Romantic Period* (New York and Basingstoke: Palgrave, 2003), pp. 71–97.

36. Southey, *Poems (1799)*, p. 183.

37. As usual with things German, the hearsay is from William Taylor: see his letter to Southey, 4 January 1799 (*Memoir of the Life and Writings of the late William Taylor*, I, p. 241).

38. Southey, *Poems (1799)*, p. 183. The allusion is probably to Gay's *Shepherd's Week*, 'Tuesday, or The Ditty', lines 27–8: 'Then first, I ween, I cast a lover's eye, / My sheep were silly, but more silly I'.

39. Taylor for his part saw the comedy, only to disapprove of it. In a letter to Southey of 4 January 1799, he writes, 'It [Gay's 'Friday'] has the fault of being witty, but has also a great share of truly bucolic merit' (*Memoir of the Life and Writings of the late William Taylor*, I, p. 243).

40. See my 'Poemets and Poemlings: Robert Southey's Minority Interest', in Lynda Pratt (ed.), *Robert Southey and the Contexts of English Romanticism* (Aldershot: Ashgate, 2006), pp. 69–86.

41. See, for example: *Robert Southey: Poetical Works 1793–1810*, V, pp. 379–80 (on the metrics of 'To a College Cat'); *Memoir of the Life and Writings of the late William Taylor*, I, pp. 271–2 (to Taylor, 15 April 1799, on Anglicising sapphics and hexameters and on the 'fetters of rhyme'); *Annual Anthology* (1799), pp. 233–6, and (1800), pp. 200–10 (on Taylor's 'The Seas', in sapphics, and 'The Show, an English Eclogue, in hexameters', both signed 'Ryalto'); *The Poetical Works of Robert Southey*, collected by himself, 10 vols (London: Longman, Orme, Brown, Green, and Longmans, 1837–8), III, p. xiv (on writing irregular Laureate odes); Francis Jeffrey, *Edinburgh Review*, 1 (October 1802), in Lionel Madden (ed.), *Robert Southey: The Critical Heritage* (London and Boston: Routledge & Kegan Paul, 1972), p. 78, on 'the singular structure of the versification' in *Thalaba*, 'which is a jumble of all the measures that are known in English poetry (and a few more), without rhyme, and without any sort of regularity in their arrangement', and which – like Southey's previous efforts at the 'naturalization' of sapphics and dactylics – is an '*experiment*' doomed to failure (my emphasis).

42. *Critical Review*, 4 (1805), pp. 118–21, opening what is in fact a generally favourable notice (in *Robert Southey: The Critical Heritage*, pp. 113–14).

43. Ibid., p. 114.

44. Southey, *Poems (1799)*, p. 85.

45. The *OED* identifies the word as 'Chiefly *U.S.*'. The first entry after that for Southey is 60 years on, and virulently racist: '1859 *Southern Lit. Messenger* 29 165/2 A ring in the nose, aided by all the brown unguent in the world, would have been powerless to negrofy the bold saxon outline of his features'. However, the verb had already come also to mean 'Favouring the advancement of the rights and interests of black people'. Coleridge is quoted for the *OED*'s first definition, 'Characteristic of a black person': '1828 S. T. COLERIDGE *Lecture Notes* Jan.–Mar. in *Coll. Wks.* (1995) XI. II. 1410 Between..the skull of a female Georgian..and most negrofied Skull of an African..no difference can be recognized but of *degree*'.

46. The *OED*, 'copper', sense 11 – 'Special comb. copper-Indian, a red Indian of N. America' – cites Southey's poem as its only example, suggesting that the phrase may originate with him. Its other racial example, Copper Eskimo, dates only from 1884. The only earlier example linking Indians and copper is '1774 GOLDSM. *Nat. Hist.* (1776) II. 229 The natives of America are of a red or copper colour'.

47. The *OED*'s first entry for 'unconge(a)lable' is dated 1611; its second is 1794, just 5 years prior to that from Southey. Both these uses are in scientific contexts.

48. See *OED* entries for both words. Platinum is 'used chiefly in chemical and other scientific processes' (*OED*, 1a).

49. The snake's name is indicative, deriving from the Greek for 'fiery (or scorching) whirlwind' (*OED*).
50. *The Botanic Garden: a poem in two parts* (London: Johnson, 1791), I, 8n. This is *OED*'s earliest entry; the second, from 1792, instead spells it 'caloric'. Southey's is the earliest cited usage outside a scientific context.
51. *The Poetical Works of Robert Southey*, IV, p. 9.
52. Ibid., IV, p. 10. See also Southey's letter to his brother Tom, 12 July 1799, in *The Life and Correspondence of Robert Southey*, ed. by C. C. Southey, 6 vols (London: Longmans, 1849–50), II, pp. 21–2, especially for the connection of experiment with new experience for which a new language is required: 'Davy has actually invented a new pleasure, for which language has no name.'
53. On Quarles, see Southey to C. W. Williams Wynn, 12 September 1797 (*New Letters of Robert Southey*, ed. by Kenneth Curry, 2 vols (New York and London: Columbia University Press, 1965), I, p. 146). On Wither, see, for example, Lamb to Southey, 8 November 1798 – 'I perfectly accord with your opinion of Old Wither. Quarles is a wittier writer, but Wither lays more hold of the heart' (*Letters of Charles and Mary Anne Lamb*, I, p. 142) – and Southey's *Letters written during a short residence in Spain and Portugal [...]* (Bristol: J. Cottle, 1797), p. 472. Since the title-page to the 1615 edition of Wither's *The Shepherd's Hunting* describes its contents as consisting of eclogues, they may be another model for Southey's excursions in that form, while Quarles is his avowed model for emblem-poetry: see *Southey's Common-Place Book*, p. 193, on 'The Holly-Tree' as 'an emblem, and somewhat in Quarles's way', and Southey's letter to John Rickman, 19 January 1803 (*New Letters*, I, p. 304).
54. Dating from the Council of Trent, 1661.
55. The *OED* gives Southey's line as its earliest entry for the transitive verb (the next citation, of Carlyle, is as late as 1843).
56. Cited by *OED*, under parasol: '1801 SOUTHEY *Thalaba* IV. Notes, Wks. 1838 IV. 163 This was a greater miracle than that of the cloud with which God defended his chosen people in the wilderness from the heat of the sun, inasmuch as it was a more elegant and fanciful parasol'.
57. See *OED*, 'mercury', sense 8.
58. Letter to William Sotheby, 10 September 1802, in *Collected Letters of Samuel Taylor Coleridge*, II, p. 865.

8
Believing in Form and Forms of Belief: The Case of Robert Southey

Bernard Beatty

Southey is a name to most readers but few read him. At the moment there seem to be three suggested approaches to his writings. The first is present in Geoffrey Grigson's anthology,[1] and has been eloquently urged by his most recent critic Christopher Smith.[2] The latter briefly reviews the first version of *Madoc* but ignores the Eastern epics and *Roderick, the Last of the Goths* because he argues, like Grigson, that we should pay particular attention to Southey's slighter poems – his parodies, ballads and domestic pieces. The other two approaches are associated with Marilyn Butler. She argues, first, for the importance of reading Southey's long poems in order to understand the better-known Romantics for the 'poets we have installed as canonical look more interesting individually, and far more understandable as groups, when we restore some of their lost peers' and Southey is a particularly helpful case of this.[3] She argues, secondly, as we might expect, for the political subtext of his Eastern epics. She is certainly right that Southey's major epics do throw real light on the poetry of Byron and Shelley in particular but my focus is of a different kind. In what sense, if any, do Southey's long poems embody religious forms of insight in their poetic processes and what relation does this have to their formal unity – that is to say to their ability to be read as such? Roughly speaking I shall argue that Southey is interested in forms of belief but he is not really interested in either belief or form. An underlying assumption will be that there is some relationship between belief and form. The secret but, I hope, increasingly manifest contention of this chapter is that the necessity of the language of form in literary and other criticism can be proven through negative examples. Southey is a good negative example of form.

Henry Crabb Robinson remarked of Southey's *Roderick*: 'the greatest fault of the poem is that it is too uniformly religious'.[4] From one point of view Crabb Robinson is certainly right; Southey seems little concerned with anything else in any of his major poems. Even his comparatively secular early poems – *Wat Tyler* and *Joan of Arc* – focus principally on a priest, John Ball, who is more central to the action and thought of the poem than Tyler himself, and a woman saint. In the argument between Ball and Piers/Tyler over the legitimacy of violence in revolutionary action we find already much of the subject matter of Shelley's *Queen Mab, The Revolt of Islam, The Mask of Anarchy* and of Byron's political tragedies. It is true that Southey's John Ball talks like William Godwin and his St Joan talks like Rousseau, nevertheless he singles out a priest and a saint as the vehicles of the two works.

On the other hand, Southey never liked priests or saints and his major religious narratives, *Thalaba, The Curse of Kehama* and *Roderick, the Last of the Goths*, utilise and advertise Moslem, Hindu and Catholic beliefs which he did not credit or practice. That this was Southey's deliberate intention is clear from his later admission on reading Picart's *Religious Ceremonies* at Westminster School: 'The book impressed my imagination strongly and before I left school I had formed the intention of exhibiting all the more prominent and poetical forms of mythology which have at any time obtained among mankind, by making each the groundwork of an heroic poem.'[5] Such 'exhibiting' of prominent mythologies in relation to ceremonies because they had 'impressed' his imagination does not sound like belief. Yet Newman singled out Southey as one of the main poets who had helped to found a revival of orthodox Christianity after the irreligious aridity, as Newman saw it, of eighteenth-century culture.[6]

How should we best approach Southey, then? Butler wants him incorporated in the, or at any rate a, canon. But it is one thing to grant his importance and therefore read him in order to discover this or that. It is another to simply read him. I do not think that it is possible to read *Thalaba, The Curse of Kehama* and *Roderick, the Last of the Goths* as we can the major poems of Byron and Shelley. They can all be read with a degree of admiration, and they are all interesting in their way, but they cannot, in my experience, and I suspect everyone else's, be re-read except as a means of finding out information of various kinds or admiring this or that short passage. Yet art is most instantly recognisable in its capacity to invite formal repetition which, in turn, proclaims the unity that such repetition presupposes. Experience falls away from us but art is acknowledged in the suspension it confers through which we are invited to re-experience the same. The question of whether we can read Southey's long poems or not is, then, a question about form.

There is in Southey's poetry, I think, a marked, almost defining, lack of integration of, or interest in the possibility of integrating, disparate or contradictory concerns. It is this lack of integration, or will to integration, which makes re-reading his poems unlikely in that they are insufficiently pleasurable or opaque or fecund. The long poems do not yield reserves of energy beyond their initiating abundance of invention because they are written in a state of apartness from any nourishing centre. They proclaim their orphan status for they are knowingly detached from the energies and credences which originally generated and sustained the mythologies and allusions upon which they depend. It is precisely for this reason, however, that they are not religious though ostensibly about very little else.

The only obstacle to the intelligibility of this thesis is Newman. He manifestly thought that Southey's epics were religious and he did re-read them. His admiration was sustained over a long period of time. Indeed, he says that 'I read *Kehama* and got it well nigh by heart'.[7] Shelley, too, 'claimed to know large parts of *Thalaba* and *Kehama* by heart from his schooldays'.[8] Newman particularly admired specifically religious emphases in Southey: 'In his use of the doctrine of a future life, Southey is admirable. Other writers are content to conduct their heroes to temporal happiness; – Southey refuses present comfort to his Ladurlad, Thalaba and Roderick, but carries them on through suffering to another world.'[9] Even if Newman were alone in these emphases, and he was certainly unusual for Southey's reputation as a poet sank markedly after about 1820, his sheer intelligence must make us pause. Hopkins was a better reader of poetry as such than Newman and he was appalled by Newman's admiration for Southey's poetry.[10] For the moment, I will assume that Hopkins was right. We begin with the problem of the integrity of Southey's vision.

Many, perhaps most, poets make their poetry out of incompatibles of various kinds. New Criticism, following out the German Romantic logic of Coleridge's doctrine of imagination and accepting wholly Keats's notion of 'negative capability', took it as axiomatic that there is an elusive but real, quasi-'organic' congruence of apparent opposites in those poems worth attending to or, more accurately, in those which attain the magic status of 'real poetry'. Later theories of reading have tended to react against such pieties and have tried to re-vindicate the purely rhetorical ways in which literary texts are stitched together and which remain therefore sites of infinitely suspended interpretation rather than being self-standing interpretable wholes. Models of reading the Scriptures can be discerned behind both these asserted emphases.

It is quite possible, however, both to accept the rhetorical, shifting and constructed nature of literary texts and still to encounter a real formal unity in them. Aristotle managed to do both. *Thalaba* is a something, a 'this-somewhat' or 'hoc aliquid' in the scholastic jargon, in as much as those constructing it and reading it necessarily find themselves assuming an intelligible sense of that which seems specifically appropriate to it. We could not for example praise an improvisation, to take an extreme instance of the ostentatiously constructed, without reacting to it as success or failure in relation to a unity of some sort and this unity would be of a palpably inferior kind if simply linked to that of the improviser as personality or to the occasion as occasion. The improvisation has to make, or appear to make, a something. That is its point. If we did not make this reference to a formal unity, there would be nothing worthwhile to attend to as such. And, in any event, this is what we do. But deconstructive scepticisms have been helpful because we can tend to over-reify the ostensive elements of a literary text and exclude that act of reading which posits the text it understands.

The whole discussion, as we can see clearly enough in Derrida, Hillis Miller and de Man, abuts on to religious territories or, at any rate, brings into view their validity or invalidity, for religions characteristically refer the multiple to the unified without necessarily denying the multiple. I suppose that Hinduism and Catholic and Orthodox Christianity are the most obvious examples. This, in itself, bears on my argument, but for the moment I simply need to establish that formal unity of some kind in works of art or 'art' is not a discredited and recent invention deriving from German theory via Coleridge but, however differently contexted, is a recognisable commodity in Lascaux, Byzantium, Urbino, Amsterdam and Salzburg as well as in Keswick and New York. Indeed we should perhaps reverse the argument which, in this new guise, has undeniable, albeit circular, force. If formal unity of some kind is ruled out, then how could we usefully distinguish between those texts, sonatas, basilicas, paintings which exhibit both incongruity and unity and those where incongruities clearly disable the possibility of any kind of working unity? Yet such discriminations have always been confidently made. There has to be a 'showing' of some sort and this showing invites a judgement not simply of this or that detail but of a totality into which a large 'Yes' or 'No' is carried. Newman was thus far right: 'To single out particular passages as "They sin who tell us etc" (in *Kehama*) is surely to evince an insensibility of the real merit of such poems – they are epics, not a string of sonnets or epigrams.'[11] Correspondingly, the business of affirming or denying the unity of a literary text is a perennially appropriate one.

In some sense Southey's Eastern epics all do have something of that formal unity which Newman claimed for them. Each has metrical, narrative and mythological consistency. But early reviewers often complained of fissures that cannot be easily accommodated. Crabb Robinson, for example, comments sharply on *Madoc*: 'There is, besides, a prevailing incongruity between the morals and the incidents of the poem. There is an exquisite purity and delicacy of moral sense which is not in harmony with the wild and romantic occurrences.'[12] His comment on *Thalaba*, apparently of a different kind, repeats, I think, the same point: 'He [Thalaba] sustains trials, but we do not see the strength that sustains him.'[13] An unsigned review of *Roderick, the Last of the Goths* in the *British Review* for November 1815 puts it more sharply still:

> we have to lament one striking inconsistency in its tone [...] the totally unqualified expression of a deeply vindictive spirit [...] the fault lies in the apparent zest and relish with which this is done [...] they are grating to the ear, because of their evident inconsistency with those high principles, the operation of which [...] forms the characteristic feature and leading interest of the poem.[14]

It is interesting that Christopher Smith produces a very similar judgement on Southey's *The Retrospect*: 'Southey's picturesque tour of the self does not seem to synthesize past and present, but contemplates the painful gap between time present and time past [...] Southey appears to have produced a picture of a fragmented self, or selves, in the attempt at autobiographical unity.' He comments insightfully on *Joan of Arc* that 'regeneration through warfare' and 'domestic stasis are literally at war in the text'.[15] Such a convergence of views by different readers at different times is striking. We can link it with two wider comments. The first is the observation by Lockhart and Whitwell Elwin that Southey's 'unadorned language equally proclaims that a command of imagery, which depends on a facility of detecting resemblances, was not among his gifts'.[16] The other is the accusation that was brought up so repeatedly against him from the time of the pirated re-publication of *Wat Tyler* onwards: that he was a renegade.

There are many ways, of course, in which this accusation is unfair. Southey held to certain preferences and to a form of social conscience throughout his life, and many pro-French English writers changed sides somewhere about the time of the Directory or, perhaps, at the resumption of warfare after the Peace of Amiens when there scarcely seemed much left of the French Revolution to support supposing that one still wished to. Nevertheless, Southey's *volte-face* can still shock the modern-day reader. To go, for instance, from Wat Tyler's confident address to Richard II – 'King of England / *Petitioning for pity* is most weak / The sovereign people ought to *demand justice*' – to Southey's confident way with Luddites – 'I would hang about a score in a county, and send off ship loads to Botany Bay' – or to go from his revolutionary enthusiasm for all things French to his wish expressed just before Waterloo – 'Buonaparte and the Marshall [Ney] to the gallows [...] and if Paris be burnt in the conflict, I for one shall acknowledge the hand of righteous retribution' – is to encounter exactly the same, apparently unknowing, inconsistency of which Crabb Robinson and Lockhart complained.[17] It is precisely 'grating to the ear'. Southey cannot see dissimilitudes because he does not habitually entertain similitudes.[18] He has rectitude but not integrity. He *was* a renegade. A comparison with the poet forever associated with Southey because of their two versions of *The Vision of Judgement* – Lord Byron – will help to make the point clear. Byron's long poems depend upon significant parallels between one section and another. Thalaba rides on a mysteriously 'self-governed courser' (42) for two days in Section 4 of the Sixth Book. Byron may well have carried over some of the details and 'feel' of this ride into his *Mazeppa*. But in Byron's poem, the ride is linked back to the opening of the poem and to Mazeppa's transgression, since the ride is the punishment for but also the expression of unbounded natural, especially sexual, life. In Southey's poem, it is simply a magic horse-ride, well done in itself and generally suggestive of Thalaba's being led by Destiny but no more. The difference is characteristic. Poetry is undoubtedly an affair of 'similitudes' for Byron but not for Southey. It would not do, I think, to justify this inconsequentiality as Ariostan, despite Southey's real admiration for Ariosto, since there exists an unconnected moral thrust in *Thalaba* which invites the similitudes which then cannot be found in it.

This indifference to similitudes (Southey, for instance, uses very few actual similes) is linked to callousness of an odd kind. I will take two striking examples from *Madoc*. In the first, Madoc determines to feed Neolin, the Aztec priest, to his own Snake God before he kills the snake itself. It is an instance of Southey's relishing his own 'vindictive spirit'. But the priest springs a surprise on us:

> Strike, man! quoth Neolin.
> This is my consummation! the reward
> Of my true faith! the best that I could ask,
> The best the God could give: ... to rest in him,

> Body with body be incorporate,
> Soul into soul absorb'd, and I and He
> One life, inseparable, for evermore.
> Strike, I am weary of this mortal part;
> Unite me to my God! (*Madoc in Aztlan*, VII, 47–55)[19]

This is the most mystical passage in Southey and we can understand why some early reviewers were bewildered by and appalled at such lines attributed to a snake priest about to be murdered by a devout proto-Protestant Welsh Christian. The phrase 'One life, inseparable, for evermore' might even stick in the throat of the Shelley who wrote 'We shall become the same, we shall be one / Spirit within two frames, oh!, wherefore two?' (*Epipsychidion*, 573–4). But whatever we do with Neolin's mystical affirmation, we cannot really read it. It is not satirical. It does not relate to any other detail in the text. It is simply borrowed life incorporated for purely local effect and then forgotten. What it borrows, on the other hand, is the Crucifixion ('my consummation'), martyrdom and both Eucharistic ('Body with body' via eating) and Pauline mystical union. Southey must presume that this borrowing does not create a similitude between donor and recipient contexts because he himself refuses to think through such a connection. This seems barely possible (it may recall the vexed question of Defoe's irony which both must be and cannot be coherently present) and yet it is the only explanation of a still more extreme case.

The Snake God is duly killed by Madoc in two stages, which are described in loving detail:

> In suffocating gulps the monster now
> Inhales his own life-blood.
>   [...] But when the Hoamen saw
> That form portentous trailing in its gore,
> The jaws which, in the morning, they had seen
> Purpled with human blood, now in their own
> Blackening, ... aknee they fell before the Prince.
>   (VII, 207–8, 226–30)

In the next Section (VIII), the Hoamen are converted. Their god after all has been killed. Their conversion, however, as the reader experiences it, is conducted via the arrival of two Christian icons and by Madoc's discourse. The first image is briefly described. It is a divine version of Southey's domestic idyll – 'Mary bends / In virgin beauty o'er her babe divine' (27–8). The second image receives much more extended description:

> who can gaze
> Upon that other form, which on the rood
> In agony is stretch'd? [. . .] his hands transfix'd,
> And lacerate with the body's pendent weight;
> The black and deadly paleness of his face,
> Streak'd with the blood which from that crown of scorn
> Hath ceas'd to flow; the side wound streaming still;
> And open still those eyes. (VIII, 30–7)

Madoc's subsequent sermon, however, though it refers obliquely to both images, seems to bear little relation to this icon of the suffering Christ. He tells the Hoamen not to offer 'blood, or life': for 'Far other sacrifice he claims, [. . .] a soul / Resign'd, a will subdued' (57–9), and they should 'Forego revenge, forgive your enemies' (65). On the other hand, some erstwhile friends should not be forgiven for 'If ever more ye worship them with feast, / Or sacrifice or dance; whoso offends / Shall from among the people be cut off, / Like a corrupted member' (77–9).

We can, just about, make a sort of sense of this. The Christian images correspond to the image of the snake which Madoc has just destroyed prior to burning and crushing the serpent. The image of the crucified Christ does in itself signify forgiveness and the cessation of Temple sacrifice and thus is quite distinct from the bloody cult of the Snake God. Christianity has long since integrated both the cult of sacrifice and its disavowal and transformation into obedience in this same single image of the Obedient Man who is also pure Sacrificial Victim and Priest. Southey relies, we must presume, on these things but the poem does not mean them and Southey does not believe them as put. The reader is bound simply to associate the two blood-soaked images, crucified Christ and bleeding snake, to which the poet seems to respond in markedly similar ways. There is, in any view, some congruence between these two images quite apart from the New Testament application of the lifting up of the serpent in the wilderness to the crucifixion of Christ.[20] That Christian collocation is associated with healing but, in Southey's text, the connection between serpent and Christ is focused on pain and torture. This could be making a satirical point, and would do so in Shelley's hands. It could be making a subtle point, or Southey could be trying to deal neutrally with Christian icons much as an Homeric or

Norse Saga image of brutal violence exists apart from any larger structure of specific signifying. But it is not in fact doing any of these things. It is not satirical, it is not profoundly Christian, it is not securely separated from Christian response, though the last of these may correspond to some sort of broad intention on Southey's part as we have seen. The sequence presents an unassimilated mixture which leaves the reader excitable and uneasy but not in an uneasiness which signifies. The poet responds to both images in similar ways but he does not think through the similitude and relies on a simple act of dissociation which is itself further vitiated by the awkwardly unmediated gap between forgiveness of enemies and cutting off corrupted members. Southey seems unaware of these problems because he is uninterested in Christian dogmas, does not interrelate images and ideas and does not think in similitudes. He has no religious reticence of any kind.[21] For this reason, he can raid any system of ideas, beliefs and images without himself being modified by or entering into, other than atmospherically, the generative connections inherent in such systems. According to some, this is what poets should do and Milton and Dante are regularly ticked off by critics in the still-continuing tradition of Walter Pater for believing in the 'myths' which they should simply use for poetic purposes. This argument is never convincing and the case of Southey disproves it.[22]

My argument has, in its different track, resembled Smith's insight that Southey cannot integrate his attraction to absolute quietist withdrawal into a book-reading, domestic stasis with his imaginative attraction to an image of world renewal through apocalyptic, blood-drenched warfare and vengeance. The corollary, we might hazard, is that a warfaring woman would be the closest imaginative embodiment of such an integration that he could muster. *Joan of Arc* is a more integrated text than *Thalaba* for this reason and, according to Edward Dowden, Southey confessed that Thalaba was 'a male Joan of Arc'.[23] Southey's play is integrated insofar as it concentrates on Joan herself but insofar as Southey finds himself punishing kings (Henry V) but also having to let Joan crown the king of France (albeit haranguing him in the manner of Madoc to be a good king and not a tyrant) we find the customary bedevilling inconsistency. The question arises whether Southey would even have wanted to cure this. Whilst writing *The Curse of Kehama*, for instance, he decided to abandon poetry for prose. He went back on this decision but prose was to be the staple of his writing life. The reason seems to have been to do with the state of excitability in which conceiving poetry placed him and the gap between his passions, thus revealed and active, and his impulse to quietness and self-control.

To surrender to the claims of writing poetry might involve madness.[24] It is clear then that Southey's remarkable facility in writing poetry is dependent upon his skirting round a massive failure to integrate incompatibles which the poems nevertheless constantly reveal. This failure is bound up directly with the gap between his increasingly explicit religious affiliations and his inability actually to entertain religious beliefs or, closely associated with this, to see religious beliefs as problematic in any way. This is what outraged Byron when he read Southey's *A Vision of Judgement*. He was appalled both by the poem as poem and by the poem as belief. The ineptness of the one is tied in with the inanity of the other.

That is the thesis as I propose it. But it leaves us with the problem of what to do with and how to explain the ostensibly religious concerns of Southey's poetry. Southey is attracted over and over again to religious images of quest based on faith and supported by invisible agencies so that he seems to give a Romance version of a Saving History. He interrupts these quests by images of domestic idylls which may be endorsed or rejected as obstacles to its completion but often, too, he presents scenes of rest and recuperation before further testing in a manner which deliberately recalls scenes from *Pilgrim's Progress*. He is fascinated by religious ceremonies and religious vocabularies. Sadistic horror for him, unlike his master Spenser, is much more readily associated with bloody religious rituals than with sexual violence. He loves to imagine shining heights and black depths which open up vast blank spaces to be traversed which, in their turn, add a spectral quality to the earthly wanderings of his protagonists, and, unlike Shelley, he normally associates divine aid with an abode to which his heroes and heroines are finally transferred.[25] Good and bad spirits correspond to these two realms (though not in the second version of *Joan of Arc* nor in *Roderick, the Last of the Goths*). Finally, his imagination is haunted by apocalyptic images of cosmic warfare and retribution. *The Book of Revelation* was amongst his favourite early reading.

Most of these preoccupations and ingredients seem to be transferable across Moslem, Hindu and Catholic mythologies but, by the same token, none of these mythologies is rendered internally coherent or interesting as a system. Indeed Southey seems almost to seek out such transferences, much as he gleefully uses the persona of a Spanish Catholic to make trenchant criticisms of English political and ecclesiastical life in *Letters from England*. Thus in *Kehama* (XIX, 172–85) he puts something like the Authorised Version on the lips of his notionally Hindu Glendoveer who is an invention as fanciful as one of Pope's sylphs in *The Rape of the Lock*.

An early reviewer complained that such a 'burlesque (for such it may possibly seem to many) is calculated to expose our holy and sublime miracles and mysteries, as written in the sacred volume, and poetically used by Milton, to all that sort of contempt, which the idle and profane wit of infidelity can heap upon it'.[26] Southey did not have much time for Christianity's 'holy and sublime miracles and mysteries' but he was not seeking to burlesque them. He is drawn to certain kinds of vision and motion, uses adroitly whatever language he has to hand and directs the whole, as it were, from the outside, to an ethic of patient, notionally Stoic, rectitude with which it is not easily in accord. He seems indifferent to the aesthetic and religious problems that this unadjusted procedure will present to any reader of any persuasion. It is a very strange set of procedures for writing poems but it seems habitual with him.

We can advance some explanations. Southey discerns, and it must be in the vaguest way possible, in religion of some kind the only possible underpinning or connecting undertow between his two poles of domestic quiet and sanctified warfare. Hence one of his best poems, 'Hymn to the Penates', which is a hymn of specific unbelief (Southey obviously reverenced no actual household gods or icons of any kind) and the utmost heartfelt devotion, rebukes the 'impious' rites defiled 'with human blood' (229–30) which were inappropriate to such familial and (at this stage in Southey's thinking) Republican pieties of 'domestic Peace and Love' (244). And yet in the definitive stages of the Revolution, Southey, who supported Robespierre to the end, must have associated, by some all too horribly familiar and pervasive sleight of hand, the calculated spilling of blood with the defence of an ideal domestic order. He cannot think straight about this. All the more reason for religious reference to cover what cannot be covered and apparently authenticate an earnestness or 'rectitude' which is not, finally, in earnest at all. He carries this vagueness across the renegade divide. At the same time, Southey's religious unearthings present him with a feast of exactly the right imagery which can, in the manner of *Revelation*, shift through fanciful visions, actual historical judgement, moral sobriety and fear-filled, blood-filled retaliations on all and sundry without raising awkward questions of integration. *Revelation* does invite belief in a revelation beyond its text but Southey, keeping the sting, conflates the vocabulary of this belief with the unontological habits appropriate to the *Arabian Nights* or Moore's *Lalla Rookh*. In the end, none of this will work and Southey's long poems, as I have suggested, do not work or, if they work, do so in the manner of a 'Western' revenge film in which some initial domestic despoliation presages an avalanche of righteous blood-letting out of all moral and formal proportion to the initiating event.[27]

And yet they did work for the young Newman as a strange, palpable confirmation of his own destiny: 'it was [...] now too, that Southey's beautiful poem of Thalaba, for which I had immense liking, came forcibly to my mind. I began to think that I had a mission.'[28] It is curious that a young atheist should found the writing of *Queen Mab* and his mission as poet in the same source text. Curious, too, that Newman, who spent a lifetime opposing Arianism should so much admire Southey, who was always an out-and-out Arian scornful of Trinitarian and other dogmas. The very lack of integration which marks Southey's poems enables them to foster opposed projects without offering resistance. Nevertheless something religious in both Shelley and Newman is activated by reading Southey's verse which, as I understand and present it here, uses religion but is not religious.

My argument has associated formal properties – the aesthetic balancing or reconciliation of opposing polarities – with intellectually and imaginatively committed religious belief. It does not follow, of course, that only those thus committed can achieve forms that will stand on their own nor that they will necessarily do so. But the connection between belief and form is real – a matter of history rather than an airy speculation. Formal unity is a matter of aesthetics but it presupposes something more than aesthetics. That is one emphasis which Southey's case negatively appears to substantiate.

Negatives help us in another way. Considerable advances have been made in understanding the relation between mental acts and parts of the brain by examining the effects of partial brain damage on speech and so on. Roman Jakobson's influential article 'Two Aspects of Language and Two Types of Aphasic Disturbances' made readers aware of the literary insights that could result.[29] Certainly, it would be very difficult to argue that there is no positive correlation given this negative evidence. But something similar might be claimed about form. It is not easy to demonstrate, though it may be easy to recognise, the unity of any form which is made up of diversities unless these are disposed in some obvious symmetry (which might be dismissed by some as merely mechanical order). We have become familiar with various kinds of demolition of the idea that form is 'there' in any sense. Form is there to be subverted or, if employed, is utilised simply as a strategy for some wholly rhetorical effect. As with Conceptual Art, not much importance attaches to what is made (the old Aristotelian insistence) as opposed to what its effects are. But what if we work the other way round? If my argument has been

followable at all then it cannot be too difficult surely to demonstrate
the lack of coherence in Southey's long poems and to link this lack of
formal coherence with a lack of intelligibility and a failure to give the
highest pleasure. It is not at all difficult to contrast this with a formal
unity that, however described or argued over, recognisably is a working
one in practice. Byron's *Mazeppa* or *Parisina* exist, please and mean in
and through their form in a way that *Madoc* and *The Curse of Kehama*
do not. Byron's *The Vision of Judgement* is a better poem than Southey's
A Vision of Judgement not only because one is sane and the other is
daft but because Byron's satirical poem is more religious than Southey's
pious one and it exists as something 'made' whereas Southey's is simply
'made up'.

Doubtless there will always be disputes, not readily decided, on which
poem falls which side of the line but to deny that there is a line is to deny
something always acknowledged and readily acted upon by everyone
irrespective of their theoretical beliefs. There is no limit to what we can
dispute but some disputes are a waste of time and, if indulged in, are to
be explained as caused by some larger misdirection surely. Would not
such a dispute be one that claimed that there was nothing at stake or
indeed nothing to determine in the question of whether Southey's major
poems hold together or not? Form is not an invention of formalists.

This has been my major argument but, as I said at the outset, I have
had an underlying assumption which this chapter may be said to both
test and support albeit less directly. To put it at its simplest, it looks
as though on this evidence there must be some kind of connection
between belief and form. The theologian Han Urs von Balthasar has
argued that the recognition of Christ as a single figure in the various
versions of the Gospel and especially across the chasm which separates life either side of the tomb is akin to, indeed is a foundational
version, of the recognition of an aesthetic form. Belief consists in seeing
real diversity as single form.[30] Any attempt to find an ur-Christ or the
historical Jesus or to confidently distinguish the Christ constructed by
the followers of James or John means that the object of attention has
disappeared and yet there can be no doubt that an object of attention is
presented and can be recognised. If we remind ourselves that the original
meaning of 'critic' is one who says 'yes' or 'no' to whatever has been
presented and that thus it would seem that approving recognition of
varied representation as single form and entrustment to it are identical,
then there is a real similitude between belief and form. The last century,
though it was in many ways obsessed with form, harried its object of
attention first because it had no extra-subjective grounds of conviction

and, latterly, either because language itself was seen as the necessary eraser of any forms that it proposed or because forms were merely the signs of rhetorical acts in different historical circumstances proposed as a means of gaining or holding on to power. In any case, the form itself could not be trusted. The one lasting addition that the last century made to the vocabulary of form was to distinguish simply between 'short' and 'long' poems. No great feat of daring involved in this perhaps and the at-hand terminology will be found in the paragraphs of this chapter. But if we keep to this niggardly and grudging division and begin with 'short poems', then it may signify that New Criticism's most influential book was called *The Verbal Icon*. W. K. Wimsatt did not wish to pick up the religious suggestions of 'icon' but must have relied covertly on the revived interest in orthodox icons at the time and the fact that to attend to an icon, to 'see' it and be seen by it, is both recognition of a form and entrustment to and through what is represented. 'Long poems', on the other hand, are *pace Essay on Man* and *De Rerum Natura*, characteristically narratives. Narratives derive from myth and myths derive from religious rituals. To read a story is to entrust yourself to it. Southey knew something of this and embarked on an ambitious programme of visiting and remaking myths from different religious cultures. The fact that no one now reads him suggests, I think, that Southey was wrong about belief and wrong about form. Wordsworth at least associates the making of a sonnet with the desire to be 'suckled in a creed outworn' ('The world is too much with us', 10). The admission presupposes a desire for a deeper unity than the aesthetic which is nevertheless linked to it. Southey wished to raid rather than be suckled by any creed and thus gives us merely forms of belief in poems that have no form.

Notes

1. See the choice of poems and introduction in *A Choice of Robert Southey's Verse*, selected with an introduction by Geoffrey Grigson (London: Faber, 1970). Some early readers of Southey made the same point: see, for instance, Herman Merivale's comments on Southey's Spanish Ballads in his review of Southey's *Poetical Works* (1838) in the *Edinburgh Review* (1839), quoted in Lionel Madden (ed.), *Robert Southey: The Critical Heritage* (London: Routledge & Kegan Paul, 1972), pp. 398–408 (p. 407).

2. See, for example, the concluding chapter of *A Quest for Home: Reading Robert Southey* (Liverpool: Liverpool University Press, 1997), where Smith quotes approvingly Kenneth Hopkins's praise for the 'clear and single voice' of Southey's shorter poems (p. 338).

152   *Believing in Form and Forms of Belief*

3. Marilyn Butler, 'Repossessing the Past: The Case for an Open Literary History', in Marjorie Levinson *et al.*, *Rethinking Historicism: Critical Readings in Romantic History* (Oxford: Blackwell, 1989), pp. 64–84 (p. 72).
4. Journal entry for 18 September 1815, in *Robert Southey: The Critical Heritage*, pp. 160–1 (p. 160).
5. *Vindiciae Ecclesiae Anglicanae* (London: Murray, 1826) pp. 6–7, quoted in Jack Simmonds, *Southey* (London: Collins, 1945), p. 25. Simmonds also quotes a letter from Southey to Cottle of August 1798 in which Southey writes that he has settled the structure of *Thalaba* and that this 'only forms part of a magnificent project, which I do not despair of one day completing, in the destruction of the Domdanyel. My intention is, to show off the splendour of the Mohammedan belief. I intend to do the same to the Runic, and Oriental systems; to preserve the costume of place as well as of religion'. (*Southey*, pp. 75–6)
6. Newman associates Southey with Coleridge and Wordsworth in this in *Apologia pro Vita Sua* (Boston: Houghton Mifflin, 1956), p. 42.
7. Letter to J. M. Capes of 22 March 1850, in *Robert Southey: The Critical Heritage*, p. 422.
8. Butler, 'Repossessing the Past: the Case for an Open Literary History', p. 79.
9. 'Poetry, with reference to Aristotle's *Poetics*', *London Review* (1829), quoted in *Robert Southey: The Critical Heritage*, p. 332.
10. See Hopkins's letter to Richard Watson Dixon of 5 October 1878, quoted in *Robert Southey: The Critical Heritage*, p. 473.
11. Letter to J. M. Capes, in *Robert Southey: The Critical Heritage*, p. 422.
12. Journal entry for 1 April 1811, in *Robert Southey: The Critical Heritage*, p. 159.
13. Journal entry for 5 August 1811 (ibid.).
14. Quoted in *Robert Southey: The Critical Heritage*, p. 190.
15. Smith, *A Quest for Home: Reading Robert Southey*, pp. 19–20.
16. Unsigned review of *The Life and Correspondence of Robert Southey* (1849–50) in the *Quarterly Review* (1850), quoted in *Robert Southey: The Critical Heritage*, p. 436.
17. *Wat Tyler (1817)* (Oxford: Woodstock Books, 1989), Act II; *Selections from the Letters of Robert Southey*, ed. by J. W. Warter (London: Longmans, 1856), II, p. 274; Simmons, *Southey*, p. 145.
18. It seems clear that Southey's own sense that *Thalaba* did not sufficiently hold together led him to take pains with *The Curse of Kehama* and, especially, with *Roderick, the Last of the Goths*, which is, indeed, much more unified than the earlier poems. But it is so only in a superficial sense. It is simpler, linked to history rather than to the supernatural, and has a more evidently dramatic plot but the gap between what deeply interests Southey and what he recommends is more evident than ever.
19. With the exception of quotations from *Wat Tyler*, all quotations from Southey's poems are taken from *Poems of Robert Southey*, ed. by Maurice H. Fitzgerald (Oxford: Oxford University Press, 1909). Line references follow quotations in the text.
20. *John* 3: 14–15.
21. For example, in Section XXIV of *The Curse of Kehama*, the 'Man-God' Kehama descends into hell (119) and Khailyal is deified and passes into a heavenly

marriage (264–83). In the most baldy explicit ways Southey borrows apparently unresisting material for his purposes.

22. This point of view is, in various guises, everywhere and is perhaps most elegantly and persuasively urged in Michael Oakeshott's 'The Voice of Poetry in the Conversation of Mankind', in *Rationalism in Politics, and Other Essays* (London: Methuen, 1962), pp. 197–247. I am not of course arguing for the subordination of form to 'ideas' and it is perfectly legitimate to protest when *Paradise Lost* or *Divina Commedia* are simply presented as vehicles for theology. It does not follow that the contrary is true. I have argued for a kinship and compatibility between belief and form.

23. 'Southey's Work in Literature', in *Southey* (London: Macmillan, 1879); reprinted in *Robert Southey: The Critical Heritage*, pp. 474–81 (p. 475).

24. See Simmons's helpful discussion of this point in *Southey*, pp. 102–3.

25. Thus in *Kehama*, the Glendoveer can climb upwards to Seeva and say, 'There is oppression in the World below [...] / Awake, O Lord, Awake' (XIX, 159, 162), which would be impossible in Shelley.

26. Unsigned review, *Monthly Mirror* (1811), in *Robert Southey: The Critical Heritage*, pp. 132–4 (p. 134).

27. Both Smith and Butler compare Southey's scenarios to film. Defoe's proto-journalistic union of morality and fictionalised vindication, again, is a recognisable antecedent of Southey's practice.

28. J. H. Newman, *Essays Critical and Historical*, 2nd edn, 2 vols (London: Basil Montagu Pickering, 1872), I, p. 16.

29. Roman Jakobson, *Selected Writings*, 8 vols (The Hague: Mouton, 1962–88), II, pp. 239–59.

30. Hans Urs von Balthasar, *The Glory of the Lord: A Theological Aesthetics*, ed. by John Riches, 7 vols (Edinburgh: T. & T. Clark, 1982). Volume I develops this argument.

9
The Seductions of Form in the Poetry of Ann Batten Cristall and Charlotte Smith

Jacqueline M. Labbe

What does it mean to be seduced by form? In this chapter, I will be exploring the ways in which, for Ann Batten Cristall and Charlotte Smith, poetic form holds attractions that are both self- and other-orientated. For each poet, there are hints and explanations regarding their poetic approaches in their paratexts: Cristall's Preface to *Poetical Sketches* (1795) plays with notions of amateurishness, while Smith's Preface to *Elegiac Sonnets* (multiple editions, 1784–1812) settles on a phrase redolent of aberration. The other – the reader – is thus teased and challenged. However, for both poets the personal allure of formal experimentation is high, and both explore the ways in which structure and meaning can coalesce. Playing with form, they exemplify a Romantic concern with the mechanics of poetry, measuring a stereotypical feminine effusiveness against a considered engagement with the composition process. Writing in the 1780s and 1790s, they demonstrate that experimentation and innovation was a function of the age, and that the enticements of 'spontaneous overflow' rely on a lengthy and attentive formal build-up.

In *Formal Charges*, Susan Wolfson notes that Byron's ironic use of the heroic couplet, which she calls 'a model of formal decorum', 'tell[s] the tale of a heroic outlaw in *The Corsair*', and points out that this 'tests the force of dominant forms (social and literary) in the poetics and politics of opposition'.[1] In this chapter, I also want to test poetic uses of form against cultural expectations of meaning. In paying so much attention to the intricacies of composition, both Cristall and Smith show an awareness of the weight of poetic form, and both demonstrate a facility with poetic structure that allows them to make meaning at the base level of form. Like Byron, they play with the nature of poetry, and, in telling their readers what they are doing and declaring the limitations of genre and their own skill, they seduce their audiences on a variety of levels: stroking readerly egos, they create a fiction of simplicity and submission. Their poetry thus disarms, even as it rewards close attention. On one level, then, Cristall and Smith show off for the attentive and appreciative reader, their poetry offering textual satisfaction.

On a more significant level, however, the two poets utilise form to investigate the nature of poetic subjectivity. Although completely contrasting in the style and content of their poetry, for both, poetic form becomes a vehicle by which they experiment with the nature of a coherent selfhood. For Cristall, the prefatory disclaimer in her *Poetical Sketches* that her verses 'were written without the knowledge of any rules' (275) allows her to depart from ordinary poetic convention with its emphasis on 'form', and facilitates the construction of a self who is simultaneously naive and worldly, innocent and experienced.[2] For Smith, the frequent departure from a strict Petrarchan/Shakespearean rhyme scheme in her *Elegiac Sonnets* signals her desire to use form to influence meaning, which here includes the identification of the speaker.[3] The Romantic subject has traditionally been seen to be based on authenticity and unity; however, poetry by women such as Cristall and Smith complicate this conclusion and raise the possibility that the unified poetic self is itself only a mask. The idea of Romantic theatricality has been well-formulated, most particularly by Judith Pascoe, who has taught us to recognise the artifice inherent in the Romantic subject.[4] In the discussion to follow, I hope to demonstrate that artifice dominates even at the level of form, and by this I mean that Cristall and Smith unpick the seemingly seamless weft of poetry even as they appear to conform to both cultural and generic expectations.

To a readership schooled in formal convention and social and poetic rules, Cristall's *Poetical Sketches* fulfils expectations of feminine artistic feebleness: she presents herself as young, ignorant and impulsive, moved to publish on an emotional rather than a thoughtful level. Throughout the text she overtly misuses poetic form, and begs her readers' indulgence for so doing. However, even as she portrays herself as incapable of attending to rules, she also establishes a poetic subjectivity only superficially 'incorrect and luxuriant'. Her volume, published in 1795 with Joseph Johnson and under her own name, is portrayed in her Preface as 'light effusions of a youthful imagination' (275). In them she reveals a sensibility finely attuned to the gendered expectations of behaviour and sexuality current in her time, infusing many of her poems with a transgressive emphasis on the power aroused sexuality wields over the female body and the female mind. Hers is a pastoral world of shepherds, swains and nymphs, of enthusiasm and ardour, of sadism, cruelty and voyeurism, naturalised in a landscape of grottoes, groves and beaches. Continually reaffirming her prefatory disclaimer that her verses 'were written without the knowledge of any rules', Cristall also constructs a poetic persona freed from, and outside, the pastoral bounds within which her poems exist. The powerful effect of her technique of artlessness is evinced by one reviewer's note that 'poesy, the child of nature, if sometimes improved, is also sometimes spoiled by the mouldring hand of art'.[5] It is not too difficult to imagine that for this reviewer Cristall herself appeared to be as much a 'child of nature' as did poesy.

To anchor her artless subject-position, Cristall sketches the rough shape of pastoral, but recombines its elements so that, for instance, Hebe pairs off with 'shallow Ned' ('Evening. Gertrude', 85–6). The emphasis she places in her Preface on her ignorance of 'any rules', moreover, directly contradicts her statement, immediately preceding, that she has 'taken much pains to *reduce* [her verse] to some degree of order' (275). Implying that conforming to the rules somehow debases or limits her verse, as the ambiguity of 'reduce' suggests, she further reveals a knowledge of what the rules are and of what 'order' consists; that, despite her pains, her 'versification [remains] wild, and still incorrect' indicates the inherent power of a naïve poetics 'inspired' by the 'beauties of nature' (275). For Cristall, a deliberately unaesthetic style suggests her manipulation of form, a knowing rejection of poetic and cultural convention. Contrasting, then, with her efforts at 'reduction' is the subversive implication that her poems cannot be held back by culture but rather assert a kind of natural strength. Cristall furthers this image of her body of work as somehow independent of poetic norms when she reflects that 'the subjects [of her poems] are not always such, as, on maturer reflection, I should have chosen, had they been originally intended for publication. The seeds scattered in my mind were casual; the productions spontaneous and involuntary' (275). It seems that what she has written has taken on a life of its own, cannot be controlled even by a Cristall now more knowledgeable, yet still, as she earlier informed us, without 'the authority of much experience', having passed most of her days in 'solitude' (275). Cristall, therefore, presents herself as an author experienced enough to be aware of the defects of her work, yet unable to correct them, almost helpless in the face of her own embodied imagination. She divests herself of poetical authority by displaying just enough knowledge to know she should do so, a preservation of modesty common to female-authored prefaces. As Richard

Sha notes, she 'excuse[s her] artistry so that [her] works might seem more proper, more persuasive, and more sincere'. But, as Sha also recognises, Cristall's 'achieved artlessness [is] rhetorically artful': she attends to the formal nature of a preface while also displaying her lack of formal knowledge.[6] Her authorial self is thus associated with a kind of charming childishness even as she maintains a strict control over her self-presentation.

Cristall thus forwards a project of independence from within a traditional feminine framework of self-deprecation, and enlivens the traditional association of the natural and the feminine with a controversial implication that this produces not the feminine object, but the voiced female subject: her implied knowledge of rules and implied denigration of 'order' presupposes a greater authorial presence than that she overtly demonstrates. Further, despite her assertion that her poems were originally private effusions not intended for publication, Cristall declines the design often used by her female contemporaries: that the admiration of 'friends' persuaded her to put her work before the public. We are not told her impetus for publishing, but rather are confronted with the act itself; as she says in the first sentence of the Preface, 'I now present [these light effusions] to such Readers whose minds are not too seriously engaged' (275). I suggest that this statement and those informing her readers of her aborted attempts at revision undermine her later assertion that she never intended to publish them; at the least, they further her construction of a contradictory persona: strong and weak, ignorant and learned, modest and self-confident. Only in the last sentence does she allude to her reason for publishing, and even here the paradoxical self she has put forward is preserved: 'A strong motive', she tells us mysteriously, 'first influenced me to the attempt [to publish], before I had sufficiently considered its boldness; and having once adventured, I found it too late to recede' (276). Asserting that she lacks control over her own work, Cristall instils a kind of ethic of helplessness at odds with the image of the adventurer ('its boldness') with which she pairs it.

Cristall's Preface therefore sells its author as simultaneously there and not there, both a present author and a passive, observing servant to the Muse, whose 'warm influence' she describes as 'flattering and seductive' (275). Embedded in the Preface, however, is a claim for originality that belies this submissive position. She tells her readers that 'what I have written is genuine and [...] but little indebted either to ancient or modern poets. With the ancient poets, indeed, my acquaintance has been but small, and only obtained through the medium of translations'

(275). Cristall constructs herself as the archetypal 'untutored youth', proclaiming her lack of learning as a strength, not a weakness. Acquaintance with the classics, she implies, makes originality difficult and 'servile imitation' (275) – her words – almost unavoidable. The genuine nature of her poems arises from the untaught nature of her mind, a situation that recalls her opening presentation of her collection to her readers' 'minds', albeit those 'not too seriously engaged'. Reflecting Cristall's concern with natural genius, then, her poems are inherently too untutored and natural to be refined into conforming to the rules of poetry. Cristall's proclaimed ignorance of her poetic forebears functions as a dismissal of the very necessity to prove one's accomplishment by copying others; her rejection of the standard poetic canon in favour of the effusions of her own mind mark her investment in her work as more 'serious' itself than 'serious minds' might be able to appreciate. Revoking the licensed authority granted to the formally educated to assume cultural power and replacing it with an authority based on the individual mind, Cristall sets aside convention and privileges her 'genuine' efforts, and this coincides with her decision, represented as involuntary, to eschew 'order' in her verse and allows its 'wildness' to stand.

Cristall espouses both the body and the mind in her Preface; she shies away from an outright declaration of her abandonment of the rules of poetry, but she does not hesitate to display her authorship. She images her authority and her relationship with the Muse physically as she concludes her Preface: 'Those who have ever felt the warm influence of the Muse, must know that her inspirations are flattering and seductive; that she often raises the heart with vanity, and then overwhelms it with fears: such will readily believe, that with a fluctuating mind, and a trembling heart, I address the Public, without any pretense for being treated with particular indulgence' (275). Although she constructs herself as the standard timid female author, complete with a fluctuating, unsteady and changeable mind, she declines the standard chivalry often appealed to by female authors in their prefaces: I refer to the kind that presents the text as offspring and the writer as parent, for instance, or that appeals to the generosity of a masculine readership to overlook the flaws that must be expected from a female pen. While such prefaces display their own challenges to convention, Cristall's states outright her desire to be treated as an author, and not as a specimen of femininity. And this connects, again, with her disregard for and unconcern with rules: this poet writes as she writes, and she – like Smith – also declares her authorship by name on the title page, in letters larger than those in the title itself. Thus we have the unapologetic display of the named self on the title page coexisting with the 'fluctuating mind' and 'trembling heart' of the Preface.

Cristall's challenges to the conventions of poetry and of presentation sparked reactions in her contemporaries that hinge on attempts to recontain her: Mary Wollstonecraft, for one, was 'afraid' that she 'g[ave] way to her feelings more than she ought to do'. As if conflating Cristall with her character Arla, whose presence in *Poetical Sketches* serves to emphasise the deforming power of 'enthusiasm', Wollstonecraft associates 'strength of mind' – that is, *not* giving way to one's feelings – with 'virtue': 'if I were to give a short definition of virtue', she says in a letter to Cristall's brother, 'I should call it fortitude.' That Wollstonecraft correlates strength of mind with strength of virtue – certainly a culturally loaded word, even in Wollstonecraft's hands – and that she fears that Cristall lacks both, suggests that Cristall was allied with her work to the point of identification; Wollstonecraft's worries over Cristall's 'uncomfortable' situation mirror her literary critics' censures over Cristall's ignorance of form.[7] Both personally and poetically, Cristall personifies a lack of control, and her body and her corpus are consequently described as requiring restraint. George Dyer echoes Wollstonecraft's tone, if not her diction, when he writes of Cristall that 'she has a very fine talent for poetry: one or two of her songs are, I think, as beautiful as any I know. She is indeed a little incorrect and luxuriant, "her poetical vine wants trimming" [...]. A. Chrystall's poetry in future, if she writes, will, I doubt not, display more judgement and correctness. But these can only be acquired by practice.'[8] Dyer softens his critique, but nonetheless he displays the same unease with her poetic luxuriousness as Wollstonecraft does with her emotional indulgences. With practice, Cristall might well become correct and conformable – that is, 'if she writes'. Dyer is chivalrous, Wollstonecraft concerned; both assume a protective attitude in keeping with the persona Cristall creates in her Preface: one whose self-confessed ignorance and inexperience also implies innocence and vulnerability. The chivalry Cristall inspires from both men and women means that she receives precisely the kind of 'particular indulgence' she says she is unmindful of; and yet, it must be noted, it also means they treat her with a condescension that works to defuse the disturbing effect of her irregular 'songs'. This is especially true of Southey:

> But Miss Christal, have you seen her Poems? A fine, artless, sensible girl! [...] Her heart is alive. She loves poetry. She loves retirement. She loves the country. Her verses are very incorrect, and the literary circles say, she has no genius, but she has genius, Joseph Cottle, or there is

no truth in physiognomy [...]. You see I like the women better than the men. Indeed, they are better animals in general, perhaps because more is left to nature in their education.[9]

Southey's enthusiasm for the physiognomy of Cristall, and his description of the naturalness of women's education, positions Cristall simultaneously exactly where she would be, via her Preface, and in the spectacularly domestic space conventionally inhabited by the 'better animals'.

Moreover, the 'nature' of women's education can also be made to account for the naturalness of Cristall's verse, and the need to 'prune' it into correctness. How, then, does form and content allow luxuriant incorrectness to manifest itself? Cristall opens her collection with a tour through the hours of the day: 'Before Twilight', 'Morning', 'Noon', 'Evening' and 'Night'. She closes the volume with poems dedicated to states of mind: 'Written when the mind was oppressed', 'The Enthusiast', 'A Song of Arla, written during her Enthusiasm'. Furthermore, she flags her own lack of structure by enlarging on her title, *Poetical Sketches*, once in the text – '*in Irregular Verse*' (1) – which chimes with Smith's 'irregular' *Elegiac Sonnets*. Cristall's verse openly flouts a concern with structure from the start, intermingling rhyme schemes, metres, stanza lengths and formats. 'Before Twilight' dramatises a conversation between Eyezion and Viza, and renders their moods and personalities poetically by varying its structure according to speaker. In this way Cristall creates poetic distinctions, subtle signals to the reader transmitted through a kind of structural code. Eyezion, then, is a pastoral songster, welcoming the dawn and modulating his versed tone of voice to suit the subject matter. As he sings of his desire for Viza in more and more complex images, Cristall varies and complicates the rhyme scheme as well, reflecting his varying and rhapsodic mood. Thus, the poem opens with Eyezion speaking a regular, repetitive rhyme scheme (*abbacc*), then, in his song, *abab*. Once he engages Viza in conversation, however, he begins to unravel the regularity of his rhyme: *aabb* becomes *aabbcdcd* becomes *abab* becomes *ababcc* becomes *abcbacddeffe*. Correspondingly, the content of his speech moves from a standard welcome to the breaking day, to a description of the excitement Viza arouses in him – a sexual excitement, as I will discuss shortly – to a rhapsody on the poetic skills this excitement awakens. Cristall even puns on Eyezion's skill when she has him say 'And every sigh I waft, and every joy I breathe, / Mix'd with seraphic airs, fly on poetic feet' (81–2). Cristall's poetic feet do indeed fly, recalling the passionate, aroused nature of her speakers, Eyezion and Viza.

It is not only through rhyme scheme that Cristall departs from regularity. She strays from the strictly correct in content as well. Viza and
Eyezion may well be allegorical, or supernatural, or pastoral, or myth-
ical characters, but what they long for is the sexual union promised by
the coming of dawn, with its intimations of unfolding and exposure.
Eyezion is 'the light poet of spring', who 'hie[s] from his restless bed,
to sing' of his desire for Viza, the embodiment of 'morning' (2, 3). The
twilight of the title occurs not at dusk, but at dawn, and its hidden,
shadowy nature invites Eyezion to rhapsodise over Viza. Eyezion feels,
not romantic love, but strong sexual desire; as he says, 'My soul, fledg'd
with desires, / Flutters, and pants for morn' – that is, Viza – while 'love
my soul oppresses' as he imagines 'Viza unfold[ing] her charms' (19–20,
32, 37). Viza responds in kind, 'open[ing] her star-like eyes [. . .] while
sweet sensations in her bosom rise' (44, 46). She wonders why Eyezion
has come, to which he replies, 'fancy paints a conscious blush / O'er thy
fair cheeks; nor need my tongue / With deeper die thy beauties flush – /
Thou know'st I'm drawn by thee alone' (93–6). Eyezion, it seems, is
the ardent pursuer, Viza the passive, shy object of desire. And yet, do
proper ladies have 'fancies' that result in 'conscious blushes'? Cristall
allows her couple to parry flirtatiously for eight more lines, but in the
end it is not the poetic Eyezion who makes a move, but Viza: 'Soon
as young light shall clear the heaven, / Urg'd by the glowing rays of
morn; / When circling mists are distant driven, / Expect me on the dewy
lawn' (105–8). Plumping for openness and clear speech, Viza arranges
their assignation, in coherent, regular *abab*, confirming the joining that
Cristall has implied, again through rhyme: the previous four lines, also
abab, have been divided between the pair.

Cristall sets a scene infused with reversals. As she does more subtly in
her Preface, here she both conforms to and undermines standard gender
roles, and enlists her poetic technique in this game. Eyezion's lust and
active search for Viza that open the poem position him as the standard
masculine figure, yet by the poem's end he has become the passive
recipient of Viza's desire; she in turn metamorphoses from the modest –
or coy? – innocent to a figure able to voice her own desire. In its position as the prefatory poem to her quartet of hours, 'Before Twilight'
suggests that the day now dawning will continue a scene based not
on the sexual and poetic standard, but sexual and poetic innovation.
Space does not permit me to discuss 'Morning', 'Noon', 'Evening' and
'Night', but I will just note that they dramatise, among other situations, ungratified desire, sexual cruelty and voyeurism, mostly played
out under the heat of a blazing sun. Structurally, the variation set

up in 'Before Twilight' continues, as Cristall introduces rhyme schemes and stanza lengths only to abandon them and replace them, creating an order based on poetic disorder. Unconcerned with regularity, she and her characters stray from the usual path of gendered behaviour, sexual propriety and poetic rules. 'Stray' is Cristall's word, but it is also frequently used by other female poets – again, Smith comes to mind – to indicate a self-conscious rejection of the path marked out for them by a patriarchal culture reliant on ordered and regular behaviour. Cristall strays – wanders – from licensed poetry; she also strays from – leaves – sanctioned male–female relations.

Cristall's seductive self-presentation allows her to disregard rules while seeming to conform to the most rigid aspects of social convention. Throughout her *Poetical Sketches*, she shadows her artless persona with a knowing misapplication of the rules of poetry. In the end, what is sketched is as much about persona as poetry: the permanency afforded by the publication process combines with the preliminary or incomplete nature of the sketch to offer a new Romantic model of formal formlessness. In her *Elegiac Sonnets*, Smith writes poetry that is much more self-consciously formal than Cristall's; indeed, she illustrates this in her Preface to the First and Second Editions. Echoing Samuel Johnson, she states that 'the little Poems which here are called Sonnets, have, I believe, no very just claim to that title: but they consist of fourteen lines, and appear to me no improper vehicle for a single Sentiment' (3). But Smith complicates the matter when she goes on to acknowledge that 'the legitimate Sonnet is ill calculated for our language' (3). The implied stress laid on 'legitimate' opens the door to the 'illegitimate' sonnet: while Smith herself calls some of her sonnets 'irregular', illegitimacy carries a different weight altogether.[10] In formal terms, the illegitimate is about what is culturally disallowed – and disavowed; it exposes the risks of the irregular, but also its fascinations. Once Smith embarks on the dark path of illegitimacy – to which she, like Cristall, 'strays' ('Sonnet IV: To the Moon', a sonnet strict in its Shakespearean rhyme scheme, line 2) – then she, too, begins to develop a new kind of poetic self, one whose attention to the possibilities of form calls into question the singleness of the sentiment the poems express.

Smith's sonnets have most commonly been read as expressions of the female experience, but they perform on a variety of more complicated levels.[11] Critics such as Stuart Curran and Judith Hawley have noted their ventriloquising tendencies, most obvious in the translation poems (from Plutarch, Goethe and Metastasio).[12] But Smith also ventriloquises in the poems reprinted from the various novels, often revoicing them as well: the male speaker of the novel, for instance, transformed into the putatively female speaker of the volume of sonnets. Most of the sonnets start off 'regular': that is, Shakespearean or Petrarchan in rhyme scheme, although these regular rhyme schemes are often disrupted by unconventional structures – as Paula Feldman and Daniel Robinson phrase it, 'many [...] are technically Shakespearean, [but] the majority are irregular in construction' (11).[13] For instance, in 'Sonnet IV: To the Moon', Smith marries the Shakespearean rhyme scheme with a reversed Petrarchan structure of a sestet and an octave, thus merging two competing forms and facilitating the transformation of the moon from a symbol of calm to the destination of lost souls. And yet it is also possible to read the structure as the more conventional three quatrains and closing couplet, in which case the moon's dual identity is smoothed and regularised and the emphasis shifted to the couplet's gloomy death wish. The suggestion is that, far from expressing a single sentiment, the sonnet has more to say than it can fit into 14 lines. Smith uses structure to flesh out the moon's potential as a symbol, while also enlarging its classical affiliations: not only is the moon the Queen of the silver bow – Diana – but it is also a double for Pluto. When Smith turns the Petrarchan structure upside down, she embeds in the poem a topsy-turvy exchange of Christian Heaven and Classical Hell. The personal tone conveyed by the repeated pronoun 'I' masks the more general thrust of a poem that rejects not only coherent poetic form but also the conventional consolations of Christianity.

Sonnet IV uses structural details to suggest a turn from convention to irregularity, but it does not call the speaker's subjectivity into question. The translation sonnets do more with this, presenting a speaker who is simultaneously a version of Smith and also recognisably the male speaker created by Petrarch, Goethe or Metastasio. In the Petrarch sonnets, Smith assumes the identity of Petrarch himself, pursuing Laura with a lover's passion. The Petrarch sonnets, XIII–XVI, are free translations based on specific Petrarchan sonnets identified by their first lines and sonnet number in the notes, and they function more obviously than do the Werter sonnets as ventriloquisms. Nonetheless, they rely on the same formulations of sensibility and sorrow as do the *Elegiac Sonnets* as a whole, and contribute more to the sense of a developing company of identities precisely because of their more open status as translations. In 'Sonnet XIII: From Petrarch', Smith assumes Petrarch's poetic identity seamlessly, writing a sonnet to Laura asserting that 'his' 'faithful heart still burns for thee!' (14). While Smith seems to make a bodily exchange – the Sonnets' familiar distressed feminine 'I' becomes the ardent masculine 'I' – she also uses poetic structure to suggest an underlying critique. Not only does this 'Petrarchan' sonnet have a strict Shakespearean rhyme scheme, but it also is written in iambic tetrameter; Smith both disrupts her readers' expectations of who speaks in the sonnets, and also confounds the very form of the sonnet. If the originator of a traditional sonnet form fails to write his sonnet correctly – that is, if he fails to embody his own corpus – then his identity is called into question. Similarly, if we read the sonnet as spoken by an *imitator* of Petrarch, someone who speaks his lines but gets them wrong, then the image of a bad actor is conjured up: the speaker is, so to speak, under-rehearsed. In fact, not one of the Petrarchan sonnets follows correct Petrarchan form. 'Sonnet XIV: From Petrarch' begins well, *abba cddc*, but then carries on with another Shakespearean quatrain, *effe*, and ends with a rhyming couplet. 'Sonnet XV: From Petrarch' is straightforwardly Shakespearean, and 'Sonnet XVI: From Petrarch' combines the two forms, laid out as two Shakespearean quatrains followed by a Petrarchan sestet with a Shakespearean rhyme scheme.[14]

Smith's translation sonnets, then, not only translate German or Italian into English, but also translate the sonnet itself, merging styles and experimenting with structure to gain maximum meaning. That this meaning often undercuts the poem's putative thrust adds to the weight she allows form. Although Feldman and Robinson identify her style as a 'more natural, freer English form' (11), they do not mention her innovations with structure that, I suggest, move her beyond merely looking for a more natural mode of expression, and place her sonnets firmly in the realm of artifice. Where the translation sonnets allow her to merge the apparently personal with the blatantly constructed, in that the sorrows of Werter, for instance, are recognisably the sorrows of Charlotte as well, other sonnets use form to call into question any kind of stable identity. For instance, Sonnet XXXVIII and 'Sonnet XXXIX: To Night' are both drawn from Smith's first novel *Emmeline*, and in the novel are written by the male protagonist Godolphin. In the novel, both speak of Godolphin's manly despair as a star-crossed lover, and are thus firmly anchored to his masculine identity. In the *Sonnets*, however, Smith does not refer openly to their source, although Sonnet XXXVIII gives readers a clue with its apostrophe to Emmeline. Sonnet XXXIX, however, is set loose from its novelistic mooring, and thus also from its original identity. Given the lengths Smith goes to convince her readers of the very personal nature of the sonnets, it is significant that in these two sonnets she elides the original male speaker.[15] Sonnet XXXVIII thus seems to be spoken by an anonymous, presumably male lover whose desire for Emmeline remains unsatisfied,[16] and Sonnet XXXIX reclaims its passion as Smith's own. Indeed, in its mention of 'sober-suited Night' (1) and its search for 'repose' 'on thy dark breast' (9), the sonnet masculinises Night and hence feminises the disembodied speaker. Where Sonnet XXXVIII, then, has Smith masquerading as the unnamed male lover, Sonnet XXXIX sees Smith masquerading as the unnamed male lover masquerading as the seeming female speaker. The poems' structures confirm these layers of identity: each is both Petrarchan and Shakespearean in form. Sonnet XXXVIII rhymes *abba baba ccd cdd*; its content shows either three quatrains and a couplet, or two quatrains and three (near) couplets (as indicated by punctuation). The rhyme is complex, self-contained (only four rhymes) and turns back on itself, almost as if it is trapped in its own limitations: a mirroring of the speaker's own repetitive despair (felt every time he wakes). Sonnet XXXIX rhymes *abab cbbc cdd cee*, which could also be seen as *abab cbbc cddc ee*. More open in rhyme than Sonnet XXXVIII, it is also more confusing, since in both rhyme and content it could be read as either three quatrains and a couplet, or an octave and a sestet. Here, repetition serves to establish familiarity, as the speaker moves deeper into depression. In other words, the sonnet is both homely (English) and unhomely (Italian), or in Freudian terms both *heimlich* and *unheimlich*. Smith's layers of sexual identity and poetic form create an uncanny scenario wherein both speaker and poem occupy multiple spaces simultaneously.

Even where a sonnet's original novel speaker is female, structure still acts to complicate identity. 'Sonnet LII: The Pilgrim' originates in *Celestina* and is there authored by Celestina herself. The male pilgrim's ('divided far from all *he* fondly loves' (3), emphasis added) unhappy situation again recalls so many of the other sonnets: Smith/Celestina identify with a male figure who exists, poetically, solely to point the speaker's woe more clearly. In a by-now familiar move, Smith begins the sonnet in Shakespearean mode, then switches to a modified Petrarchan mode: *abab cdcd efefef*. She gives eight and a half lines to a description of the pilgrim, and five and a half lines to her speaker's own sorrows: a modified octave/sestet that more strongly than in other sonnets suggests a Petrarchan structure.[17] The poem's part-Shakespearean/part-Petrarchan composition thus chimes with the speaker's part-Smith/part-Pilgrim (/part-Celestina) identity. Looking more closely, however, another kind of generic dissonance emerges:

lines 1, 8, 11 and 14 contain more than 10 syllables.[18] Breaking out of iambic pentameter, the lines encode their own unruliness:

Line 1: Faltering and sad the unhappy Pilgrim roves (12 syllables)
Line 8: And hears, with ear appall'd, the impetuous surge
(12 syllables)
Line 11: By Friendship's cheering radiance *now* unblest (11 syllables)
Line 14: That, trembling at the past – recoils from future woe
(12 syllables)

Roving and surging out of shape, stumbling over their own feet, the lines' refusal to conform to convention illustrate the speaker's aliena- tion, which is integral to the poem. Now even the split between an eight-and-a-half-line octave and five-and-a-half-line sestet, which had provided a brief, if unbalanced, respite, breaks down under scrutiny: the sestet is also a quatrain/couplet by punctuation. It becomes impossible to assign a poetic identity to this poem, which is only the most extremely mixed of the five *Celestina* sonnets. Of the four remaining, three are both Shakespearean and Petrarchan in structure.[19] The fifth, 'Sonnet LIII: The Laplander', is perfectly Shakespearean until the last, 13-syllable, line, which only serves to underscore its unique lack of a personal referent.

The formal irregularity of Sonnets XLIX–LIII thoroughly compromises the gender match between Smith and Celestina; in the same way, irregu- larity emphasises the other novel-sonnets' gender mismatch. But gender is only one aspect of identity. In 'Sonnet LXXXVII: Written in October', from *The Young Philosopher*, the original female speaker commits suicide and the sonnet reflects her hopelessness. Once in the *Elegiac Sonnets*, the ascendant speaker Smith evokes 'Sonnet II: Written at the close of Spring' (which exists in the *Sonnets* but not in the novel) when she concludes, 'Nature delights *me* most when most she mourns, / For never more to me the Spring of Hope returns!' (LXXXVII, 13–14). This is the flipside of Sonnet II: 'Another May new buds and flowers shall bring; / Ah! why has happiness – no second Spring?' (13–14). Smith lives on, unlike Sonnet LXXXVII's original speaker, but the sonnet itself shows signs of injury: a fairly regular rhyme scheme (*abab cddc effe gg*) cannot compensate for the structure dictated by punctuation: five lines, one line, six lines, two lines. It is as if the poem is shaking itself to pieces: decomposing. The sonnet begins to self-destruct, to kill itself. Smith writes Death into this sonnet's being, as she does even more strongly when reflecting on her lost daughter Augusta. Several of Smith's sonnets about her dead daughter position the bereaved mother as a kind of bereft lover. Sonnet LXXIV is one of these, and as it progresses we can see the similarities of tone and imagery to Sonnets XXXVIII and XXXIX. As with the novel sonnets, Smith sometimes identifies the lost love and sometimes not. Here the only additional information she gives is a note attached to 'ancient towers' in line 6: 'These lines were written in a residence among ancient public buildings' (64). Again, in terms of identity the speaker is Smith writing as the (hidden) bereaved mother writing as the (apparent) bereaved male lover. The poem rhymes *abba cdcd efef gg*; or does it rhyme *abba acac dede aa*? The progression of near-rhymes (care/prepare to hear/drear to deplore/more) encloses the poem even as the 'ancient public buildings' enclose the speaker's residence. Further, in structure this poem abandons form altogether: 5 lines, 6 lines, 4 lines, adding up to 15 since line 5 both ends and begins a sentence. The uncertain rhyme scheme and lack of a clear sonnet structure reflect the speaker's grief and detachment in a life of despair, while the care with which Smith dispenses with the conventions of sonnet form attests to her attention to the ramifications of form. Like Sonnet LII, this is a sonnet that refuses to be a sonnet while also functioning recognisably as a sonnet.

The point of looking so closely at Smith's experiments with the sonnet is that the more one looks the more one sees that Smith moves far beyond 'irregularity'. The illegitimacy that many of her sonnets embody confronts issues of identity and selfhood, emphasising that for all their seamless grief the sonnets are about how identity is lost, multiplied and complicated. Feldman and Robinson note that, during the Renaissance, the sonnet was a vehicle 'by which poets could prove their virtuosity and technical skill' (11). Smith's sonnets show that this virtuosity was not confined to the Renaissance. Chided by Anna Seward, among others, for her experiments with illegitimacy, Smith tinkered repeatedly with the formal elements of the sonnet, under the spell of its charms: 'I wish to make as much *variety* of verse in this book as possible – & have studiously varied the measure of the quatrains &c.'[20] Her readers, too, returned again and again between 1784 and 1803, but gradually their fascination gave way to revulsion and they professed themselves fatigued with what Seward characterised as Smith's 'hackneyed scraps of dismality'.[21] Even Smith, at the end of her life, grew sated: 'I am tired of Sonnets, & mine you know are almost all illegitimate & must go to the foundling Hospital'[22] – the usual destination for the usual consequence of seduction. Smith's innovative handling of the sonnet is overshadowed by the more familiar Romantic experiment that is the

Lyrical Ballads, but it is nonetheless central to the period's manipulations of poetic form.

In her excess, Cristall too disturbs a poetic status quo that is only more famously disrupted by Wordsworth and Coleridge. But whereas they introduce experiments more of content than of form – after all, the lyric and the ballad are traditional, although not traditionally joined – Cristall refuses the very nature of Enlightenment poetry. Looking back at her Preface, we notice that she does not so much apologise for her lack of learning and knowledge of poetic rules as declare it as fact. Linking the state of nature she claims for her mind with the natural, uncultivated state of her poetry, she emphasises its 'casual', 'spontaneous' and 'involuntary' character. It is this language that encourages her readers to propose 'trimming her poetical vine'. Cleverly playing on the cultural assumption of feminine disorder and intellectual indiscipline, Cristall creates poetic scenarios remarkable for their transgression and subversion, and implants her own defence when she implies in her Preface that she cannot control her own verse: it is 'wild', 'irregular'. Faced with the choice of deliberate poetic innovation and considered disregard of the established rules, or a 'trembling', 'untutored', 'light' approach, it seems that most of Cristall's readers gallantly considered her merely young and inexperienced. And yet, shadowing the admissions of amateurism is another voice with which Cristall overlooks, or resists, the established norms of the literary aesthetic. Together, in their separate ways, Cristall and Smith promote the necessity of giving in to the fascinations of poetic form.

Notes

1. Susan Wolfson, *Formal Charges: The Shaping of Poetry in British Romanticism* (Stanford: Stanford University Press, 1997), p. 29.
2. All quotations from *Poetical Sketches* are taken from *Romantic Women Poets*, ed. by Duncan Wu (Oxford: Blackwell, 1997). Line/page references follow quotations in the text.
3. All quotations from Smith are taken from *The Poems of Charlotte Smith*, ed. by Stuart Curran (New York: Oxford University Press, 1993). Line/page references follow quotations in the text.
4. See *Romantic Theatricality: Gender, Poetry and Spectatorship* (Ithaca: Cornell University Press, 1997).
5. *Analytical Review*, 21 (1796), p. 282, quoted in Richard Sha, *The Visual and Verbal Sketch in British Romanticism* (Philadelphia: University of Pennsylvania Press, 1998), p. 123. See Wu, pp. 273–4, for a useful selection of quotations from reviews.
6. *The Visual and Verbal Sketch in British Romanticism*, p. 121.

7. Letter to Cristall's brother Joshua, 9 December [1790?], in *The Collected Letters of Mary Wollstonecraft*, ed. by Janet Todd (London: Allen Lane, 2003), p. 185.
8. Quoted in Roger Lonsdale, *Eighteenth-Century Women Poets* (New York: Oxford University Press, 1990), p. 485.
9. In Joseph Cottle, *Reminiscences of Samuel Taylor Coleridge and Robert Southey* (Highgate: Lime Tree Bower Press, 1970), p. 204.
10. In the Romantic period, of course, 'legitimate' and 'illegitimate' in a poetical context refer simply to how well a sonnet or other poem conforms to the strictures of its genre. The social context of the words, however, pertains, especially if we remember how upset Anna Seward, for example, felt over the irregularities of Smith's sonnets.
11. See my *Charlotte Smith: Romanticism, Poetry and the Culture of Gender* (Manchester: Manchester University Press, 2003) for a full discussion.
12. See: Curran, 'Introduction', *The Poems of Charlotte Smith*; Judith Hawley, 'Charlotte Smith's *Elegiac Sonnets*: Losses and Gains', in Isobel Armstrong and Virginia Blain (eds), *Women's Poetry in the Enlightenment: The Making of a Canon, 1730–1820* (Basingstoke: Macmillan, 1999), pp. 184–98.
13. Paula R. Feldman and Daniel Robinson (eds), *A Century of Sonnets: The Romantic-Era Revival* (New York: Oxford University Press, 1999). Page references are given in the text.
14. Sonnet XVII and the Werter sonnets also follow Shakespearean form. Moreover, they ally their male speakers with the *Sonnets'* putatively female persona through imagery: in Sonnet XVII, the 'beauteous tree' (2) of love shelters the dove and the nightingale, both birds emblematic of the sonnets' distressed 'I'. The Goethe sonnets, XXI–XXV, which follow Werter from despair to death, contain references to: the nightingale as a 'sweet songstress' (Sonnet XXII, 12), echoing Sonnet III ('songstress sad', 13); the 'maniac' (Sonnet XXI, 5), anticipating Sonnet LXX (the 'Lunatic' sonnet); and 'the tempests drear' (Sonnet XXIII, 5), mirroring Sonnets LXVI and LXVII (as the last two are drawn from *Montalbert*, where they are written by the male hero Walsingham, a provenance not noted by Smith, something of a double-blind seems to operate). Werter even envisages the sorrow of 'Charlotte' at his death. But Smith writes all the Werter sonnets in perfect Shakespearean rhyme, Anglicising Goethe's sentiment as much as her use of 'Charlotte' Anglicises 'Lotte'.
15. See Chapter 1 of *Charlotte Smith* for full discussion of Smith's technique of embodiment.
16. It should be noted that in some of her sonnets about her dead daughter Anna Augusta, Smith's tone is as much romantic as maternal (see discussion of Sonnet LXXIV below).
17. As I suggest in my discussion of Sonnet LXXIV, this also can be seen to give the sonnet 15 lines.
18. Some of the other sonnets under discussion here also contain lines of more than 10 syllables: line 14 of Sonnet XXXVIII and Sonnet LXXXVII both contain 12 syllables, for instance. But Sonnet LII seems to make a point of this irregularity.
19. Sonnets XLIX, L and LI. In 'Sonnet XLIX: Supposed to have been written in a church-yard, over the grave of a young woman of nineteen', the rhyme scheme is simple – *abab baab bcbc dd* – but the 'b' rhymes create a vast 12-line

170 The Seductions of Form

group divided by punctuation into the Petrarchan two-quatrain octave and sestet.

20. Letter to Thomas Cadell Jr and William Davies, 28 April 1797, in *The Collected Letters of Charlotte Smith*, ed. by Judith Stanton (Bloomington: Indiana University Press, 2003), p. 269.

21. *Letters of Anna Seward, written between the years 1784 and 1807*, 6 vols (London: Longman, Hunt and Rees, 1811), II, p. 287.

22. Letter to Sarah Rose, 26 April 1806, in *Collected Letters of Charlotte Smith*, p. 731.

10

'Seldom Safely Enjoyed by Those Who Enjoyed it Completely': Byron's Poetry, Austen's Prose and Forms of Narrative Irony

Caroline Franklin

> The writer is a person who knows how to work language while remaining outside of it; he has the gift of indirect speech.
>
> (Mikhail Bakhtin, *The Dialogical Principle*)[1]

> Irony, however, has no purpose [...] If, for example, the ironist appears as someone other than he actually is, his purpose might indeed seem to be to get others to believe this; but his actual purpose still is to feel free.
>
> (Søren Kierkegaard, *The Concept of Irony with Continual Reference to Socrates*)[2]

In his 1983 polemic against Romanticists' 'uncritical absorption in Romanticism's own self-representations', Jerome McGann selected as illlustration a special issue of *The Wordsworth Circle* on Jane Austen. Rather than recognising that not all great Romantic-period literature is necessarily 'Romantic', the contributors had attempted to rectify Austen's marginalisation from the canon simply by identifying 'Romantic' aspects of her novels.[3] *Persuasion* drew particular notice, for scholars have often commented on its lyrical and melancholy tone.[4] Such readings, however, had the effect of qualifying without really displacing the orthodox view of Austen as a Johnsonian moralist. Marilyn Butler's political reading of Austen as an Anti-Jacobin writer also left in place this impression of Augustan rather than Romantic ideological and aesthetic affiliations.[5] However, recent scholarship shows Austen was far from an anomaly. A whole spectrum of writers of the period continued to produce topical literary parodies, comedy and satire.[6] The question of how to relate irony such as Austen's to 'Romantic' writing is therefore rendered all the more pertinent.

Byron was of course McGann's other premier example of a major Romantic-period writer who failed to meet the Romantic paradigm as defined by Meyer Abrams. The bleakness of Byronic scepticism, McGann asserted, was underestimated by critics such as Anne Mellor, willing to widen the definition of Romanticism to include 'Romantic irony', but only such celebrations of creative chaos as could be compared with Friedrich Schlegel.[7] If Austen was too light then Byron was too dark to fit the Romantic spectrum, seemingly.

The exclusivity of the traditional Romantic canon has long been breached, and no one could now regard Byron or Austen as relatively neglected. In fact they are the two writers of the period who generate particular fascination within popular culture, biography and film as well as scholarship both amateur and professional. Yet the question of their anomalous position has not altogether been answered merely by recognising that irony did not vanish with the passing of Augustanism. This chapter will pay close attention to literary form to demonstrate that Byron and Austen both pioneered narrative forms of irony which were developed to contain or frame the 'Romantic' as much as to dispel it.

I will focus first on Austen's parody of the Byronic. My title alludes to Anne Elliot's first conversation in *Persuasion* with Captain Benwick, who is in mourning for his fiancée who had died 5 months previously. The pair discuss the 'richness of the present age' in poetry, instanced in the verse romances of Scott and Byron. The tale of the Giaour, a renegade Venetian adventurer who dragged out the rest of his life in perpetual mourning for his one and only love, the murdered odalisque of a Turkish pasha, affords the British sailor, making polite conversation to a strange Englishwoman in off-season Lyme Regis, access to 'impassioned descriptions of hopeless agony':

> He repeated, with such tremulous feeling the various lines which imaged a broken heart, or a mind destroyed by wretchedness, and looked so entirely as if he meant to be understood, that she ventured to hope that he did not always read only poetry; and to say, that she thought it was the misfortune of poetry to be seldom safely enjoyed by those who enjoyed it completely; and that the strong feelings which alone could estimate it truly, were the very feelings which ought to taste it but sparingly. (93–4)[8]

The 'larger allowance of prose' (94) that the Christian stoic, Anne, recommends to help Benwick control his emotions consists of epistolary and biographical conduct literature. Of course, it was out of these very genres that courtship fiction such as *Persuasion* itself had been gestated. Concentration on the view of one protagonist, to whose interior monologue we are privy, via free indirect discourse, was a narrative form Austen had developed out of epistolary first-person meditations on the past self, while the exterior plotline of a *bildungsroman* derived from the linear time and causality of the moralised life.[9]

The very aptness of the heroine of such a novel endorsing didactic prose over popular poetry should make us suspect tongue-in-cheek, and turn to consider how far the authorial voice endorses Anne's nervousness about Romantic verse. The narrator describes Captain Benwick as 'a young man of considerable taste in reading, though principally in poetry' (93). The cautionary note sounded by 'though' surely belongs to Anne's inward view, rendered through occasional touches of free indirect discourse here, for her 'indulgence' of his fondness for poetry is contrasted and opposed to her utilitarian purpose: the 'real use' of her 'suggestions as to the duty and benefit of struggling against affliction' (93). Having stoically coped with loss herself, Anne considers herself possessor of 'the right seniority of mind'.[10] Despite this, the indirect account of Anne's introspective examination of her own conduct encourages the reader to see the protagonist and her didactic view of literature in a gently ironic light:

> When the evening was over, Anne could not but be amused at the idea of her coming to Lyme, to preach patience and resignation to a young man whom she had never seen before; nor could she help fearing, on more serious reflection, that, like many other great moralists and preachers, she had been eloquent on a point in which her own conduct would ill bear examination. (94)

In the midst of this representation of the heroine's guilty awareness of her hypocrisy, the passing comparison of Anne with the 'other great moralists and preachers' who do not practise what they preach is the narrator's interpolation, for it suggests the very conduct-book authors Anne has been recommending. This teases the reader with the semi-serious proposition that the courtship novel they are reading is more edifying fare than the new competition of male-authored romances, yet both more entertaining and true to lived experience than a conduct book.

This metafictional edge to the heroine's suspicion of Romantic poetry is comparable to the narrator's chauvinist defence of the art of the novel in the fifth chapter of *Northanger Abbey*. The subtext is a literary war of the sexes expressed in gendering of the genres. Scott's and Byron's phenomenally popular verse romances were in the process of masculinising verse by introducing martial adventure as the principal theme, though both poets consciously set out to attract women readers, now a crucial test of success in *belles-lettres*. Until Scott's publication of *Waverley* in 1814, the year in which *Persuasion* is set, women writers' largely didactic fiction dominated the novel, and it is clear that Austen's *Persuasion* intends to demonstrate that patriotic support for the British forces during wartime was not a masculine monopoly. Her own realistic fiction of contemporary life could more directly address the issues than the mystifying invocation of the medieval in the Burkean verse romance, *Marmion*. Her sharpest satire yet, in the shape of Sir Walter Elliot, of the preening vanity yet obsolescence of the Regency aristocracy targeted the glamour bestowed by both male poets on the aristocratic values of past times.

In the character of Captain Benwick, *Persuasion* singles out for particular mockery the fashionable appeal of Romantic *weltschmertz*, the Byronic indulgence of melancholy which Peacock, too, satirised in *Nightmare Abbey*, in the same year that saw the publication of *Persuasion*.[11] Benwick, as an example of a young man modelling himself on the Byronic hero, and, like Childe Harold and his author, consciously or unconsciously attracting sympathetic young women to him with his air of melancholic inconsolability, is a type ripe for satire. Thus it is a delicious blackly comic twist when Benwick removes Louisa Musgrove as a block to Anne's own marriage with Frederick Wentworth: becoming engaged to her within weeks of his conversations with Anne, confirming her suspicion that he had been attracted to her too – 'He had an affectionate heart. He must love somebody.' (157)

The Byronic Benwick, who wears his mourning heart on his sleeve, is of a piece with that vein of anti-Romantic parodic comedy threading through Austen's novels, from the excesses of the lachrymose Marianne in *Sense and Sensibility*, and the quixotic Gothic fantasist Catherine Moreland in *Northanger Abbey*, to the satire of hypochondria in *Sanditon* – and not forgetting the endless rehearsals of *Lovers' Vows*, Elizabeth Inchald's translation of Kotzebue, which reinscribe the characters' repressed sexual desires in *Mansfield Park* into sentimental terms. As Adela Pinch has commented, 'readers in the eighteenth and nineteenth centuries took seriously the emotions derived from books, both taking consolation in and deploring their effects',[12] and *Persuasion* is particularly concerned with the power of books to channel, to refine and to train the emotions.

However, the case of Captain Benwick is not introduced merely to debate the moral usefulness of literature, though that is a side issue. As Peter Knox-Shaw has argued, Byron's work is 'discussed with the seriousness due to a "first-rate poet" in an age remarkable for its poetry', and 'he is at once the butt of criticism and an index to the novel's quick'.[13] For Austen's novel takes up the philosophical question underlying *The Giaour*: does human love have an absolute value and should a bereaved lover remain constant after the death of the beloved? James Benwick and William Elliot are both in mourning yet will soon be seen obtaining new wives, while Sir Walter, Lady Russell, Mrs Clay and Mrs Smith have retained their widowed status, we suspect, rather out of an inability to improve their financial status through a second marriage than out of overwhelming grief. Anne considers herself as bereft as one whose lover has died, and compares herself to Benwick: 'And yet [...] he has not, perhaps, a more sorrowing heart than I have' (91). She prides herself on keeping sacred the memory of her broken engagement to Captain Wentworth eight years previously.[14] In selecting the theme of undying love for *Persuasion*, Austen was not only responding to the Byronic Romanticism of *The Giaour*, but also answering Scott's review of *Emma* which had chastised 'authors of moral fiction' for coupling Cupid 'indivisibly with calculating prudence' instead of endorsing first love.[15]

Knox-Shaw rightly points out the fact that Austen 'restores the enduringly sorrowful heart to womanhood', and is concerned to stress the Christian fortitude of her heroine in contrast to Benwick's Byronic repining.[16] But Austen's narrator is also capable of treating her own heroine's Giaour-like belief in undying love with a degree of scepticism, and this is an aspect of, not separate from, her affinity with Romanticism. Sceptical questioning of the absolute value of human love relates Austen to the later Byron of *ottava rima*, rather than a Wordsworthian Romanticism. Søren Kierkegaard, in his critique of sceptical irony from a Christian perspective, acknowledges the role irony plays in qualifying subjectivity, but also points out the paradox that Romantic irony tended to reassert subjectivity in another less obvious form: that of an 'intensified subjective consciousness'.[17] The assumption that there is always a clear-cut distinction between 'Augustan' irony, relying on shared moral standards, and philosophical 'Romantic irony' perhaps needs re-examining if Austen is to be claimed not as backward-looking but a writer intensely but sceptically engaged with Romantic subjectivity.[18] Indeed, as William Galperin has suggested, rather than a conservative defence of the status quo, we should consider Austen's irony as 'a *post*-romantic gesture whose opposition to romanticism more properly reflects the extent to which the latter and its revolutionary agenda have been assimilated, not rejected'.[19]

In his recent study of the comedy of Romantic irony, Morton Gure-witch provocatively asks himself the rhetorical question whether it is plausible 'to describe the conflict between romantic urge and anti-romantic control in Jane Austen's *Sense and Sensibility* as proof of romantic irony'.[20] Plainly the answer should be no, as that novel's didactic origins are still discernible, and much of its social satire has a firm moral basis. The same could be said for all of Austen's fictions, none of which remotely approaches the ambivalently presented vision of a chaotic universe that characterises the Romantic irony of Friedrich Schlegel or Byron's *Don Juan*. Nevertheless, the ambivalent presentation of Marianne does allow for the juxtaposing of idealism with scepticism. However, the more sophisticated dualism of the later fiction, such as *Persuasion*, lies in the entwining of sceptical narrator and Romantic protagonist within the narrative style of free indirect discourse. Galperin argues that the 'sympathetic treatment' of the heroine of this novel marks 'a temporary reprieve' from the 'regulatory work of direct narrative', in other words the didacticism to which free indirect discourse lends itself.[21] One could go further: the ironising of such a 'good' protagonist marks an increasingly secularised vision.

Byron's *The Giaour* and Austen's *Persuasion* may be closely compared in terms of the way their narrative forms simultaneously project Kierkegaard's 'intensified subjective consciousness' yet subject it to ironic qualification. Both authors construct narratives which subor-dinate plot to character. Contemporary readers were puzzled by Byron's having left out the connecting links of the story and disrupted its temporal sequence, and reviewers commented that nothing really happened in Austen's novels.[22] Both foregrounded speech instead: Austen's novels were dialogic, though mainly focalised through the prot-agonist, and Byron's poem consists of a series of monologues by different speakers. Both minimalised the omniscient author, in favour of letting the characters speak/think and thus show us their contrasting person-alities in action. In doing this, both were pioneers in expanding the possibilities of existing literary forms in order to present one individual's psyche in detail: their innovations, in prose and poetic narrative respect-ively, would be taken up by the premier writers of the later nineteenth century.

Byron was arguably the major inspiration behind the reshaping of the dramatic monologue from the classical form of the complaint or expression of grief, into the nineteenth-century poetic character study of central importance to the oeuvres of Hemans, Landon, Browning and Tennyson.[23] Crucially, it was the philosophical sceptic, Byron, who developed the form in the direction of moral relativism by exploring the beliefs of extraordinary individuals from other cultures or ages.

Austen's extensive use of free indirect discourse to represent the psyche of the protagonist constitutes her major claim to be considered a Romantic. Austen was crucial in the development of this major technique of fictional narrative, laying the ground for Flaubert and George Eliot in the nineteenth century. Though it is usually considered a purely literary phenomenon, Sylvia Adamson has convincingly argued that the practice of empathetic deixis (the technical transfer of the egocentric subject position to another person) is rooted in normal spoken practice.[24] She relates the empathetic dislocations of space and time to a speaker's effort to entertain simultaneously two viewpoints which the movement of time should have set apart, citing as a literary example the concluding lines of Wordsworth's 'Tintern Abbey', in which the poet combines his immediate experience with the perspective of his sister's future memories. While Austen is arguably as interested as Wordsworth in developing forms of narrative that enable the subjective and the empathetic to be voiced together, what she has in common with Byron is the exploitation of a double narrative voice also capable of juxtaposing sympathy with judgement, producing irony. Austen fuses the inner voice of the perceiving mind with that of a sometimes sceptical narrator. *Erlebte rede, le style indirect libre* or free indirect discourse does not report speech literally, but is a condensation of what passes through the character's mind, whose language and ordering is determined by the narrator, producing what Roy Pascal's study terms 'a dual voice'.[25] In *Persuasion* it engages in a sceptical questioning of various certainties, including even the protagonist's own moral idealism: a scepticism quelled but not entirely dispelled by the comic resolution of plot.[26]

Both free indirect discourse and the dramatic monologue are literary forms produced by the advent of Enlightenment relativism, and therefore conducive to ambiguity. In both *The Giaour* and *Persuasion*, for example, new forms are being forged in order to present a central character who believes in the absolute value of Romantic love in contrast to his/her society, whose view is presented sympathetically yet also specifically as a subjective one and therefore open to question. Both works centre on loss and the impossibility of recapturing the past. Both protagonists reflect on the story of a love affair which is already over when the narrative begins, and which is recounted to us through their memory. As Byron's antihero puts it,

> My memory now is but the tomb
> Of joys long dead – my hope – their doom. (1000–1)

In both cases that love was perceived as transgressive by the authority figures of the society in which the individuals live, thus representing existential freedom on the one hand yet threatening social alienation on the other. Byron's protagonist, typically, broke the rules, and Austen's, typically, did not, yet both now mourn for the lost lover. The philosophical problem is posed as to whether they should remain constant to the feelings of the past or remain open to future experience: the reader experiencing the pathos of human subjectivity beached by the flux of time.

The Giaour foregrounds and makes strange the act of narration by presenting as 'disjointed fragments' the story or fabula summarised in the Advertisement, which Byron claims in the notes to have heard 'by accident recited by one of the coffee-house story-tellers, who abound in the Levant, and sing or recite their narratives', to have imperfectly remembered, and thus to be presenting only parts of it with 'additions and interpolations by the translator'.[27] Because the poem opens with a declamatory Western Philhellenist voice (1–167), presumably that of the 'translator', the next piece of narrative (the memories of a fisherman who witnessed the central events) is emphasised as the performance of a Turkish point of view. This signalling of the exotic to the reader distances him/her sufficiently that s/he may view the fragments of dramatic monologue which follow with some degree of irony, even though not guided to do so by any rhetorical asides of the narrator/translator. The technique anticipates that of Browning's historical dramatic monologues, which may be perceived ironically by some readers, as examples of culturally 'other' ways of thinking. The effect is achieved because the reader is implicitly expected to contextualise by being thrown *in medias res* and denied any other factor but the speech for judgement of character.

As Linda Hutcheon argues in *Irony's Edge*, it is a pre-existing, shared cultural context that allows irony to come into being, where a play between the said and the not-said tests out particular assumptions.[28] So when Byron's readers are briefly reminded of their Philhellenist preconceived notion of Greece as the site of long-entombed classical heroism (3), they perceive the contrast with the Turkish fisherman's voiced hatred of Westerners with a shock which transforms Greece from a familiar scholarly idea into a strange, *unheimlich* place, Islamic and Oriental. The uncanny effect is heightened by the Philhellenist narrator's famous extended simile where present-day Greece is compared to the corpse of a beautiful girl (68–102): 'We start – for soul is wanting there' (93). The 'form' of the dramatic monologue is obliquely related by this image to 'form' in its theological sense, mere matter which will be transformed by sacred utterance into sacramental substance. The poet will make Greece speak for us and thus help her rise again – as he will in a later monologue raise Dante from the dead to voice his prophecy for a free Italy. These are typically Romantic, even visionary claims for the power of poetry, yet simultaneously hedged with the darkest pessimism in which contemporary Greece is mordantly viewed as mere clay.

The reader is then plunged from the Utopian into the present-day 'here and now' of the fisherman's world, as conveyed by the use of the present tense in both the third-person presentation of the fisherman narrator – 'He shuns the near but doubtful creek' (169–79) – and the latter's first-person subjective view of the Giaour: 'I know thee not, I loathe thy race' (191). This together with the drumming hoof beats of driving octosyllabic couplets gives the performance the immediacy and energy for which Byron's verse is renowned. So although the section describing Hassan's hall as ruinous in present time (288–351) will shortly make it plain that the events described happened in the past and that Hassan was murdered by the Giaour, the fisherman-narrator creates mystery by substituting performative spontaneity for omniscience, challenging the auditor/reader to impose coherence. Instead of always using the past tense to imply retrospection, we notice that fisherman uses the past tense (200–7) interspersed with the present historic (208–15), then past (216–20), present historic again (221–33) and so on, and we realise that either the fisherman himself is reliving the memory of the moment the Giaour galloped past him, or the coffee-house bard is ventriloquising his doing so. The sections in the past tense often recount the stranger's actions while the counterpointing present tense often enacts the fisherman's questioning thoughts at the time when he had no knowledge of the outcome (180, 228–31, 267–8). In other words, the narrator and the perceiving mind of the character are merged together in a dualism comparable to Austen's technique of free indirect discourse. Alan Sinfield's comments on the peculiar effect of dramatic monologue are apposite here:

What we experience in dramatic monologue – and it is a quality which is not easily gained in other modes – is a divided consciousness. We are impressed, with the full strength of first-person presentation, by the speaker and feel drawn into his point of view, but at the same time are aware that he is a dramatic creation and that there are other possible, even preferable perspectives. This condition is a precise consequence of the status of dramatic monologue as feint: we are obliged to posit simultaneously the speaking 'I' and the poet's 'I'.[29]

The form necessarily complicates moral judgements. Condemnation of the Giaour's adultery is also problematised by the juxtaposition of different cultural mores, but it is not until the Giaour is himself allowed to recount his story, in the long final section (970–1334), that the reader perceives the irony of the only name we know him by, which means 'infidel'. The renegade has now abjured Islam as well as Christianity, so is judged a heretic by both faiths. A Muslim curse predicts he will become a vampire feeding on his own womenfolk (747–86) and, directly juxtaposed with this, he is feared as another wandering Cain by the monks, in whose monastery he chooses to stage his lack of repentance and refusal to take communion (787–970). Such a plethora of judgement has the effect of undermining that of the reader. This is in addition to the structural irony that, despite the cultural chasm between East and West, they produce similar codes of behaviour. Both Hassan and the Giaour commit murder, neither repents; they mirror each other in rivalry, possessiveness, rapaciousness and violence:

> Yet did he but what I had done
> Had she been false to more than one. (1062–3)

But whereas the orthodox believer, Hassan, was on his way to obtain another bride for his harem when he was ambushed by the Giaour's band (519–36), the Giaour's unrepentant 'confession' shows that, as a Romantic sceptic, personal love is now the only source of belief for him. It is so sacred that it has become his religion, and he can never take a second mistress (1166).

> Yes, Love indeed is light from heaven –
> A spark of that immortal fire
> With angels shar'd – by Alla given,
> To lift from earth our low desire. (1131–4)

The absence of Leila herself, except as she is recalled in memory and seen by him as a spirit beckoning him to his death (1257–1301), indicates that it is the Giaour's moral freedom to love rather than the object of that love that is important in the poem. The urgent re-constituted speech-acts which make up the poem themselves project the ideology of the Giaour: that his absolute commitment to love constitutes the freedom to act spontaneously from passion 'like the lava flood' (1101), not prudence (1230), and to bear in alienated solitude the solipsism of his self-determinism. The time-bound framework that was mystified by the fragmentary narration of the poem frustrates the Utopian desire for absolute value with which the Giaour tries to exert his will. His determination to live in the past and refusal to accept change or the limited nature of human love after Leila's death express a nihilistic philosophical scepticism which sees life as a curse. The moral relativity implied by the contrasting points of view with which his story is told and heard dooms his attempt to achieve complete coherence and selfhood, turning his very identity to a 'broken tale' (1331–2) of evanescent moments which can only temporarily be relived in utterance.

If form is the performance of speech in *The Giaour*, we turn to *Persuasion* to find a protagonist spending the whole text learning to find her voice. Instead of a partial narrator with limited knowledge, we have an omniscient one who gives access to the main characters' motivations and inner thoughts. Indeed, as Marvin Mudrick commented 50 years ago, the novel 'marks the most abrupt turn in Jane Austen's work: it shows the author closely attentive to personal feeling [...] for the first time'.[30] The novel is extremely close to a first-person viewpoint in its focalisation through the heroine, and indeed Anne herself may be seen as Romantic in her love of poetry and her melancholic identification with autumnal landscapes. Her subjective thoughts are forms in a Kantian sense, apprehending and synthesising external reality. But *Persuasion* is not concerned with natural religion or how the imagination determines its own reality, though Anne herself, as a Romantic, might well have been. The novel's viewpoint is sociological rather than philosophical, and, as in the novels of George Eliot later in the century, deals with a religious heroine but from a secular perspective.

Anne is always presented in society. The technique of free indirect discourse enables her to be viewed simultaneously from within and without, objectively and subjectively, as a character with strong beliefs but limited social status. We vicariously experience her attempts to withstand the pressures of social determinism, as she negotiates the outer shows that society demands of her day by day. Her unappealing family, whose obsession with their genealogy emphasises the dead hand of the past on the present, upholds and attempts to enforce conformity, the merely formal manners and conventions of a society empty of feelings. The careful precision in time and space and straightforward onward movement of the retrospective narrative provide a strong outline, in contrast to the provisional inchoate nature of the inner world as we see the protagonist's psyche struggling to retain its integrity. A radical pessimism has produced this disjunction between the alienated individual and the community which no longer endorses and enforces her morality. As Julia Prewitt Brown points out, *Persuasion* is Austen's most modern work, portraying a post-revolutionary world in which confidence has been lost in the traditional ruling class, and self has been dislocated from social role:

> In its general structure, *Persuasion* registers an almost Weberian crisis of belief in the legitimacy of social structures.[31]

Gary Kelly argues, however, that the formal structure of Austen's Romantic comedies 'is consistent with an Anglican reading of human history as a form of romance journey in which an omniscient yet benevolent deity presides over a historical plot of human error, fall and redemption by both free will and grace, and which instructs the reader to hope for and aspire to redemption'. He suggests that a didactic purpose impels Austen's ironic narrative form: 'to tempt the reader [...] into error by misreading [...] by ignoring the narrator's ironic distance from the protagonist', so that the naïve reader experiences with the heroine 'her journey through error and suffering'.[32] However, in *Persuasion* the reverse seems to be the case. It is the protagonist who sees her life in providential terms while the narrator ironises her idealism, often by juxtaposing it with bubble-pricking mundane social realism. And readers have tended to misread Anne as a touchstone of moral authority rather than noting her human fallibility, and the pathetic fallacy of each individual thinking s/he is the centre of the universe. Tara Ghosal Wallace has rightly challenged the assumption of many critics that Anne is 'the infallible and dependable locus of authority'.[33] For even Anne's faith in her own permanent unchanging love, which seems endorsed and celebrated at the conclusion, is actually ironically presented through inconsistencies and vacillations at many points. Wallace also notes that free indirect discourse is by its nature imprecise: continually varying the distancing of character from narrator, throwing into question the source of narrative authority for every viewpoint expressed and challenging a nimble reader to recognise differing layers of irony through contextualisation.

If we examine the thoughts of Anne as registered in free indirect discourse we see that her strong sense of her own individualism is related to her spiritual belief in practical Christianity. Though her belief in absolute truths and values is sometimes ironised, it is also used to show up the hollowness of the Regency society amongst whom she moves. So when her father is bankrupted yet feels it would be demeaning to his rank to economise, Anne 'considered it as an act of indispensable duty to clear away the claims of creditors [...] and saw no dignity in any thing short of it' (13). The word 'duty' is again emphasised by being used twice in Anne's mental embracing of the temporary role of family mediator, favourite aunt and nurse amongst the empty-headed squirearchy at Uppercross, feeling the 'satisfaction of knowing herself extremely useful there' (32, 113).

Bereft of a mother or any relative who cares for her, bereft of her suitor, and now bereft of her home, Anne is in search of a role. The momentary attraction of Mr Elliot lies in 'the idea of becoming what her mother had been; of having the precious name of "Lady Kellynch" first revived in herself; of being restored to Kellynch', but this dream is then cancelled out by Anne's doubts as to whether Mr Elliot possesses genuine religious fervour:

He certainly knew what was right, nor could she fix on any one article of moral duty evidently transgressed; but yet she would have been afraid to answer for his conduct. [...] She saw that there had been bad habits, that Sunday-travelling had been a common thing; that there had been a period of his life (and probably not a short one) when he had been, at least, careless on all serious matters. (151)

Anne is obviously an Evangelical for she looks for signs of a religion of the heart:

There was never any burst of feeling, any warmth of indignation or delight, at the evil or good of others. This, to Anne, was a decided imperfection. (151)

Such passages led to Austen being described as 'evidently a Christian writer' by Richard Whately in his review of *Persuasion* in the *Quarterly Review*.[34] But this is to confuse the view of the protagonist with that of the novel. Anne's religiosity is not presented uncritically.

Like many Evangelicals, she embraces suffering as beneficial to the soul. Despite the advice to Benwick, we have seen her indulge her own melancholy through dwelling on 'the influence so sweet and so sad of the autumnal months in the country' (32), and witness on the walk to Winthrop the comic irruption of Wentworth and Louisa's flirting into Anne's recall of 'some tender sonnet, fraught with the apt analogy of the declining year, with declining happiness, and the images of youth and hope, and spring, all gone together' (79). The narrator, however, points out that the reality of the ploughs at work in the landscape before her eyes 'spoke the farmer, counteracting the sweets of poetical despondence, and meaning to have spring again' (79). This implies that a second spring is what is natural, and indeed the admiration of Benwick and then Mr Elliot, and Anne's enjoyment of their attentions, allows us to predict that the turn of the year will see Anne's own revival.

> She had been forced into prudence in her youth, she learned romance as she grew older – the natural sequence of an unnatural beginning. (29)

Anne sees woman's role as that of 'ministering angel', in the words of Scott's *Marmion*. When her small nephew suffers a painful dislocated collar-bone and possible back injury, and both parents want to go out to dinner and quarrel about who should stay with him, Anne enjoins her sister: 'Nursing does not belong to a man, it is not his province. A sick child is always the mother's property, her own feelings generally make it so' (53). She relishes taking on the role herself when Mary is unmoved by this (55). Indeed, Anne proves herself capable in a crisis twice in the novel when serious accidents occur: little Charles's fall (50) and Louisa's head injury on the Cobb (102–6). While her humanity and common sense are admirable and bear comparison with men of action, some of whom have seen battle, Anne is later ironically portrayed ardently rhapsodising about the scenes in a sickroom which nurses witness, as spiritual arenas in which the soul is truly tested:

> What instances must pass before them of ardent, disinterested, self-denying attachment, of heroism, fortitude, patience, resignation – of all the conflicts and all the sacrifices that ennoble us most. A sick chamber may often furnish the worth of volumes. (146)

Anne's friend, Mrs Smith, herself an invalid, is sceptical, giving physical causes of behaviour, such as debility and fatigue, their due:

Here and there, human nature may be great in times of trial, but generally speaking it is its weakness and not its strength that appears in a sick chamber; it is selfishness and impatience rather than generosity and fortitude. (147)

Mrs Smith, though suffering the worst that life can throw at her, is endowed with 'elasticity of mind [...] which was from Nature alone' (145), according to Anne. The fact that Mrs Smith does not dwell on her suffering and can take pleasure in such mundane pleasures as knitting and hearing her nurse's gossip gently brings out the comparative self-indulgence in Anne's melancholy musings.

The narrator can be much more brutally sceptical about the capacity of suffering and bereavement to ennoble the soul, and the idealisation of the family as nurturing true feeling. Anne's maternal devotion to nursing her nephew is spliced with remorseless mockery by the narrator of Mrs Musgrove's mourning for her drowned son (48). Byron himself could not have been more cynical in comically portraying the mother's 'large fat sighings over the destiny of a son, whom alive nobody had cared for' (63). That this is no mere aberration may be shown by the earlier, longer passage where the unsentimental narrator declares roundly that Dick 'had been very little cared for at any time by his family' and his death was 'scarcely at all regretted' (48). The depiction of the drama on the cob is similarly undercut. The narrator uses melodramatic language to describe Wentworth 'staggering against the wall for his support' and exclaiming 'in the bitterest agony, "Oh, God! her father and mother!"' (102). Yet tragic sentiment is momentarily punctured when the narrative enters the minds of the workmen who gathered 'to enjoy the sight of a dead young lady, nay, two dead young ladies, for it proved twice as fine as the first report' (103). The clashes between tragic and comic registers, between empathetic and distanced satiric narrative voices, should not be seen as stylistic infelicities but as occasional manifestations of a dualistic irony, holding moral idealism and scepticism in play.

Not only does the enveloping of the protagonist's subjectivity in third-person narrative enable an ironic perspective, but the twofold structure of Anne and Wentworth's romance also allows us a dual vision of it. Anne views romantic love as unique and spiritual, and to her the fact that their union has been deferred suggests the greater importance of spirituality than the desires of the body for the lovers. However, when the flirtation between Louisa and Wentworth re-enacts just the path the younger Anne had followed (60), this suggests how common and easily replicated their story really was. The radical pessimism infecting the novel is questioning the providentialism of Anne's idealised view of romantic love by placing the story within a deterministic universe where common social and environmental conditions shape experience.

So the narrator explains the origin of Anne and Captain Wentworth's love in terms of material circumstance rather than spiritual essence:

> Half the sum of attraction, on either side, might have been enough, for he had nothing to do, and she had hardly anybody to love. (26)

Similarly, limited social opportunities are suggested as the main reason for Anne's constancy since that time:

> No second attachment, the only thoroughly natural, happy, and sufficient cure, at her time of life, had been possible to the nice tone of her mind, the fastidiousness of her taste, in the small limits of the society around them. (28)

Anne herself realises how circumstances brought together Benwick and Louisa Musgrove:

> Where could have been the attraction? The answer soon presented itself. It had been in situation. [...] of course they had fallen in love over poetry. (157)

Indeed, the novel even implies that an individual's character and temperament is not a fixed essence but may be conditioned by physical causes such as injury, when Charles Musgrove reports how, after her fall, Louisa 'is altered: there is no running or jumping about, no laughing or dancing' (205).

The narrator's emphasis on the social and material determinants of individuals' behaviour is in direct contrast to indications in free indirect discourse of the heroine's own self-belief in her individualism, her capacity for making moral decisions and for remaining true to her ideals. Anne does realise that the 'extraordinary circumstances' of their accidental meeting at Lyme and 'everything in situation' have created a favourable and 'flattering' opportunity to fall in love with her cousin, but her thoughts twist away from recognising the possibility of interpreting this providentially. The original plot, featuring her 'eternal constancy' to Wentworth, would then have to be re-written:

> How she might have felt, had there been no Captain Wentworth in the case, was not worth enquiry; for there was a Captain Wentworth: and be the conclusion of the present suspense good or bad, her affection would be his for ever. Their union, she believed, could not divide her more from other men, than their final separation.

> Prettier musings of high-wrought love and eternal constancy, could never have passed along the streets of Bath, than Anne was sporting with from Camden-place to Westgate-buildings. It was almost enough to spread perfume and purification all the way. (181)

Even such an exemplary and constant heroine is not quite enough to sanctify the streets of pleasure-loving Bath, as the narrator dryly notes.

The famous debate between Captain Harville and Anne on the relative capacity of men and women for constancy in love in a way replicates the situation of free indirect discourse. For Captain Wentworth is an auditor, allowed to overhear Anne's thoughts as expressed to Harville, who plays the part of the sceptical narrator in subjecting them to question. Their discussion as to whether the capacity for enduring love is an aspect of nature in a specific individual, such as Fanny Harville or Anne herself, or an aspect of woman's nature, whether induced by circumstances or by innate feminine capacity for sensibility, is contested and ultimately left unresolved. Yet the moral idealism of Anne seems, if anything, braver and more full of pathos when opened to such sceptical scrutiny and the possibility of fallacy. Anne's words seem to have been taken up by Byron in the letter of Donna Julia in Canto I of *Don Juan*, published the year following *Persuasion*:

> Man's love is of his life a thing apart,
>   'Tis woman's whole existence; man may range
> The court, camp, church, the vessel, and the mart,
>   Sword, gown, gain, glory, offer in exchange
> Pride, fame, ambition, to fill up his heart,
>   And few there are whom these can not estrange;
> Man has all these resources, we but one,
> To love again, and be again undone. (st. 194)

The poet may well have read the novel as it was published by his own publisher, John Murray, at the very beginning of 1818 and Byron received a large parcel of new books and reviews from him that February in Venice.[35] Finding Austen's parody of the Byronic Benwick may have spurred him into taking up the debate, though such claims for women's special capacity for enduring love are also found in Madame de Staël's *Corinne* and other texts of the time. Literary debates over men and women's relative capacity for constancy had raged for a century, and by the nineteenth century the older stereotype of woman as changeable and fickle had metamorphosed into an endorsement of her superior capacity for love.

The self-made man, Captain Wentworth, represents a different type of Romantic individualism, complementing that of Anne's religion of the heart. His belief in firm characters resisting outside influences is exemplified in his parable of the hazelnut which keeps its shape 'while so many of its brethren have fallen and been trodden underfoot' (81). He mistakenly thought Anne lacked such moral strength because she listened to Lady Russell's advice in refusing his proposal, yet the reader is aware that such a decision could equally be seen as having demonstrated Anne's independence of judgement by not being persuaded by him. Her ability to overrule personal desire at that time indicates Anne's belief in a stable inner self resisting the demands of the body and surmounting physical change. Though Wentworth judged her 'altered beyond his knowledge' in the eight years which have robbed her of her physical bloom (57), Anne prides herself on remaining essentially the same. So when they are reunited, and he then declares, 'to my eye you could never alter', Anne is more flattered that his perception of her beauty is thus demonstrated as entirely subjective, 'the result, not the cause of a revival in his warm attachment' (228), than if his love had been prompted by physical attraction. In fact the replaying of their love story, this time with a happy ending, confirms them both in their belief that this predestined unique Romantic love of two particular individuals transcends the merely physical as they were 'more tender, more tried, more fixed in a knowledge of each other's character, truth and attachment' (225). It is their words which make sacred this actual time when they confess their love:

> the power of conversation would make the present hour a blessing indeed; and prepare it for all the immortality which the happiest recollections of their own future lives could bestow. (225)

But, even here, the ironic use of the word 'immortality' lightly indicates just how far from immortal human love is, limited as it is by the finite constraints of one's lifetime and memory.

Byron and Austen both endorsed the claims of their own sex to greater capacity for heroic constancy in love: a way of asserting selfhood and affirming meaning in the face of time and transience. The literary forms of *Persuasion* and *The Giaour*, however, foregrounding but framing the heroine's unspoken thoughts and hero's speech, are imbued with relativity. The very form of free indirect discourse – subjectivities voiced but contained within the narrator's overarching design – demonstrates the limitations of human consciousness to know and judge the truth. Byron's poetic fragments in *The Giaour* are epiphanies, tableaux frozen in time, an acknowledgement of the transience and evanescence of human life against which human claims to constancy pit themselves in vain.

Notes

1. Tzvetan Todorov, *Mikhail Bakhtin: The Dialogical Principle* (Manchester: Manchester University Press, 1984), p. 68.
2. Søren Kierkegaard, *The Concept of Irony with Continual Reference to Socrates*, ed. and trans. by H. V. Hong and E. H. Hong (Princeton: Princeton University Press, 1989), p. 256.
3. Jerome J. McGann, *The Romantic Ideology: A Critical Investigation* (Chicago and London: University of Chicago Press, 1983), pp. 18, 29.
4. On Jane Austen and the Romantic, see *The Wordsworth Circle*, 7:4 (Autumn, 1976) and Susan Morgan, 'Jane Austen and Romanticism', in J. D. Grey (ed.), *The Jane Austen Handbook* (London: Athlone Press, 1986), pp. 364–8. On *Persuasion*, see: Barbara Hardy, *A Reading of Jane Austen* (New York: New York University Press, 1976), pp. 56–8; Nina Auerbach, 'O Brave New World: Evolution and Revolution in *Persuasion*', *ELH*, 39 (1972), pp. 112–28; Jon Spence, 'The Abiding Possibilities of Nature in *Persuasion*', *Studies in English Literature, 1500–1899*, 21 (1981), pp. 625–36; S. M. Tave, 'Jane Austen and One of her Contemporaries', in John Halperin (ed.), *Jane Austen: Bicentenary Studies* (Cambridge: Cambridge University Press, 1975), pp. 61–74; A. Walton Litz, '*Persuasion*: Forms of Estrangement', in Halperin (ed.), *Jane Austen: Bicentenary Studies*, pp. 221–34; Keith G. Thomas, 'Jane Austen and the Romantic Lyric: *Persuasion* and Coleridge's Conversation Poems', *ELH*, 54:4 (Winter, 1987), pp. 893–924; Peter Knox-Shaw, '*Persuasion*, James Austen and James Thomson', *Notes and Queries*, 49:4 (2002), pp. 451–3.
5. Marilyn Butler, *Jane Austen and the War of Ideas*, 2nd edn (Oxford: Oxford University Press, 1987).
6. See: John Strachan (ed.), *British Satire 1785–1840*, 5 vols (London: Pickering & Chatto, 2003); Steven E. Jones (ed.), *The Satiric Eye: Forms of Satire in the Romantic Period* (New York: Palgrave, 2003); Gary Dyer, *British Satire and the Politics of Style, 1789–1832* (Cambridge: Cambridge University Press, 1997); Marcus Wood, *Radical Satire and Print Culture 1790–1822* (Oxford: Oxford University Press, 1994).
7. McGann, *The Romantic Ideology*, pp. 21–4; Anne K. Mellor, *English Romantic Irony* (Cambridge Mass.: Harvard University Press, 1980).

8. Jane Austen, *Persuasion*, ed. by Gillian Beer (London: Penguin, 1998). All quotations are taken from this edition and page references follow quotations in the text.

9. Joe Bray persuasively argues that the duality of narrator and character that generates free indirect style's key meanings, including irony, had its origins in the dramatised consciousness of eighteenth-century epistolary novels, in 'The Source of "Dramatized Consciousness": Richardson, Austen and Stylistic Influence', *Style*, 35:1 (Spring, 2001), pp. 18–33. See also: Graham Hough, 'Narration and Dialogue in Jane Austen', *Critical Quarterly*, 12 (1970), pp. 201–29; Frances Ferguson, 'Jane Austen, *Emma*, and the Impact of Form', *Modern Languages Quarterly*, 61:1 (March 2000), pp. 157–80.

10. Jane Austen wrote of Anne to Fanny Knight on 23 March 1817: 'You may *perhaps* like the Heroine, as she is almost too good for me' (*Jane Austen's Letters to her Sister Cassandra and others*, ed. by R. W. Chapman, 2 vols (Oxford: Oxford University Press, 1932), II, p. 487).

11. Thomas Love Peacock, *Novels of Thomas Love Peacock* (London: Pan, 1967), p. 150.

12. Adela Pinch, *Strange Fits of Passion: Epistemologies of Emotion, Hume to Austen* (Stanford: Stanford University Press, 1996), pp. 136–63.

13. Peter Knox-Shaw, '*Persuasion*, Byron and the Turkish Tale', *Review of English Studies*, 44:173 (1993), pp. 47–69 (p. 48). This article provides a lively discussion of *Persuasion* in the context of Austen's reading of Byron's Oriental tales, and is especially sharp on both authors' reaction to Wollstonecraftian feminism.

14. On this topic, see: Loraine Fletcher, 'Time and Mourning in *Persuasion*', *Women's Writing*, 5:1 (1998), pp. 81–90; Jill Heydt-Stevenson, ' "Unbecoming Conjunctions": Mourning the Loss of Landscape and love in *Persuasion*', *Eighteenth-Century Fiction*, 8:1 (October, 1995), pp. 51–71.

15. *Quarterly Review*, 14 (March 1816), pp. 188–201; reprinted in B. C. Southam (ed.), *Jane Austen: The Critical Heritage* (London: Routledge & Kegan Paul, 1968), pp. 58–69.

16. Knox-Shaw, '*Persuasion*, Byron and the Turkish Tale', p. 52.

17. Kierkegaard, *The Concept of Irony with Continual Reference to Socrates*, p. 242.

18. Clara Tuite concentrates, instead, on the way the canonised Austen has been perceived in Burkean terms in *Romantic Austen: Sexual Politics and the Literary Canon* (Cambridge: Cambridge University Press, 2002), p. 63. Knox-Shaw makes a powerful case for relating Austen to the intellectual tradition of the sceptical Enlightenment in *Jane Austen and the Enlightenment* (Cambridge: Cambridge University Press, 2004), p. 248.

19. William H. Galperin, 'Byron, Austen and the "Revolution" of Irony', *Criticism*, 32:1 (Winter 1990), pp. 51–80 (p. 60).

20. Morton Gurewitch, *The Comedy of Romantic Irony* (Lanham, Maryland and Oxford: University Press of America, 2002), p. 11.

21. William H. Galperin, *The Historical Austen* (Philadelphia: University of Pennsylvania Press, 2003), pp. 13, 215.

22. The reviewer of *Northanger Abbey* and *Persuasion* for the British Critic commented, 'so little narrative is there in either of the two novels [...] that it is difficult to give any thing like an abstract of their contents' (*British Critic*,

9 (March 1818), pp. 293–301; reprinted in *Jane Austen: The Critical Heritage*, pp. 79–84 (p. 80)).

23. As well as *The Giaour*, Byron experimented with the dramatic monologue in many of the Hebrew Melodies, his poems on Napoleon's defeat 'from the French', *The Prisoner of Chillon*, *The Lament of Tasso* and *The Prophecy of Dante*. Byron is not indexed in Alan Sinfield, *Dramatic Monologue*, in the Critical Idiom series (London and New York: Methuen, 1977), and the 2003 text in the same series by Glenys Byron does not discuss Byron's dramatic monologues either, whilst the dramas are the only poems of Byron's mentioned in Robert Langbaum, *The Poetry of Experience: The Dramatic Monologue in Modern Literary Tradition* (London: Chatto & Windus, 1972).

24. Sylvia Adamson, 'Subjectivity in Narration: Empathy and Echo', in Marina Yaguello (ed.), *Subjecthood and Subjectivity: The Status of the Subject in Linguistic Theory* (Paris and London: Ophrys, 1994), pp. 193–208 (p. 201).

25. Roy Pascal, *The Dual Voice: Free Indirect Speech and Its Functioning in the Nineteenth-Century European Novel* (Manchester: Manchester University Press, 1977), p. 26.

26. For a different view, see Mary A. Favret, who argues that 'nowhere else in her novels does the narrator bolster the heroine's voice and perspective so consistently and without irony', in *Romantic Correspondence: Women, Politics and the Fiction of Letters* (Cambridge: Cambridge University Press, 1993), p. 175. Knox-Shaw comments, 'From the perspective of its close, the novel provides an unqualified celebration of undying love, and it is interesting to find the narrator toying a trifle nervously, in the last pages, with the language of full-blown romance' ('Persuasion, Byron, and the Turkish tale', p. 54).

27. *Lord Byron: The Complete Poetical Works*, ed. by Jerome J. McGann, 7 vols (Oxford: Clarendon Press, 1980–91), III, p. 423. All quotations from Byron's poetry are taken from this edition and line or stanza references are given in the text.

28. Linda Hutcheon, *Irony's Edge: The Theory and Politics of Irony* (London and New York: Routledge, 1994), pp. 89–101.

29. Sinfield, *Dramatic Monologue*, p. 32.

30. Marvin Mudrick, *Irony as Defence and Discovery* (Princeton: Princeton University Press, 1952), p. 240.

31. Julia Prewitt Brown, 'The Radical Pessimism of Persuasion', in Judy Simmons (ed.), *New Casebooks: Mansfield Park and Persuasion* (Basingstoke: Macmillan, 1997), pp. 124–36.

32. Gary Kelly, 'Religion and Politics', in Edward Copeland and Juliet McMaster (ed.), *The Cambridge Companion to Jane Austen* (Cambridge: Cambridge University Press, 1997), pp. 149–69 (pp. 165–6).

33. Tara Ghoshal Wallace, *Jane Austen and Narrative Authority* (Basingstoke: Macmillan, 1995), pp. 100–16.

34. *Quarterly Review*, 24 (January 1821), pp. 325–76; reprinted in *Jane Austen: The Critical Heritage*, pp. 87–105 (p. 95).

35. See Byron's letter to Murray of 20 February 1818, in *Byron's Letters and Journals*, ed. by Leslie A. Marchand, 13 vols (London: John Murray, 1973–94), VI, p. 11.

11
'What Constitutes a Reader?' *Don Juan* and the Changing Reception of Romantic Form

Jane Stabler, Martin H. Fischer, Andrew Michael Roberts and Maria Nella Carminati

'Byron's poetry is the most striking example I know in literary history of the creative role which poetic form can play', Auden wrote in 'The Shield of Perseus'.[1] The question of what role, exactly, Byron's ironically hailed 'gentle reader' plays in the reception of poetic form has been approached in a number of ways since the Romantic period. There have been studies of the economics and politics of reception and close analysis of various scenes of reception such as Lucy Newlyn's examination of Romantic poets' responses to hearing each other's work.[2] On a different front, profiles of the wider reading public have been constructed through analyses of guides and educational books to see how the ideal reader was envisaged while other scholars have traced the aesthetic horizons of the different groups that make up a readership, for example, women, children and working-class readers. Since Jon P. Klancher's *The Making of English Reading Audiences, 1790–1832* (1987), and Lee Erickson's *The Economy of Literary Form: English Literature and the Industrialization of Publishing, 1800–1850* (2000), particular attention has been paid to the shaping of readerly taste through the direction of the reviewers and editors. In diverse studies of the Romantic period, marginalia, literary table talk and memoirs have been scrutinised for what they can tell us of reactions to poems in the run up to, and immediate aftermath of, publication. William St Clair's recent magisterial survey, *The Reading Nation in the Romantic Period* (2004), reminds us that we cannot 'recover the range of actual responses to the reading of printed texts without information from outside the texts', but that anecdotal information raises methodological difficulties of other kinds. When records are plentiful, it is easy to slip into the belief that they are a reliable record of actual acts of reception. It is easy to forget that, however many of such reports are found and collected, they can never be, at best, anything beyond a tiny, randomly surviving, and perhaps highly unrepresentative, sample of the far larger total acts of reception which were never even turned into words in the mind of the reader let alone recorded in writing.[3]

The situation as regards Romantic period readers is exactly as St Clair describes and we cannot, of course, hope to capture historical 'acts of reception' in anything other than a subjective and piecemeal way. Nevertheless, the vibrancy of some of these records gives us tantalising information about the affective power of poetry on individual readers. When these readers are reviewers or essayists we know that they will have influenced many other readings, as Klancher has demonstrated the ways in which nineteenth-century readers internalised the reactions of the leading reviews.

Different readers, different readings

This chapter concentrates on the reception of Byron's most controversial use of poetic form during the Romantic period – that is, his employment of *ottava rima* – and examines some continuities with and differences from the reception of that form today. The chapter diverges from the other chapters in this book in its approach to the analysis of poetic form: it reports the results from an interdisciplinary research project that has been using the methods of cognitive psychology to obtain empirical data about readers' responses to Romantic-period poetry and late-twentieth-century poetry.[4] In some ways, we are following in a long line of Romantic critics such as I. A. Richards and Georges Poulet who have striven to make literary criticism more psychologically accountable. In *Science and Poetry* (1926), Richards asked: 'What can the dawning science of psychology tell us about poetry?' His approach to poetry was one that emphasised the dichotomy between poetry and science ('In its use of words most poetry is the reverse of science'), but which remained alert to the possibility of defining precisely what happens when a properly attuned reader encounters a poem.[5]

This approach has its root in a Romantic (more precisely, Coleridgean) sense that science and poetry are both explorations of human consciousness and that poems often take the form of 'experiments'.[6]

Empirical responses to poetry include a wide range of reader response criticism, pedagogic accounts of the experience of teaching poetry in the classroom, literary sociology, communication theory and phenomenological criticism.[7] More recently Peter Manning, Susan Wolfson and Richard Cronin have examined the historical meanings of various Romantic forms but, as Gunnar Hansson remarks, we still know

> shockingly little of what constitutes response to literature. There are almost no limits to the amount of research that is needed before we know even the gross outlines of what goes on in the reading processes when the latent meanings, qualities, and structures of works of literature are realised in the minds of readers.[8]

We have been using an innovative approach that brings together the disciplines of literary criticism, psychology and neuroscience. Considerable barriers remain between these fields because of the disciplinary structures of the modern academy. To begin with, psychologists and literary critics work with very different ideas of what 'reading' is: for psychologists it is the activity of scanning a page in which the points of eye fixation indicate the focus of cognitive processing (the eye–mind assumption), and the length of those fixations reflects the duration of cognitive processing of that material (the immediacy assumption). For literary critics reading is the way we describe our perception, comprehension, meditation around and interpretation of a text. Psychologists accustomed to working with small artificial segments of text that can be easily manipulated are disconcerted by the plethora of variables presented by a poem: the complexity of poetry threatens to compromise the principle of scientific 'control' guaranteed by the isolation and manipulation of the element under observation. By contrast, literary critics are unused to the rigorous experimental design and statistical analysis required to produce verifiable scientific data and tend to mistrust claims for experimental objectivity. But the attraction of seeing exactly what paths real readers follow with their eyes through real texts is strong for both parties. For literary critics, this interdisciplinary approach confronts the often overlooked theoretical issue of who (or what) constitutes 'the reader'; it also removes the obvious disadvantages of talking about Culler's 'ideal reader', Fish's 'informed reader', Riffaterre's 'super-reader' or the 'implied reader' of Booth or Iser; all of whom seem to boil down to the literary critic himself or herself on an above-average day.[9]

An example of the sort of affective response to Romantic poetry that we set out to examine in more detail is A. C. Swinburne describing the experience of reading Byron's *Don Juan* as a whole rather than through extracts:

> Here and here alone the student of his work may recognise and enjoy the ebb and flow of actual life. Here the pulse of vital blood may be felt in tangible flesh. Here for the first time the style of Byron is beyond all praise or blame: a style at once swift and supple, light and strong, various and radiant. Between *Childe Harold* and *Don Juan* the same difference exists which a swimmer feels between lake-water and sea-water: the one is fluent, yielding, invariable; the other has in it a life and a pulse, a sting and a swell, which could touch and excite the nerves like fire or like music. Across the stanzas of *Don Juan* we swim forward as over 'the broad backs of the sea': they break and glitter, hiss and laugh, murmur and move, like waves that sound or that subside. There is in them a delicious resistance, an elastic movement, which salt water has and fresh water has not.[10]

This is distinctively Swinburnian, but its evocation of the restlessness and 'resistance' of the poem has much in common with the reviews that greeted (or condemned) the publication of *Don Juan* (1819–24). Byron's first readers reported a sense of palpable disruption, issuing from the sensation of being 'hurried' from one area of experience to another (or what Hazlitt called an 'utter discontinuity of ideas and feelings' and a desire to 'astonish the reader by starting new subjects and trains of speculation').[11] The subject of the poem no longer causes outrage in a secular postmodern audience. But what about the form, and that indefinable point at which style and form merge? Can the disturbing aesthetic effects attributed to form by literary critics be traced by more empirical research methods? Our initial aim was to examine the historical accounts of readers' responses to Romantic poetry, draw out the salient responses to poetic form and then deploy the methods of cognitive science to provide empirical data to enable a comparison with the reactions of readers today.

Although it is obviously extremely difficult to isolate the surface features of a text during a reading of 'real poetry' – or poetry which has not been manipulated or controlled – this was an important objective for the interdisciplinary nature of our project. We wanted to overcome the problem voiced by Eugene R. Kintgen in 1985 when he observed ruefully that 'there seems to be no way to study the dynamics of reading without interrupting or otherwise altering the act'.[12] Psychological experiments examine one thing at a time in very carefully controlled conditions. As this chapter will show, if experimental psychology is to contribute anything substantive to our knowledge of what happens when we read poetry, more than one methodology needs to be employed to enable an incremental assembly of tightly focused studies on all facets of the reading experience (for example: recognition of genre, syntactical and lexical processing, metrical awareness, recreation of metaphor, response to form, recognition of allusion, aesthetic evaluation, emotional response). The early stages of our research involved the relatively simple measurement of readers' speeds through timed readings and assessment of sensory or emotional impact through questionnaires; we then moved on to use eye-tracking technology as a way of assessing preliminary cognitive processes during the reading of poetry. In the next phase of our work we shall investigate the use of functional magnetic resonance imaging (fMRI) to supplement findings about the auditory effects of form on specific areas of the brain. The results help to show that critical assumptions about the effects of form are often based on imaginary narratives of reading (such as Swinburne's swimming), rather than a report of observable events.

Reasoning rhyme

In an investigation of the visual impact of form the role of rhyme was an obvious place to begin. Literary critics are certain that rhyme perceived on the page plays an important role in reading. Gillian Beer summarises this: 'Line ending provides an architectonics. Rhymes stress across those line endings.'[13] Cognitive research into the ways in which readers of poetry process rhyme is scanty, inconclusive and tends to concentrate on the aural reception of rhyme.[14] In the mid-1990s Johan Hoorn, for example, set out to test Roland Barthes's claim that rhyme creates a tension between the congenial and the dissimilar, making a kind of 'structural scandal'.[15] Hoorn measured the electrical activity of the cerebral cortex (electroencephalography or EEG) while participants heard lines of poetry where the last word was manipulated according to four conditions: rhyme/semantically plausible, non-rhyme/semantically plausible, rhyme/semantically implausible and non-rhyme/semantically implausible. Interestingly, the main effect of rhyme resulted when, during the first processing of texts, rhyming expectations were not satisfied. This certainly shows that some recognition of the rhyming structure of a poem takes place in the very early stages of reading. It also suggests that readers construct an internal representation of the structure of the rhyme scheme and that they might use this representation to guide them in the subsequent stages of reading. Hoorn's study was a promising point of departure for our research where the notoriously tricky compound rhymes of Byron's *Don Juan* might be expected to provoke responses similar to those elicited by rhyming violation. For psycholinguists, the question of whether the rhyming information is retained in memory is still controversial.[16]

While Byron's passages of political satire, autobiographical scandal, sexual innuendo and profanity succeeded in outraging many of his first readers, the *ottava rima* form was clearly responsible for some of the disrupted reading experiences. *The Literary Gazette* in 1819 explained the disjunctive tendencies of the rhyme scheme for its readers: 'the first six lines and the last two usually alternate with tenderness or whim'.[17] As Donald Wesling points out, 'the Romantics reinvent existing forms with a fine sense of how the device is limited and enabled by previous work':[18] Byron started to use the *ottava rima* form for long comic poems at exactly the point when the literary *cognoscenti* and shapers of taste were congratulating English poets for having chastened, corrected, mellowed and harmonised the barbarity of the original Italian.[19] Contrary to the assumptions of Russian formalism that innovative aesthetic devices over time lose their ability to surprise, a strong effect of violated expectation was still detected by Byron's readers in the twentieth century. R. D. Waller's classic description of *ottava rima* in English focuses on the final *cc* couplet: 'The style which varies naturally with the poet, abounds in pointed wit, epigrams, and sudden bathos (here assisted by the structure of the octave with its home-striking final couplet).'[20] Anne Barton's authoritative guide to *Don Juan* identified the final couplet in the *ottava rima* rhyme scheme as a significant source of readerly disruption. Considering the infamous 'beside the river/Guadalquivir' rhyme of *Don Juan*, I, stanza 8, Barton remarks,

> The poem is filled with such ingenious traps, some of them – as becomes especially apparent when read aloud – designed to bring the reader to an abrupt halt while he or she reconsiders how to articulate a particular word in the light of the two (or one, in the case of the concluding couplet) with which it is rhymed. To find 'Indigestion' paired with 'question' amuses; the introduction of 'rest eye on' as the third rhyme (XI, st. 8) produces temporary dismay, modulating after a telling moment of uncertainty into delight. What is to be made of 'rattles'/'battles'/'what else', another show-stopper, apart from its

obvious intention to diminish the dignity of the central noun? *Don Juan's* readers are continually being forced to interrogate a rhyme's imperfection: a casual flaw, or an unsettling joke with the language and their own assumptions?[21]

Jerome McGann also finds the concluding couplet to be of key importance for both the poet and the reader:

> The final couplet of Byron's *ottava rima* has been much commented upon. In truth, it is an extraordinary device in the poem. On the one hand, it is the place for summary and sententiousness, where the easy shifts of the stanza's first six lines can be nailed down. But it serves, simultaneously, as the pivot of change and movement in the poem. It is a moment of pause and poise, a sort of stanzaic caesura, and Byron handles it in a great variety of ways. [...] The couplet is the sting in the tail of Byron's *ottava rima* which he will dart back, comically or satirically, into the desperate brain of the first six lines. The final couplet can be used to make a turn upon what has gone before, and so it is rightly seen as a locus of Byron's management of tonal shifts.[22]

As the above quotations illustrate, discussion of Byron's *ottava rima* is a strong instance of the critical assumption that emotive and semantic effects can be attributed to specific technical features of poetry, with the apparent implication that such effects have at least part of their impact during the initial process of reading. These critics regard Byron's rhymes as exerting temporal control over the reading process and enforcing a 'moment of pause' or an 'abrupt halt'. Barton shrewdly notes the probability that this effect will be more pronounced when the reader reads aloud. As far as the dynamics of surprise in visually encountering a rhyme are concerned, the effects of reading aloud and re-reading ask to be studied in their own right, but these were outside the scope of our initial project. We began by asking whether it was possible to detect destabilising effects in present-day first silent readings of *Don Juan*.

Self-paced reading experiment

Our research question was simply to ascertain by empirical research whether the concluding *cc* couplet of Byron's *ottava rima* stanza had the disruptive effect on silent readers that literary critics had claimed. As a comparison we selected Thomas Gray's 'Elegy Written in a Country Churchyard' (1751). This is written in quatrains of alternating rhyme (*abab cdcd*), which could easily be run together to form an eight-line freestanding unit of sense. The 'Elegy' is traditionally seen as a masterpiece of meditative symmetry and balance. Dr Johnson famously claimed that the 'Elegy' 'abounds with images which find a mirror in every mind, and with sentiments to which every bosom returns an echo'.[23] The metaphor of the returning echo itself echoes the rhyme structure of the 'Elegy' while indicating that the poem (unlike Byron's) was not expected to unsettle its readers. Roger Lonsdale writes of 'the balancing effect of the basic quatrain unit', while Philip Hobsbaum described Gray's 'slowness of rhythm' in the 'Elegy', 'largely brought about by [...] the alternating rhymes'.[24] In an essay which focuses on Gray's poetic diction, Richard Terry notes in passing that the 'tranquillizing effect of the poem stems not just from the reiterated certainty of the iambic quatrains but also from the co-operative nature of the poem's lexis: words of like association being clustered to produce a concerted effect. The technique is itself complemented by a tight-knit acoustical pattern produced by alliteration.'[25] This last comment in particular demonstrates how interwoven various poetic techniques are within one poem, but it also shows that the rhyme pattern of the 'Elegy' is believed to contribute significantly to its 'tranquillizing effect'. While recognising that Gray and Byron have different poetic styles and voices, our experiment was designed to focus on the rhyme patterns of their work as the literary critics whose claims we were testing regard these patterns as being at the forefront of the reader's mind during reading or, at least, one of the most obvious surface features that affects the reader's perception of and reaction to the poem.

The experiment employed the method of self-paced reading to measure the reading times of readers who had been presented with several stanzas composed by Byron and Gray.[26] Unlike Hoorn's study we were following the way in which a reader might respond to a rhyme scheme that repeated itself over a sequence of stanzas. Thus, our focus was not merely on whether readers pay attention to rhyme but more importantly on whether they construct an internal representation of the structure of the rhyming scheme they are reading and whether they are using this internal representation to guide them in the subsequent stages of reading.

First, readers were repeatedly exposed to only one type of poetry (either Byron's *ottava rima* or Gray's alternating rhyme). This was designed to induce a familiarity or 'habituation' with that particular rhyme scheme, as indicated by their progressively more efficient reading.

Following this habituation phase, readers were presented with stanzas written by the other author and using a rhyming pattern that diverged from the one to which they had become accustomed. We were interested in any effect of these changes on their reading speed. The critical reputation of Byron's *ottava rima* would lead one to expect a disruption or a slowing-down in reading speed in the last two lines of each *ottava rima* stanza, but not in the last two lines of the alternating rhyme stanza.

The second aim of the experiment was to discover what role a rhyming scheme has in the immediate reception of poetry. To what extent are readers aware of the formal dynamics of a rhyme scheme? Are they more attuned to collective effects of style or a poetic 'voice'? The inclusion of two different poets and rhyming schemes in the experiment helped to avoid a possible experimental confound. It is well known that in reading experiments readers become more efficient in the task of reading as they proceed through a text. This increased efficiency is reflected in a gradual increase in reading speed as the experiment progresses (the so-called 'practice' effect). If the task in the experiment were simply to read a certain number of stanzas in the same rhyming scheme and by the same poet, and an increase in reading speed were observed as readers read through the experimental stanzas, it would be impossible to say for sure whether this increase was due to readers habituating to a poet (and/or rhyming scheme) or simply becoming more efficient in the general task at hand as they progress through the experiment. To avoid this confound, the experiment was designed in such a way that evidence for habituation would come indirectly from a possible detection of a *new* rhyming pattern or poet. That is, one group of participants first had to read seven examples of Byron's *ottava rima* from *Don Juan*; they were then presented with stanzas in alternating rhyme from Gray's 'Elegy'. If readers slowed down as soon as they encountered the other poet (at the start of the eighth stanza), we would have evidence that habituation is style-based, but if they slowed down only when the rhyme scheme shifted from one form to another (near the end of the eighth stanza), we would have specific evidence for the pervasive power of rhyme in its own right. Finally, we gave each reader either a rhyme instruction or a neutral instruction, to explore whether a reader's focus of attention would influence our results. The rhyme instruction asked the reader to pay close attention to the rhyme scheme. The neutral instruction simply asked people to read. The effectiveness of this instruction was verified after the experiment by asking readers in a questionnaire to identify the rhyme schemes they had read and to classify the emotional impact of each rhyme scheme.

Our results showed that there was a greater unevenness in the length of time taken to read a line of iambic pentameter in Byron's stanzas compared with Gray's stanzas and that, overall, participants in both instruction groups read line 7 faster than line 6, and line 8 faster than 7. The interaction between line and position in experiment was not significant, implying that the tendency for line 7 to be read faster than line 6 and for line 8 faster than seven is present in *all* stanzas of the habituation block, irrespective of their order of presentation in the experiment. In sum, there was an incremental increase in reading speed as readers read the last three lines of the *ottava rima* stanzas. This occurred independently of the type of instructions they had been given so being told to pay attention to the rhymes did not retard the increase. Indeed, there was a marginal tendency for readers who had been assigned *ottava rima* as their habituation rhyme to read faster when they received rhyme instructions than when they received neutral ones, while readers who were assigned alternating rhyme as their habituation rhyme showed an opposite trend.

Although the influence of instructions on rhyme was not strong enough to give full statistically robust results, it is nevertheless worth commenting on an interesting trend in the data. Asking readers to concentrate on the rhyming pattern of a poem may encourage 'shallow' processing of the semantic content of the poem – this would lead to faster reading times for rhyme instructions than neutral instructions, on the assumption that with neutral instructions readers focus on semantic comprehension and do not pay much attention to the rhyme. In view of our results, it would seem that Byron's *ottava rima*, as a rhyming pattern, is easier to process than Gray's alternating rhyme. However, when closer attention to meaning is asked for, *ottava rima* becomes much harder to read.

Awareness that we read in different ways according to pre-established codes of decision is not a new discovery. Charles Lamb in his 'Detached Thoughts on Books and Reading' identified an amusing variety of modes of reading:

> Books of quick interest, that hurry on for incidents, are for the eye to glide over only. It will not do to read them out. I could never listen to even the better kind of modern novels without extreme irksomeness. A newspaper, read out, is intolerable.[27]

Lamb was doubtless responding to the increasing number of different formats of publication as well as the proliferation of 'two-penny trash' in the 1820s. The *OED* dates the sense of skim reading ('to read rapidly or carelessly; to glance over without close attention') to Hannah More's disapproval of this form of reading in 1799, and Byron's use of it, 'skimming a charming critique' in *The Blues* (I, 22), is also noted in 1820. The relatively new concept of skim reading may lie behind Byron's image of the compositional process of *Don Juan* ('But at the least I have shunned the common shore, / And leaving land far out of sight, would skim / The Ocean of Eternity' (X, st. 4)) and it may be that if Byron's *ottava rima* rhyme scheme always encourages skimming as opposed to deep processing (as it appeared to do in our selection of readers), this may account for the sensations of speed or being 'hurried on' that early nineteenth-century readers associated with their first readings of *Don Juan*.

Both the results of the on-line reading task and the questionnaire show that our readers did not experience any seriously unsettling disruption at the change in rhyming pattern in the last couplet of *Don Juan*'s stanza. In the self-paced reading experiment, these lines were read faster than the preceding line (line 6), suggesting that readers increased their reading rate as they approached the end of the stanza. This behaviour was not fundamentally different from that observed when participants read the last two lines of alternating rhyme, where there is no such change in rhyme. The responses to the questionnaire were in agreement with the on-line finding: the great majority of readers did not find the change in rhyming scheme in the last couplet of *ottava rima* disruptive or unpleasant, although when readers reflected on their reading experience they did detect an element of 'surprise' in the couplet of the *Don Juan* stanzas. A large proportion agreed with the idea that this change adds an element of interest to the poem and that it produced an effect of completeness. Thus, these results do not support the general claims made by some literary critics that the *ottava rima* rhyming structure *per se* has an unsettling effect on readers, especially the assumption that the couplet prompts a moment of pause in the flow of reading.

There could be several reasons for this unexpected result. First, it is possible that critics may have overstated or misconstrued the impact of the couplet on the stanza form as a whole making a generalised claim for Byron's *ottava rima* based on a few controversial instances of the couplet rhyme. Interestingly, it is consistent with the nature of the reception of Byron's fame that some details of his work should achieve a disproportionate emphasis in public memory. If the disruptive or unsettling effect of Byron's *ottava rima* is limited to a few notorious instances in *Don Juan*, our criterion in selecting the experimental stanzas may have made it difficult to observe the disruptive effect of the last couplet. The stanzas we selected had to be freestanding for the purpose of the experiment, and to minimise the distance between Byron's and Gray's subject matter we chose more sententious or philosophically contemplative stanzas rather than the infamous *éclats* in the narrative.

Furthermore, it may well be that today's readers are less sensitive to sudden changes in rhyming pattern within a stanza than Byron's classically-educated contemporaries and highly-educated literary critics. Familiarity with free verse may have led to a decrease in sensitivity to the processing of the regularity of traditional rhyme and to an increased tolerance of deviant rhyming patterns. Perhaps this may be attributed to the likelihood that twenty-first-century readers are more used to sudden change and fragmentation in the rapidly changing media of television, film and advertising. In addition and more importantly, our readers of poetry are likely to have been exposed to examples of modern and contemporary poetry, where rhyming patterns are either not found or employed on a more irregular basis than in traditional poetry.

There is considerable evidence to suggest that readers who are familiar with the devices of modernist free verse and avant-garde poetry adopt a distinctive reading strategy for poetry (as compared with prose genres) that involves suspending the usual imperative drive to resolve syntactic ambiguity. Interestingly this suspension of the usual reading strategies for clearing away doubts and uncertainties accords with Romantic views that literature in general and poetry in particular is capable of enthralling or casting a spell over the reader.[28] The effect of reading of poetry (as the most concentrated form of literary language), and its ability to possess the mind of the reader connects the philosophical inheritance of the Romantic period with the psychological literary criticism of the early twentieth century. In his *Dialogues Concerning Natural Religion* (1779), Hume's Demea suggests the distance between the Deity and a human mind by referring to the discourse of literature and the susceptibility of the reader's mind to authorial influence:

When I read a volume, I enter into the mind and intention of the author; I become him, in a manner, for the instant; and have an immediate feeling and conception of those ideas, which revolved in his imagination while employed in that composition. But so near an approach we never surely can make to the Deity. His ways are not our ways.[29]

Demea's orthodoxy is all the more important here for pointing out the way in which the power of reading to draw the mind of the reader into correspondence with the author was an accepted part of eighteenth-century thought. Demea's normative view of reading anticipates the act of attention sought by I. A. Richards and the same process of surrender is echoed with startling clarity in Georges Poulet's account of reading:

> Reading is [. . .] a way of giving way not only to a host of alien words, images, ideas, but also to the very alien principle which utters them and shelters them [. . .] how could I explain, without such take-over of my innermost subjective being, the astonishing facility with which I not only understand but even *feel* what I read [. . .] it is important to note that this possession of myself by another takes place not only on the level of objective thought, that is with regard to images, sensations, ideas which reading affords me, but also on the level of my very subjectivity.

The sensations of rapid movement recorded by Byron's contemporaries and the accelerating reading pace exhibited by the readers we tested suggest that Poulet's 'take-over' has indeed taken place in both cases. On the other hand, the resistance that Poulet associates with a failure on the reader's part to read 'without mental reservation, without any desire to preserve [. . .] independence of judgment' may have been experienced by those readers of *Don Juan* who could not, for moral or political reasons, read with 'the total commitment required of any reader'.[30]

A third viable account of our results is that some of the effects claimed by critics, notably the generation of new semantic and inter-pretative possibilities, depend upon more extensive re-reading. The line-by-line presentation in our first experiment did not allow such re-reading. If these interpretations are only acquired by a gradual process of thinking over the text then what critics are describing as effects realised during reading may need to be re-conceived of as effects of combined re-reading and reflection. This raises interesting issues about the terms of critical discourse and the different definitions of reading touched on at the beginning of the essay.

Subsequent paths of enquiry

Up until the late nineteenth century, most people assumed that reading proceeds as a series of regular sweeps from left to right and top to bottom across the page. Eye movements have been measured since 1879 when a student of Professor Javal at the University of Paris first made observations about the discontinuous movements of the eye.[31] The end of the nineteenth century saw some fascinating experiments when scientists watched readers through telescopes or fitted readers with ivory cups on the cornea with little brushes attached to trace reading patterns on smoked glass, and all the basic features of eye movements were discovered with these and other early methods. However, it was not easy to apply these methods to the study of reading processes. From the 1970s onwards new technology, including the use of computers to collect and process vast amounts of data, made it possible to track eye movements millisecond by millisecond by analysing the reflections of an infra-red light beam that was trained on the pupil. Reading in a strict cognitive psychology definition consists of a series of jumps forward, rests and returns by the eyes: forward jumps are known as 'saccades', backward ones are 'regressions' and the resting points are known as 'fixations'. Readers typically fixate (keep their eyes on one spot in the text) for about a quarter of a second and saccade forward about eight character spaces with 10–15 per cent of fixations being regressions to earlier points in the text. Difficult texts or readers with a condition like dyslexia produce longer fixations, more frequent regressions and more cautious short saccades.[32] Literary texts complicate psychological paradigms to the extent that, as teachers, we encourage readers to pause, re-read and dwell on a literary text to appreciate its richness. Thus a full, slow, thoughtful reading of a poem will produce all the characteristics of reading that a psychologist would recognise as typifying an impediment.

In one of our experiments, we found that the same text when laid out as poetry (with line breaks) and as compared with prose (no line breaks) produced all these standard indications of 'difficulty', even when the two texts were identical in content. Readers of poetry fixate for longer and regress more often, not because the information contained in the text is more 'difficult', but because they are reading for something in addition to 'lexical information'.[33] Conversely, knowledge that psychologists take for granted (about the discontinuous scanning of the page) complicates standard critical accounts of the way a formal device like rhyme works. Beer summarises a common critical assumption about the dynamics of reading verse:

We read forwards; we rhyme backwards [...] rhyme relies on backward allusion. Rhyme is de-formation; a first, apparently rationally sanctioned word, is tripped and changed (both semantically and aurally) by the rhyme word. For rhyme is always retrospective. It *is* not until it is seconded. The second word invades, splices to itself engrafted signs, charges the boundaries of the single term. Pounce or slide, the second word moves in on the first and tricks it into rhyme, claims kinship against the odds.[34]

A further example of the assumption that rhyme directs the reader backwards is to be found in an article by Marjorie Perloff:

> rhyme plays a significant role as a metrical and rhetorical marker, signalling the ends of lines and organizing lines into larger stanzaic units [...]. The pleasure produced is that of sameness in difference: the syntax of a given stanza propels us forward even as the metrical repetition and rhyming pulls us back and makes us aware of the verse unit itself.[35]

This reads like a description of a dynamic process, and it seems likely that the sensation of being 'pulled back' would happen while reading, rather than being a *post-hoc* conceptual construction. Indeed, most critical accounts of the effects on the reader of formal poetic elements such as rhyme, rhythm and layout all sound as if they are describing the process of reading in real time (usually a first reading) which involves an element of surprise. It is likely that rhyme works as an aural echo in the memory as well as a visual recognition even during silent reading. Building on the suggestions of Beer and Perloff, we might hypothesise that readers are pulled backwards by the memory of a sound while the visual cue of a rhyme pulls them forwards. According to the eye–mind assumption of psychologists, the processes of being propelled forward and pushed back described by literary critics would be registered in some way as eye movements. Our observation of an increased percentage of regression eye movements for poetry compared with prose (see above) supports this prediction.

Following the self-paced reading experiments, we used eye-tracking technology to map individual readings of stanzas of *Don Juan*. The eye maps displayed below show the scan paths of individual readings of *Don Juan*, canto I, stanza 8. There are a number of regressions at line endings, moments where the reader pauses and re-reads a segment of text, but in several instances the rhyme seemed equally likely to catch the eye and propel the reader forwards. In one case (not recorded in this data set), the eye path of an experienced poetry reader encountering the infamous couplet rhyme showed that the reader's eye jumped forward to take in 'Guadalquivir' immediately after landing on the last word ('river') of line 7. It seems likely that 'Guadalquivir' at the end of line 8 was detected in parafoveal vision and triggered a downward saccade before the reader even attempted the final line by initiating a return sweep. Although this works against the accounts of rhyme lagging behind by Beer and Perloff, it accords with Barton's account of the 'temporary uncertainty' provoked by individual words in Byron's rhymes.

The scan paths below (Figure 11.1) show how nine readers navigated the same stanza: the maps show that these readers were also tripped up by (or paused to revel in) the 'pleasant city / much to pity' and 'quite agree / soon may see' rhymes as well as the final couplet.

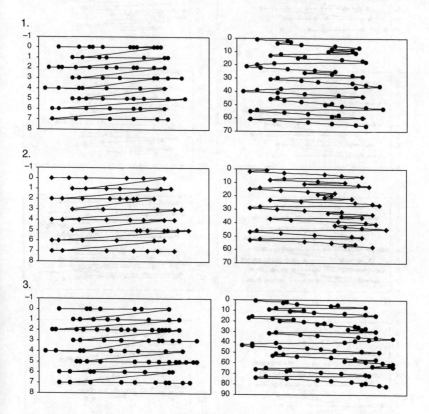

Figure 11.1 Figures showing how nine individuals read *Don Juan*, I, st. 8, 'In Seville was he born'

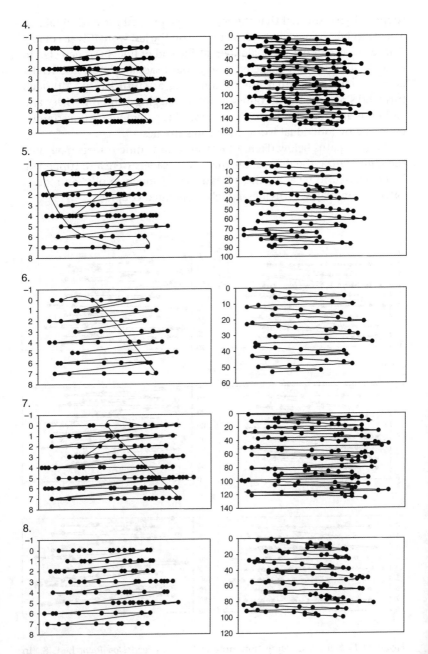

Figure 11.1   (Continued)

9.

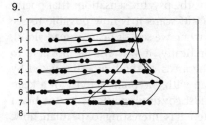 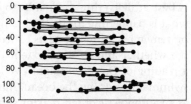

Figure 11.1 (Continued)

All the images map the spatial extent of the text on their horizontal axis and each pair of images shows the same person's reading in two ways: in the left-hand image, the vertical axis corresponds to the line numbers and thus the dots show the points where the eye rested on each line of the stanza (the indentation of the second, fourth and sixth lines of Byron's *ottava rima* stanza is clearly visible). In the right-hand image, the vertical axis merely reflects the sequential order of events and so the dots record the eye fixations in time (measured in milliseconds). Readers 1 and 2, for example, read the stanza once but readers 4–9 show more extensive re-reading.

Furthermore the range of different possible approaches to the same stanza was evident: as well as the left-to-right, top-to-bottom trajectory of reading, certain points in the poem induced individual readers to leap back (from 'Spanish' to 'Seville', from 'agree' to 'women' and from 'so says' to 'oranges'). The question for psychologists and literary critics is, to what extent were these regressions prompted by difficulty or delight or a complex mixture of both? Eye tracking can tell us exactly what was read, but not what was thought; it can tell us exactly where a reader hesitated and the precise word they went back to, but not why.

'I want a form that's large enough to swim in', Auden wrote in 1936 as he contemplated the shape of his homage to *Don Juan* and the concomitant 'fascination of what's difficult'.[36] If we take the materiality of reading seriously and admit the sort of empirical evidence generated by diverse, real readers, the form of *Don Juan* may call into question many long-lived formalist accounts of reading. Seeking to unite the materiality of reading with the more aesthetic concerns of conventional formalist criticism we could do worse than return to Swinburne's impressionistic plunge into the poem. A recent study of the art and craft of poetry from the perspective of practising poets observed that 'comparatively little has been written on the mental changes that take place in the consciousness of the reader of poetry, the psychic sensations that poetry is best at delivering'.[37] Thanks to fMRI scans it is now possible to see what is happening inside the brain when we see, or hear, or read aloud, or remember different texts. Theoretically, it will also be possible to see whether and to what extent the areas of the brain stimulated by a reading of *Don Juan* might overlap with the brain activity of a keen swimmer imagining the ocean. Amidst continuing interest in the brain as an autopoietic or self-making system it is interesting to speculate how, on a micro-level, the self-making of individual poetic readings might interact with this larger organic process.[38] The relationships between difficulty, pleasure and memory in our experience of poetic form present a fascinating field for future interdisciplinary research.

Notes

1. Auden, *The Dyer's Hand and Other Essays* (London: Faber, 1963; repr. 1975), p. 394.
2. Lucy Newlyn, *Reading, Writing, and Romanticism: The Anxiety of Reception* (Oxford: Oxford University Press, 2000).
3. William St Clair, *The Reading Nation in the Romantic Period* (Cambridge: Cambridge University Press, 2004), p. 5.
4. The project was initially funded for the period 2002–3 by an award from the AHRB Research Innovations Scheme to the Departments of English and Psychology at the University of Dundee for the project, 'The effects of form and technique on cognition, aesthetic response and evaluation in reading poetry'.
5. Reissued as *Poetries and Sciences* (London: Routledge & Kegan Paul, 1970), pp. 32, 46.
6. See, for example, the 1802 Preface to *Lyrical Ballads*: 'The knowledge both of the Poet and the Man of Science is pleasure; but the knowledge of the one cleaves to us as a necessary part of our existence, our natural and unalienable inheritance; the other is a personal and individual acquisition, slow to come to us, and by no habitual and direct sympathy connecting us with our fellow-beings' (*Lyrical Ballads*, ed. by R. L. Brett and A. R. Jones, 2nd edn (London and New York: Methuen, 1991), p. 259).
7. See, for example, Roger J. Kreuz and Mary Sue MacNealy (eds), *Empirical Approaches to Literature and Aesthetics* (Norwood: Ablex, 1996).
8. Gunnar Hansson, 'Verbal Scales in Research on Response to Literature', in Charles R. Cooper (ed.), *Researching Responses to Literature and the Teaching of Literature: Points of Departure* (Norwood: Ablex, 1985), pp. 212–32 (p. 226).
9. Eugene R. Kintgen discusses the problems of relying on an individual reader's reconstruction of his or her reading in *The Perception of Poetry* (Bloomington: Indiana University Press, 1983), pp. 4–19.
10. Andrew Rutherford (ed.), *Byron: The Critical Heritage* (London: Routledge & Kegan Paul, 1970), p. 375.

11. *The Complete Works of William Hazlitt*, ed. by P. P. Howe, 21 vols (London: Dent, 1930–34; repr. Tokyo: Yushodo Booksellers, 1967), XI, pp. 70, 75.
12. Eugene R. Kintgen 'Studying the Perception of Poetry', in Cooper (ed.), *Researching Responses to Literature and the Teaching of Literature: Points of Departure*, pp. 128–50 (p. 128).
13. Gillian Beer, 'Rhyming as Comedy: Body, Ghost, and Banquet', in Michael Cordner, Peter Holland and John Kerrigan (eds), *English Comedy* (Cambridge: Cambridge University Press, 1994), pp. 180–96 (p. 185).
14. In 'Rhyme and Cognitive Poetics', R. Tsur argued for the application of cognitive psychology to acoustics and phonetics to analyse the effects of rhyme (*Poetics Today*, 17:1 (1996), pp. 55–84). D. C. Rubin, in *Memory in Oral Traditions: The Cognitive Psychology of Epic, Ballads and Counting-out Rhymes* (New York: Oxford University Press, 1995), examined the interaction between human memory and rhyming patterns in determining the shape of oral poetry.
15. Johan Hoorn, 'Psychophysiology and Literary Processing: ERPs to Semantic and Phonological Deviations in Reading Small Verses', in Kreuz and MacNealy (eds), *Empirical Approaches to Literature and Aesthetics*, pp. 339–60 (p. 341).
16. In an off-line study David Hanauer did not find convincing evidence that readers direct attention to phonetic information in the reading of poetry, where the measure of attention was the degree of verbatim recall of the text. Instead, verbatim recall was significantly increased by the textual layout of the original poem, that is, by its format of short lines and stanzas. See 'Reading Poetry: An Empirical Investigation of Formalist, Stylistic and Conventionalist Claims', *Poetics Today*, 19 (1998), pp. 565–80.
17. Donald Reiman (ed.), *The Romantics Reviewed: Contemporary Reviews of British Romantic Writers, Part B: Byron and Regency Society Poets*, 5 vols (New York and London: Garland Publishing, 1972), IV, p. 1412.
18. Donald Wesling, *The Chances of Rhyme: Device and Modernity* (Berkeley: University of California Press, 1980), p. 50.
19. See Ugo Foscolo, 'Narrative and Romantic Poems of the Italians', trans. by Francis Cohen, *Quarterly Review*, 21 (1819), pp. 486–556 (pp. 508–9).
20. John Hookham Frere, *The Monks and the Giants*, ed. by R. D. Waller (Manchester: Manchester University Press, 1926), p. 22.
21. Anne Barton, *Byron, Don Juan* (Cambridge: Cambridge University Press, 1992), p. 17.
22. Jerome J. McGann, *Don Juan in Context* (London: John Murray, 1976), p. 96.
23. Samuel Johnson, *Selected Writings*, ed. by Patrick Cruttwell (Harmondsworth: Penguin, 1988), p. 480.
24. Roger Lonsdale (ed.), *The New Oxford Book of Eighteenth-Century Verse* (Oxford: Oxford University Press, 1987), p. 115; Philip Hobsbaum, *Metre, Rhythm and Verse Form* (London: Routledge, 1996), p. 129.
25. Richard Terry, 'Gray and Poetic Diction', in W. B. Hutchings and William Ruddick (eds), *Thomas Gray: Contemporary Essays* (Liverpool: Liverpool University Press, 1993), pp. 73–110 (pp. 94–5).
26. For a detailed description of the methodology of this experiment and a full statistical analysis of the results, see Maria Nella Carminati *et al.*, 'Reader's

responses to sub-genre and rhyme scheme in poetry', *Poetics*, 24 (2006), pp. 204–18.

27. Charles Lamb, *Elia and the Last Essays of Elia*, ed. by Jonathan Bate (Oxford and New York: Oxford University Press, 1987), p. 198.

28. For a recent view of this process, see Billy Collins, 'Poetry, Pleasure and the Hedonist Reader' in David Citino (ed.), *The Eye of the Poet: Six Views of the Art and Craft of Poetry* (New York and Oxford: Oxford University Press, 2002): 'The pacing of the voice, the careful phrasing, the affinity of sounds, and the lineation of the words control the speed of our reading and cast a modest spell over us' (p. 4).

29. David Hume, *Dialogues Concerning Natural Religion*, ed. by Nelson Pike (Indianapolis: Bobbs-Merrill, 1970), p. 38.

30. Georges Poulet, 'Criticism and the Experience of Interiority', in Jane P. Tompkins (ed.), *Reader-Response Criticism from Formalism to Post-Structuralism* (Baltimore and London: Johns Hopkins University Press, 1980), pp. 41–49 (p. 45).

31. Edmund Burke Huey, *The Psychology and Pedagogy of Reading with a Review of the History of Reading and Writing of Methods, Texts, and Hygiene in Reading* (Cambridge, Mass.: MIT Press, 1908), pp. 18–23. See also N. J. Wade and B. W. Tatler, *The Moving Tablet of the Eye* (Oxford: Oxford University Press, 2005), p. 136

32. See Keith Rayner, 'Eye Movements in Reading and Information Processing: 20 Years of Research', *Psychological Bulletin*, 124:3 (1998), pp. 372–422.

33. Fischer *et al.*, 'Eye movements during Prose and Poetry Reading', submitted to the *British Journal of Psychology*.

34. Beer, 'Rhyming as Comedy: Body, Ghost, and Banquet', p. 181.

35. Marjorie Perloff, 'Homeward Ho! Silicon Valley Pushkin', *The American Poetry Review*, 15:6 (November–December 1986), pp. 37–46 (p. 37).

36. W. H. Auden, *The English Auden: Poems, Essays and Dramatic Writings 1927–1939*, ed. by Edward Mendelson (London: Faber & Faber, 1977), p. 172.

37. David Citino, Preface, *The Eye of the Poet*, pp. vii–x (pp. vii–viii).

38. Humberto Maturana and Francisco Varela coined the word 'autopoiesis' to describe living organisms as systems that continually remake themselves. See Humbert R. Maturano and Francisco J. Varela, *Autopoiesis and Cognition: The Realization of the Living* (Dordrecht: D. Reidel, 1980) and *The Tree of Knowledge: The Biological Roots of Human Understanding* (Boston and London: Shambhala, 1998), pp. 43–52. For recent discussion of the ways in which this theory might be applied to consciousness, see John McCrone, *Going Inside: A Tour Round a Single Moment of Consciousness* (London: Faber, 1999).

Afterword: Romanticism's Forms

Susan J. Wolfson

> People respond to easily processed information [...]. For example, they are more likely to believe an aphorism that rhymes ('woes unto foes') than one with an identical meaning that does not rhyme ('woes unto enemies').
>
> (Nicholas Bakalar, The New York Times)[1]

> We read forwards; we rhyme backwards [...]. Rhyme is deformation; a first, apparently rationally sanctioned word, is tripped and changed (both semantically and aurally) by the rhyme word. [...] The second word invades, splices to itself engrafted signs, charges the boundaries of the single term. Pounce or slide, the second word moves in on the first and tricks it into rhyme, claims kinship against the odds.
>
> (Gillian Beer, 'Rhyming as Comedy')[2]

What is the agency of form, and how might it matter in processing information? Nicholas Bakalar and Gillian Beer suggest, in a line that some recent critiques of formalism might endorse, that the force of form is surreptitious: it invades the field of information, plays its tricks, slips its influence under the radar of conscious consideration. Rhyming a slogan greases the rails of information, sliding the tenor on a seductive vehicle. And though Nicholas Bakalar does not mention this, metre matters, too: the briskly accented rhyming of '*woes* unto *foes*' is more felicitous than the clunky double-dactyl '*woes* unto *ene*mies'. Just so, we say: snappy rhyme and rhythm are the signature of commercial, political or courtroom sloganeering – the foes might be cockroaches or criminals (it scarcely matters). Johnny Cochran deployed the formal force at the O. J. Simpson murder trial: 'if it doesn't fit, you must acquit', he proposed to the jury considering the glove-exhibit. Gillian Beer nicely assays the cagey work of the device: the wit of rhyme is to re-seed the semantic field, re-organise meaning-making, re-conceive it, even, in its verbal yokings.

It is such pressures on the presumed binary, content, that motivate the critiques of form as an underhanded, nefarious business. Yet the very fun of encountering language in form also testifies to what might be a wiring of human consciousness for pleasure in excess of function or necessity. The ongoing critiques of formalism, though not as dominant as they were in the 1980s and 1990s, are still with us, and have been especially persuasive to a generation that never seems to have attended to literary form and the best formalist criticism in the first place, that prefers the attacks of 'far reading', trained on determinative ideological formations, to the resources of skills trained by 'close reading'.

Reading close or far, can we say what is at stake in the aesthetic forms of language? While all language, by virtue of material presence, has form and organisation to speak of, readers who like literature (or any art 'form') respond to forms as a kind of content as well as containment. Yet, as the wide terms of this orientation might already suggest, to ask 'What is form?' is to court no congruent set of answers, even in the plural. After one agrees about the pressures of form on information, the franchise for attention seems wide open, as the essays in *Romanticism and Form* demonstrate in their ranging from local events such as rhyme and metre, to rhetorical figures such as apostrophe, to generic and conceptual figures, such as the ruin or the fragment, to the ambitions and failures of architectonic design, to the literary consequences of attitudes such as faith and conviction, satire and irony, and even to the readerly attention that measures all these forms of meaning, and more.

To feel that the question 'What is form?' – or, more specifically, 'What is Romanticism and Form?' – is endlessly productive is to recognise a vitality that is no less durable than renewable, with a scene of lively activity throughout the Romantic era. Here is one careful reader, and participant, on the subject:

> The reader should be carried forward, not merely or chiefly by the mechanical impulse of curiosity, or by a restless desire to arrive at the final solution; but by the pleasurable activity of mind excited by the attractions of the journey itself. Like the motion of a serpent, which the Egyptians made the emblem of intellectual power; or like the path of sound through the air; at every step he pauses and

half recedes, and from the retrogressive movement collects the force which again carries him onward.[3]

Except for the assumption of a he-reader and a perhaps overly prescriptive 'should', Coleridge conveys the durable impulse of literary over informational reading, of reading for pleasure, surprise, excitement, of going back and forth over words, inefficiently and attentively. And for one who is reading Coleridge, there is the entertainment of sentences enacting what they describe, wheeling on a surplus of metaphors, the burgeoning syntax doubling back on itself, of similes reining in a surge to inspired expansion – all a busyness of language that is hardly businesslike about getting to the syntactic destination, *onward*. Coleridge's sentences carry us pleasurably backwards as they move forward, with no loss of value. There is no point to speed-reading.

Poetry – the mode that draws the attention of every chapter in this book – is the meta-form of this recognition. At the outset of *Biographia Literaria*, the autobiography about the growth of the reader's mind that houses the description of reading above, Coleridge recalls a stern but inestimably important teacher (Reverend James Bowyer) who insisted that in truly great poetry 'there is a reason assignable not only for every word, but for the position of every word'.[4] Thus, too, Wordsworth urges his readers, at the close of the Preface he felt he had to add to *Lyrical Ballads* (1800), that 'if Poetry be a subject on which much time has not been bestowed, the judgment [of what it says and how it says it] may be erroneous, and [...] in many cases it necessarily will be so'. The indicator of 'much time' is not just advice about the advantage of habitual study, that 'long continued intercourse with the best models of composition'; it is also advice about the value of silence and slow time in reading.[5] If one is inclined to think of form as an atemporal structure (analogous to those 'beautiful and permanent forms of nature'), Wordsworth proposes an investment that accrues richness across time.[6] Even those signifiers of poetry, rhyme and metre, though these can be schemed out as structures, work their effects in the time of reading.[7]

It is in this syntax of reading that form makes its claim to critical attention. I have always liked W. K. Wimsatt's analysis of the effect and its power:

> It is something like a definition of poetry to say that whereas rhetoric – in the sense of mere persuasion or sophistic – is a kind of discourse the power of which diminishes in proportion as the artifice of it is understood or seen through – poetry [...] is a kind of

discourse the power of which – or the satisfaction which we derive from it – is actually increased by an increase in our understanding of the artifice.[8]

You might want to press this a bit: some poetry is primarily in the business of rhetoric, as Wimsatt describes it; and other genres can do the work of poetry (Wimsatt might be willing to call them 'poetic' in this respect) in presenting the artifice as a focus for critical inquiry and readerly pleasure. And I take it that Wimsatt means by 'understanding' not totality of comprehension, but rather an intellectual apprehension. Yet whatever quarrels or refinements we might want to administer to Wimsatt's proposal, and whatever allowances or judgements we might want to apply the historical and institutional situation of his instruction, we can appreciate the point that artifice is what form supplies to attention. Any view of poetic artifice that argues only its power to occlude and mystify misses the canniness of Wimsatt's remarks: the capacity of poetry to strengthen critical understanding by engaging attention with its structure, making a reading of its forms fundamental to any reception of or quarrel with its power.

Certainly (or uncertainly), Romantic-era writers were quickened by the possibilities of producing a semantics of form. Whether in Miltonic blank verse, in ballads, in romance couplets, or the syntactic extravagances of personal essays, the writers asserted their modernity, their departure from the eighteenth century. Like all modernisms, their flaunted newness is a debatable differential; but noting this modernist gesture of self-constitution is less important here than noting the chosen ground: formal practice. The sense of its significance generated more than a few ventures in literary theory, among the most famous, Coleridge's proposal (with A. W. Schlegel's fingerprints) of a difference between the 'mechanical regularity' of 'a pre-determined form' (the imposition of tradition) and the unpredictable vitality of organic form: 'it developes itself from within [...]. Such is the Life, such the form.'[9] Such is the Romanticism that wants to ally imagination with the pulse of nature over and against the dictates of cultural formations.

Coleridge's formulation developed its own tradition, ironically to the detriment of both Romanticism and form. The idea was taken up by an American New Criticism interested in isolating the 'organic' from the environments of history (literary and social) to claim for literary form an iconicity, unity and intrinsic totality. And this claim has been cited, in turn, to indict both a 'Romantic Ideology' and to stigmatise any care for form that is not sceptical, suspicious, ultimately anti-formalist in agenda. Yet for all the anti-formalist rigour, there has been no *rigor mortis* in the capacity of aesthetic forms to engage our fascination, our imagination, our critical attention.

Can we historicise the ideological contours of New Criticism, and retain a productive formalist criticism? This is the challenge taken up by the essays in *Romanticism and Form*, all written in the wake of New Criticism, deconstruction and new historicism, variously in conversation with their challenges but also with the challenges of an adventurous Romanticism. As if to say that the proof is in the reading, editor Alan Rawes has book-ended this volume with essays on the reader: Paul Curtis on the situations in which Romantic poets place (or displace) their readers; Jane Stabler, Andrew Roberts, Maria Nella Carminati and Martin Fischer on how present-day readers process Byron's brisk new form for the nineteenth-century epic, the *ottava rima* extravaganza of *Don Juan*.

Curtis takes up what seems to be an anti-form, moments of reading in which hopes of linear unfolding (plot, meaning, information) run athwart indirections. Shakespeare's Polonius is the ghost of this procedure, but curiously, too, its ironiser, for the indirections are always calculated to find directions out. Curtis's chapter itself catches the impulse – crossing from text to text to develop an essay in which linear progress is almost an arbitrary determination, and the fun is in the suggestions and inspirations of contingency. The shifts in chronography (prolepsis, anticipation, retrojection) that play against chronology inspire his exposition, and find their hero (as, too, for Caroline Franklin and Jane Stabler's team) in the Byron of *Don Juan*, a *liber* of libratory successions.

To see Byron as the new godfather of Romantic form – at least in this libratory aspect – is already to see that *Romanticism and Form* has refused the New Critical map, for which Coleridge supplied the terms and from which Byron was erased. It is even to see how far we are from the natural/supernatural metaphysics of M. H. Abrams' Romanticism that had to exile Byron.[10] Satiric, ironic Byron was always a confirmed formalist: 'Good workmen never quarrel with their tools', says the poet of *Don Juan* (I, 201), in disdain of rhyme–disdaining blank verse. Byron is back in this book as a formalist of self-ironising multiplicity, the avant-garde of modernism.

Like Paul Curtis, Michael O'Neill exercises a critical liberty of exposition: an excursion to a half dozen or so landmarks of Romantic self-consciousness about poetic form that amount to a period genre. O'Neill finds his quarry in the mimetic formal practices of Wordsworth, Byron, Shelley, Beddoes and Hemans, working, variously, in blank verse, *ottava rima*, romance couplets (non-Augustan) and heroic lines. *The Prelude*, naming its subject as the growth of a poet's mind, finds its animating medium in blank verse that glances at Milton's epic but works its modernism through the mirroring of a poet's self-discovery in the reflexive forms of his poetry. For Byron, it is rhyme that is the expansive poetic – endlessly productive, playing its wit with contingencies and surprise, a local effect, O'Neill proposes, that is a synecdoche for modern epic. Keats and Hunt declare themselves with couplets that flout Augustan protocols, while Shelley unrolls the couplets of *Epipsychidion* (it is hard to remember that this poem is in this form) as virtual blank verse in its swells and surges, without sacrificing the resources of rhyme as a trope of harmonies, achieved or in collapse. It devolves to Beddoes, in *Pygmalion: The Cyprian Statuary*, to put the promised harmony of the couplet form to devastatingly ironic effects, of desire as fulfilled, or mocked in, verbal form.

Gavin Hopps re-opens the question of invocation, that stagey performance of voice mostly treated as retro-artifice by the Romantics (or embarrassing, and prone to parody if not so supervised). Refusing Jonathan Culler's rehabilitation of the Romantic stage of this rhetoric as self-constituting figure (invocation is a declaration of vocation), Hopps charts a middle space between naïve sincerity and conscious mystery in a form of invocation that he terms 'stammering': a hesitant, uncertain voice, in tacit relation with some addressee, illuminated by the I–Thou protocols of religious ritual. From this perspective, invocation operates like prayer, and its hesitations express authentic humility. The wavering stances of invocation (now aspiring, now stammering) trace out, Hopps argues, the intertextual semiotics of liturgy, a discourse in which conflicting impulses are normative, even constitutive, in the face of mystery.

If Hopps reads a semiotics of transcendence in the haltings of liturgical poetics, Mark Sandy finds intertextuality in the semiotics of the fragment poem – the binary site here not a transcendent mystery, but a future reader. Neither the signifier of existential crisis, nor a truckling to a commercial taste for the alluring relic or portent, the fragment thus figures into Sandy's interpretive architecture as a double-charged form: at once the signifier of conceptual undecidability (such is its authenticity), and a canny strategy to thwart a reader's interpretive authority, and so protect authorial possession (such is its self-interest). One of the surprises of this formalism is the way it takes us to under-reported fields, in this case Keats's little fragment that is also an allegory of mysterious reading, *The Eve of St Mark*. Sandy sets this fragment suggestively against

Shelley's *Triumph of Life*, a progress interrupted by Shelley's death, but
with this end scarcely mattering, since the *Triumph* was always about
the defeat of understanding in ceaselessly self-replicating, self-ironising
forms.

A romance that is hard to mark and a triumph that is defeat are some
of the signposts of attenuated organic formalism. Another Romantic site
in which organic form not only will not hold, but seems never to have
had a foothold to begin with, argues Steven Jones, is the satiric print.
The formal logic of this lively culture is 'combinatoric' – a portmanteau
Jones coins to join combinings to a rhetoric that is always pointing
towards new combinations. Jones's combinatoric form is as tempor-
ally fraught as Sandy's canny fragment. In Jones's story, however, the
forward thrust is not to seed a defeat of interpretation, but to guarantee
the dispersals and surprising recombinations of its elements across time.
In the world of print media, word and image proliferate in parodic or
satiric detachments from original sites to produce a complex collage
of vernacular meanings. The printmaking that is the material vehicle
for this promiscuity, Jones proposes, is another site of the Romantic
grotesque – materials wrenched out of context, with revelatory effects,
about both the prior context and the new situations. If Coleridge tagged
mechanical form as lifeless copying on prescribed patterns, Jones shows
a lively mechanical formalism in print culture, where accretions, appro-
priations and combinations flourish. In Jones's account of Romanticism
and form, form matters not as something to be refined into a synchronic
understanding, but as a diachronic aesthetic of excess, of the successive
play and re-play of re-combinative imaginations.

History is the virtual agent of Jones's formalism. And history has
been the enemy of Wordsworth's idealising formalism in one influential
critique of Wordsworth, of 'Tintern Abbey' in particular. Complicating
this unforgiving view of the poet who used to name the age, Rawes
recovers a seemingly elided history, elided not by Wordsworth but by
his critical interrogators. This is the history of the ode in the eighteenth
century, across the tracks of which 'Tintern Abbey' appears far more
critically pointed than we would guess from indictments of its 'Romantic
Ideology'. Under that sign, Jerome McGann exposed historically located
issues getting translated into ideal abstractions, Marjorie Levinson traced
back into view the non-represented public world and Kenneth Johnston
fanned faintly legible embers, reporting the churning charcoal-works
beneath the sight-line of half unreal, picturesque wreathes of smoke.
Against these indictments, Rawes summons a formal-generic history to
see what Wordsworth's 'Lines' look like against the rural idealism of the

eighteenth-century ode. His keynote (in the teeth of arguments against using Romantic representations to read Romanticism) is Wordsworth's 'Essay, Supplementary' to the Preface of 1815. Here Wordsworth reports shaping his poetry from 'the shocks of conflicting feeling and successive assemblages of contradictory thoughts'. Taking the present participles as seriously as the terms 'successive' and 'contradictory', Rawes disputes the new historicist story of a poet seeking and failing to leave history behind, and illuminates instead a poem of visionary desire confronting social anxiety. In so far as this confrontation involves a critical reaction to the eighteenth-century odes that project rustic idealism in retreat from contemporary society and politics, Wordsworth enacts new historicism *avant la lettre*, writing 'Tintern Abbey' as just such a critique of these forms of displacement.

Material particularities in contention with idealising agenda turn out to be the haunt, if not the main region, of Robert Southey's songs – a surprise encounter, especially after his incineration in Byron's unforgiving *ottava rima*. We do know that Southey prided himself as a practitioner of form. That notorious Preface to his *Vision of Judgement* was more devoted to clucking over his heroic hexameters than to ranting his unheroic Tory politics. Nicola Trott and Bernard Beatty leave Byron's Southey behind, and return to an early, quirkier Southey. Trott finds a poet in vigorous experimentation with, and satirically against, the tropes that would later be codified as 'Romanticism'. The 'combinatoric forms' described by Jones find a kin in Southey's coinage of new words and syntaxes to wring his satires. Or like Hood, he will bring a literalising formalism to extreme situations, often by punning in a practical-jokey way against 'the one Life within us and abroad' ('The Eolian Harp', 26): how different this one life looks when we turn from wild breezes, dancing sunbeams and honey-dropping flowers, to maggot-infested nuts, horseflesh hanging for dogmeal and little pigs destined for the table alongside the produce snatched from yon beanfield. In a dazzling reading of Southey's 'Cool Reflections during a Midsummer Walk', Trott shows Southey playing chemist Davy against poet Coleridge, physics against theology, the universal impulse to experiment against a universal faith, all in the laboratory of language invigorated by contact with the new disciplines within us and abroad. Beatty's Southey is also caught between discourses, between religious beliefs and poetic revelations, between quiet faith and the excitement of apocalyptic warfare. If the oscillations, as they play out in *Thalaba, The Curse of Kehama, Madoc* and *Roderick, the Last of the Goths*, baffle any sure rapprochement between multiple events and unified meaning, the vibrant template is given by contemporaneous models for reading Scripture, itself a text of historically fraught contradictions.

Jacqueline Labbe's formalist for the age is Charlotte Smith, a ceaseless experimenter in her signature form, the sonnet. In a genre in which poets make their mark by tracking and troping the form, all within the budget of 140 syllables, Smith and another female poet, Ann Batten Cristall, break out with the production of paratexts, surrounding their sonnets with prefaces and notes. A poetics of female subjectivity is at stake in these projects, insofar as the poetic 'I' defines herself in relation to traditional expectations, and her capacity to make new discoveries. Not the least of these discoveries is a confrontation with subjectivity as a production of form. Cristall artfully exploits her pose as artless artist to liberate a poetic persona who may transgress normative feminine proprieties (usually, ritual self-deprecation). Her manipulations of poetic form argue for a kind of unruled and unruly natural strength. Smith becomes a skilled practitioner of the 'illegitimate sonnet', mingling forms, conventions and personae, Petrarchan and Shakespearean elements, sometimes trans-sexually. 'I wish to make as much *variety* of verse in this book as possible – & have studiously varied the measure of the quatrains &c', she assured her publishers (Cadell and Davies) in 1797.

While Labbe focuses closely on sonnet variations, Caroline Franklin shows the widest uses of formalist self-consciousness in the variable forcefield of narrative irony, a terrain she maps out in a surprisingly persuasive comparison of Jane Austen's *Persuasion* and Byron's own adventures in *Don Juan*. Franklin uncovers a mode of irony that vexes the formal dispersals of *The Giaour* with the same force as it does the alternating forms of interiority and plot development in the novel. In the fragmented poetic tale, Sandy's dynamics of non-possession return: all Byron gives us is fragmented, often conflicting, points of view on the central agons – Hassan's murder of harem-favourite Leila, the Giaour's murder of Hassan, the profound melancholy of the Giaour's shattered idealism. We know that Austen read this tale, because she puts a discussion of it in *Persuasion* (with reservations about the seductive effect of its lovelorn melancholy Byronism). Byron, moreover, may have read *Persuasion*, because one of the novel's key, concluding conversations (about the different modes of man's love and woman's love) gets reprised in the first canto of *Don Juan*. Observing the relative (partial, as well as related) knowledges that issue from Byron's tale in fragments, Austen (Franklin proposes) works a similar effect in her novel. She does this by setting her signature form, that 'free indirect discourse' by which we come to know a character's consciousness, in relay with the ironising pressures of linear narrative, or plot design. Working this double-view, Austen can even take Byronic agonists, such as Captain Benwick, as occasions for sceptical regard, an interval of scrutiny not dispelled by the comic resolutions of the plot design. Moral relativity – the modern temper that haunts both the fragmented narrative of Byron's romance and the alternating modes of Austen's late romantic novel – is the achievement of an ironised management of form as the proposed conveyer of coherent meanings.

Jane Stabler, Andrew Roberts, Maria Nella Carminati and Martin Fischer ask in a very analytical way how events of form register in the work of reading *Don Juan* – a famously breezy, elastic poem, seemingly propelled forward and wittily pivoting on its signature *ottava rima* stanza. Without getting into the re-reading, reflection and synchronic attention that is the usual business of critical study, the team uses cognitive psychology to measure, with empirical data, the pause of the eye over events of form. Byron is a canny choice for this inquiry – since there is such momentum in the sequencing of the *ottava rima* yet punctuated by the periodic couplet closings that may arrest the pace.

I was intrigued by what the team had to report, and it is a measure of their study's interest that it raised a host of related, follow-up questions. I found myself wondering about whether the experiments might be continued into measures of what we do as critical readers. What happens in re-reading? How is it is accelerated by familiarity, or slowed by curiosity? And what happens when listening, or listening while reading, is engaged? If one of the elements of concern in the team's inquiries is rhyme, what happens in actual audition in contrast to the silent audition of reading? And does reading out loud matter? We can all report anecdotes of our students saying that poetry snapped into sense when they heard us read it. Why might this be so (beyond our inclination to perform the forms)? Does social or institutional context affect a reader? What if one is reading in a situation that encourages slow reading, pausing, reflection, instead of a laboratory intent on measuring flutters and eye movement and not particularly interested in the fun of Byron, in the challenges of Romanticism or the (not to put too fine a point on it) inestimable rewards of slow reading?

So here, anyway, is Byron as a test case not only for Romanticism these days, but Romanticism in its formal activity. What are the forms of Romanticism shaping this book? Keats and Shelley, two of the most meticulous and witty articulators of poetic form, now sit alongside some old but neglected favourites such as Beddoes. Coleridge makes his marks and Wordsworth, though with stature, shows up only here and there; but both seem outpaced by fellow-Laker Southey, the subject of two chapters. Byron is everywhere, while Blake – there was never a more conspicuous formalist – scarcely anywhere. Smith and Cristall compel meticulous attention for effects that might be observed in other skilled practitioners of the sonnet, male and female, even with the class and performative interests applied here. And Austen takes a Byronic turn. This population and its variable presence may be just the accident of this book, or may remind us that even that reified and contested category, Romanticism, which we use to identify a historical phase, a sensibility and/or their convergences, is one of the linguistic forms that is always transforming what it names and what it does.

Under the sign of 'Romanticism and Form', Rawes's readers refute the much vaunted turn against formalism as an unrewarding aversion. With a fresh appreciation for thinking through forms, these readers give us new encounters with the densities and surprises of Romantic literature. The encounters are not set against historical and cultural information, but neither are their interests reducible to, or contained by, these mandates. What survives, in exuberance, are all those energies of language that make a reflective reading of literature worthwhile in the first place.

Notes

1. Nicholas Bakalar, 'What's in the Name? Researchers Suggest it's Money', *The New York Times*, 30 May 2006, p. 6.
2. Gillian Beer, 'Rhyming as Comedy: Body, Ghost, and Banquet', in M. Cordner, P. Holland and J. Kerrigan (eds), *English Comedy* (Cambridge: Cambridge University Press, 1994), pp. 180–96 (p. 181).
3. S. T. Coleridge, *Biographia Literaria, or Biographical Sketches of My Literary Life and Opinions*, ed. by James Engell and W. Jackson Bate, 2 vols (Princeton: Princeton University Press, 1983), II, p. 14.
4. Ibid., Chapter 1, I, p. 9.
5. The Preface is quoted from *'Lyrical Ballads' and Other Poems, 1797–1800, by William Wordsworth*, ed. by James Butler and Karen Green (Ithaca: Cornell University Press, 1992), p. 759.
6. Ibid., pp. 743–44.
7. The difference from other arrangements of language with which he gives his poetry affinity of diction, Wordsworth admits (then insists), abides in the pleasure principle of rhyme and metre. I've written about the complexity of metre in Romantic theorising in 'Romanticism and the Measures of Meter', *Eighteenth-Century Life*, 16:3 (1992), pp. 221–46.
8. W. K. Wimsatt, 'What to Say about a Poem', in *Hateful Contraries: Studies in Literature and Criticism* (Lexington: University Kentucky Press, 1966),

pp. 215–44 (pp. 240–1). One need not endorse Wimsatt's strong (though not absolute) affection for designs of 'unity' and 'coherence' in service to 'truth and significance', in order to appreciate the nuance and care of his interest in 'structures of forms which are radiant or resonant with meaning' (p. 240). It is that possibility that is the field in which ruptures and discontinuities become legible and counter-significant.

9. *Lectures 1808–1819, On Literature*, ed. by R. A. Foakes, 2 vols (Princeton: Princeton University Press, 1987), I, p. 495.

10. 'Byron I omit altogether', M. H. Abrams announced in his Preface to *Natural Supernaturalism* (New York: Norton, 1971), explaining that his greatest work (*Don Juan*) produces 'an ironic counter-voice' that 'deliberately opens a satirical perspective on the vatic stance of his Romantic contemporaries'; even Keats has to be vaticised, or Wordsworthianised out of his ironic modes to qualify for inclusion, worthy 'insofar as he represented [...] the growth and discipline of the poet's mind, conceived as a theodicy of the individual life' (p. 13).

Select Bibliography

Armstrong, Isobel, *The Radical Aesthetic* (Oxford: Blackwell, 2000)

Austin, J. L., *How to Do Things with Words* (Cambridge, Mass.: Harvard University Press, 1967)

Balfour, Ian, *The Rhetoric of Romantic Prophecy* (Stanford: Stanford University Press, 2002)

Balthasar, Hans Urs von, *The Glory of the Lord: A Theological Aesthetics*, ed. by John Riches, 7 vols (Edinburgh: T. & T. Clark, 1982)

Beer, Gillian, 'Rhyming as Comedy: Body, Ghost, and Banquet', in Michael Cordner, Peter Holland and John Kerrigan (eds), *English Comedy* (Cambridge: Cambridge University Press, 1994), pp. 180–96

Blanchot, Maurice, *The Infinite Conversation*, trans. by Susan Hanson (Minneapolis: University of Minnesota Press, 1993)

Bray, Joe, 'The Source of "dramatized consciousness": Richardson, Austen and Stylistic Influence', *Style*, 35:1 (Spring, 2001), pp. 18–33

Chrétien, Jean-Louis, *The Call and Response*, trans. by Anne A. Davenport (New York: Fordham University Press, 2004)

Citino, David, (ed.), *The Eye of the Poet: Six Views of the Art and Craft of Poetry* (New York and Oxford: Oxford University Press, 2002)

Clark, Michael P. (ed.), *Revenge of the Aesthetic: The Place of Literature in Theory Today* (Berkeley: University of California Press, 2000)

Cooper, Charles R. (ed.), *Researching Responses to Literature and the Teaching of Literature: Points of Departure* (Norwood: Ablex, 1985)

Culler, Jonathan, *The Pursuit of Signs: Semiotics, Literature, Deconstruction* (London: Routledge, 1981)

Curran, Stuart, *Poetic Form and British Romanticism* (New York: Oxford University Press, 1986)

Cox, Philip, *Gender, Genre and the Romantic Poets* (Manchester: Manchester University Press, 1996)

de Man, Paul, 'Epistemology of Metaphor', *Critical Inquiry*, 5 (1978), pp. 13–30

——, *Allegories of Reading: Figural Language in Rousseau, Nietzsche, Rilke, and Proust* (New Haven: Yale University Press, 1979)

——, 'The Dead-End of Formalist Criticism', in *Blindness and Insight: Essays in the Rhetoric of Contemporary Criticism*, 2nd edn (London: Routledge, 1983), pp. 229–44

——, *The Rhetoric of Romanticism* (New York: Columbia University Press, 1984)

Derrida, Jacques, 'Signature Event Context', in *Margins of Philosophy*, trans. by Alan Bass (Chicago: University of Chicago Press, 1982), pp. 307–30

Eagleton, Terry, 'Ideology and Literary Form', in *Criticism and Ideology: A Study in Marxist Literary Theory* (London and New York: Verso, 1978), pp. 102–63

Frye, Northrop, *Anatomy of Criticism* (Princeton: Princeton University Press, 1957; repr. 1973)

Hanauer, David, 'Reading Poetry: An Empirical Investigation of Formalist, Stylistic and Conventionalist Claims', *Poetics Today*, 19 (1998), pp. 565–80

Hartman, Geoffrey, *Beyond Formalism: Literary Essays 1958–1970* (New Haven and London: Yale University Press, 1970)

Hollander, John, *Melodious Guile: Fictive Pattern in Poetic Language* (New Haven: Yale University Press, 1988)

Jakobson, Roman, 'Linguistics and Poetics', in Lucy Burke, Tony Crowley and Alan Girvan (eds), *The Routledge Language and Cultural Theory Reader* (London: Routledge, 2000), pp. 334–9

Jameson, Fredrick, *The Political Unconscious: Narrative as a Socially Symbolic Act* (Ithaca: Cornell University Press, 1981)

Jones, Steven E. (ed.), *The Satiric Eye: Forms of Satire in the Romantic Period* (New York and Basingstoke: Palgrave, 2003)

Keach, William, 'Cockney Couplets: Keats and the Politics of Style', *Studies in Romanticism*, 24 (1986), pp. 182–96

Kreuz, Roger J., and Mary Sue MacNealy (eds), *Empirical Approaches to Literature and Aesthetics* (Norwood, New Jersey: Ablex, 1996)

Levine, George (ed.), *Aesthetics and Ideology* (New Brunswick: Rutgers University Press, 1994)

Levinson, Marjorie, *The Romantic Fragment Poem: A Critique of a Form* (Chapel Hill: University of North Carolina Press, 1986)

Marks, Herbert, 'On Prophetic Stammering', *The Yale Journal of Criticism: Interpretation in the Humanities*, 1:1 (1987), pp. 1–20

McGann, Jerome J., *The Romantic Ideology: A Critical Investigation* (Chicago: Chicago University Press, 1983)

——, *The Beauty of Inflections: Literary Investigations in Historical Method and Theory* (Oxford: Oxford University Press, 1985)

Mitchell, W. J. T., *Picture Theory: Essays on Verbal and Visual Representation* (Chicago and London: University of Chicago Press, 1994)

Newlyn, Lucy, *Reading, Writing, and Romanticism* (Oxford: Oxford University Press, 2000)

Oakeshott, Michael, 'The Voice of Poetry in the Conversation of Mankind', in *Rationalism in Politics, and Other Essays* (London: Methuen, 1962), pp. 197–247

O'Donnell, Brennan, *The Passion of Meter: A Study of Wordsworth's Metrical Art* (Kent, Ohio: Kent State University Press, 1995)

O'Neill, Michael, *Romanticism and the Self-Conscious Poem* (Oxford: Clarendon Press, 1997)

Pickstock, Catherine, *After Writing: On the Liturgical Consummation of Philosophy* (Oxford: Blackwell, 1998)

Rawes, Alan, *Byron's Poetic Experimentation: Childe Harold, the Tales and the Quest for Comedy* (Aldershot: Ashgate, 2000)

Rajan, Balachandra, *The Form of the Unfinished: English Poetics from Spenser to Pound* (Princeton: Princeton University Press, 1985)

Rajan, Tilottama and Julia M. Wright (eds), *Romanticism, History and the Possibilities of Genre* (Cambridge: Cambridge University Press, 1998)

Richards, I. A., *Poetries and Sciences* (London: Routledge & Kegan Paul, 1970)

Richter, David H. (ed.), *Ideology and Form in Eighteenth-Century Literature* (Lubbock: Texas Tech University Press, 1999)

Ricks, Christopher, 'William Wordsworth 1: "A Pure Organic Pleasure from the Lines"', in *The Force of Poetry* (Oxford: Oxford University Press, 1984), pp. 89–116

——, *Allusion to the Poets* (Oxford: Oxford University Press, 2002)

Ricoeur, Paul, *Time and Narrative*, trans. by Kathleen McLaughlin and David Pellauer, 3 vols (Chicago and London: University of Chicago Press, 1984)

Roe, Nicholas (ed.), *Romanticism: An Oxford Guide* (Oxford: Oxford University Press, 2005)

Said, Edward W., *Beginnings: Intention and Method*, new edn (London: Granta, 1998)

Sandy, Mark, *Poetics of Self and Form in Keats and Shelley: Nietzschean Subjectivity and Genre* (Aldershot: Ashgate, 2005)

Sha, Richard, *The Visual and Verbal Sketch in British Romanticism* (Philadelphia: University of Pennsylvania Press, 1998)

Soderholm, James (ed.), *Beauty and the Critic: Aesthetics in an Age of Cultural Studies* (Tuscaloose: University of Alabama Press, 1997)

Stabler, Jane, *Burke to Byron, Barbauld to Baillie 1790–1830* (Basingstoke: Palgrave, 2002)

——, *Byron, Poetics and History* (Cambridge: Cambridge University Press, 2002)

Tetreault, Ronald, *The Poetry of Life: Shelley and Literary Form* (Toronto: University of Toronto Press, 1987)

Wesling, Donald, *The Chances of Rhyme: Device and Modernity* (Berkeley: University of California Press, 1980)

Wimsatt, W. K., 'What to Say about a Poem', in *Hateful Contraries: Studies in Literature and Criticism* (Lexington: University Kentucky Press, 1966), pp. 215–44

Wolfson, Susan J., *The Questioning Presence: Wordsworth, Keats and the Interrogative Mode in Romantic Poetry* (Ithaca and London: Cornell University Press, 1986)

——, 'What Good is Formalist Criticism? Or: "Forms" and "Storms" and the Critical Register of Romantic Poetry', *Studies in Romanticism*, 37 (1988), pp. 77–94

——, *Formal Charges: The Shaping of Poetry in British Romanticism* (Stanford: Stanford University Press, 1997)

—— and Marshall Brown (eds), *Reading for Form*, Special Issue of *Modern Language Quarterly*, 61:1 (March 2000); new expanded edn (Seattle: University of Washington Press, 2006)

Wood, Gillen D'Arcy, *The Shock of the Real: Romanticism and Visual Culture, 1760–1860* (New York: Palgrave, 2001)

Zimmerman, Sarah, *Romanticism, Lyricism and History* (New York: State University of New York Press, 1999)

Index

Abrams, M. H., 100, 172, 217
Adamson, Sylvia, 177
Akenside, Mark, 104
Armstrong, Isobel, xv n3
Arnold, Matthew, 45–6
Auden, W. H., 36, 192, 209
Austen, Jane, 171, 223
   Mansfield Park, 174
   Northanger Abbey, 174
   Persuasion, 171, 172–7, 179, 181–9, 221–2
   Sanditon, 174
   Sense and Sensibility, 174, 176
Austin, J. L., 20 n8

Bagehot, Walter, 34
Bakalar, Nicholas, 213
Bakhtin, Mikhail, 171
Balfour, Ian, 12, 21–2 n27
Balthasar, Hans Urs von, 52, 150
Barrell, John, 109–10, 111
Barthes, Roland, 196
Barton, Anne, 197–8, 207
Bate, Jonathan, 34
Beatty, Bernard, xiv, 19, 220–1
Beddoes, Thomas Lovell, xiii, 217, 222
   'Pygmalion: The Cyprian Statuary', 31–2, 218
Beer, Gillian, 196, 205–6, 207, 213, 214
Blake, William, 78, 223
   Jerusalem, 42
   Milton, 42
Blanchot, Maurice, 57
Bloom, Harold, xv n1, 42, 63, 75 n12, 76 n31
Boydell Shakespeare Gallery, 78, 92
Bradshaw, Michael, 31
Bray, Joe, 190 n9
Brown, Julia Prewitt, 182
Brown, Marshall, xv n3
Buber, Martin, 56
Burroughs, William, 85

Butler, Marilyn, 138, 139, 171
Byron, George Gordon, Lord, 13, 139, 143, 147, 154, 172, 173, 175, 192, 193, 193, 217, 218, 220, 222
   Beppo, 13
   The Blues, 202
   Childe Harold's Pilgrimage, 2, 35, 43–4, 61
   The Corsair, 154
   Don Juan, 4, 13–20, 25–7, 55, 56, 84, 176, 187–8, 194–203, 204, 206–9, 217, 221, 222
   The Giaour, 172, 175, 176–7, 178–81, 189, 221
   Manfred, 60–3, 70, 74
   Mazeppa, 143, 150
   Parisina, 150
   The Prophecy of Dante, 22 n29
   'Stanzas to [Augusta]', 35–7
   The Vision of Judgement, 143, 150

Carminati, Maria Nella, 217, 222
Chatterton, Thomas, 66
Chrétien, Jean-Louis, 55, 59 n24
Clare, John, xiii
   'I Am', 34–5
   'To the Rural Muse', 42–3
Clark, Michael P., xv n3
Cohen, Ralph, 103, 104
Coleridge, Samuel Taylor, 13, 83, 93, 98, 119, 120, 121, 122, 124, 132, 133, 134 n21, 140, 141, 168, 216, 217, 219, 220, 222
   Biographia Literaria, 6–8, 116–17, 118, 123, 214–15
   The Ancient Mariner, 124, 128
   'Dejection: An Ode', 99
   'The Eolian Harp', 2, 120, 220
   'Frost at Midnight', 10, 11–12
   'Kubla Khan', 9, 84
   'This Lime-Tree Bower my Prison', 122
   'To a Young Ass', 119

228